FOUNDATION
CENTER
Knowledge to build on.

NCNE

National Center on Nonprofit Enterprise

WISE DECISION-MAKING IN UNCERTAIN TIMES

Using Nonprofit Resources Effectively

Dennis R. Young, Editor

Library of Congress Cataloging-in-Publication Data
Wise decision-making in uncertain times.
    p. cm.
    ISBN 1-59542-099-1 (pbk. : alk. paper) 1. Nonprofit organizations—Management.
2. Decision making. I. Young, Dennis R., 1943- II. Foundation Center.
    HD62.6.W57 2006
    658.4'03—dc22
                                                          2006021335

Table of Contents

Preface

The genesis of this book was the second national conference of the National Center on Nonprofit Enterprise (NCNE), held in Washington, DC in January of 2004. At that time, the theme of the conference, "Wise Economic Decision-Making in Uncertain Times," seemed to choose itself. The events of 2001, and their wake in the years immediately following, caught nonprofit organizations up in a maelstrom of damaging forces beyond their control. The bursting of the economic bubble of the 1990s and government's new preoccupation with terrorism created multiple difficulties—reallocations of public resources away from traditional nonprofit priorities, squeezing of foundation philanthropy and investment income as a result of stock market losses, dampening of giving by individuals as a consequence of the slowing economy, and difficulties in making up the difference through fees and commercial activity as purchasing power of relevant groups of consumers and clients waned. At the same time, during this tempest demands on nonprofits to deliver their essential services were only magnified.

If nothing else, this experience highlighted the fact that nonprofits were not well prepared for economic turbulence. In its first national conference in 2002, NCNE had examined a spectrum of basic nonprofit economic decisions, resulting in a set of helpful principles that executives could use to think through pricing, compensation, investment, outsourcing, and other economic choices, strategies, and policies (see *Effective Economic Decision-Making by Nonprofit Organizations.* New York: The Foundation Center, 2004). Rather than simply revisit and extend this set of deliberations, it seemed sensible, for our second conference, to explicitly add a dynamic dimension to the discussion. How indeed could nonprofits best approach their economic challenges in the context of a rapidly changing and uncertain world? Once framed in this way, it became clear that the challenges of uncertainty and change were not temporary issues associated with the confluence of events at the turn of the millennium, but rather a chronic condition of nonprofit life and one which nonprofits needed to be able to address more effectively in the foreseeable (and unforeseeable) future.

As has become NCNE's custom and *modus operandi,* the conference featured multiple expert panels consisting of leading academic researchers, practicing nonprofit leaders and managers, consultants, business sector executives, and foundation officers. Each panel was given a topic, the list of which is essentially coincident with the chapters of this book. At the conference, each panelist was asked to define the nature of the particular challenge at hand, and to offer ideas for how nonprofits could best think about and approach that challenge. Audience members were encouraged to participate in the discussions. For the most part, the panels were chaired by the academic member who was charged to consider the ideas put forth in the session and then to write a chapter based on this discussion, on the knowledge available from the literature, on his or her own research, and on the experiences and thoughts of the panel members. The chapters were not to be merely a synthesis of session discussions but rather a fresh coherent look at the issue, based on all relevant and available information. The authors here took up that mandate with grace, enthusiasm, and seriousness of purpose, with little compensation except the pride of contributing to an important body of work.

Roughly following the four tracks of the conference, this book is divided into four main topical areas. The first focuses on operating decisions, with emphases on performance, risk, and fiscal stress management. The second focuses on building capacity in order to cope more effectively with risk and change over the long term. The third explicitly highlights foundation decision-making—reflecting to some degree the extraordinarily heavy contemporary pressures on foundations to help struggling nonprofits. The fourth part focuses on relationships between nonprofits and business, another potential source of support as well as stress for nonprofits in a rapidly changing economy. These four streams are bracketed in this volume, at the front end with introductory chapters that set the stage for the substantive analytical chapters that follow, and at the back end by a chapter that addresses needs for future research.

The book, and the conference that preceded it, were collaborative efforts dependent on the contributions of many different people and institutions. The authors who took leadership in crafting the chapters are listed elsewhere in the volume, and so are acknowledged here only as a group. In addition, the members of the panels are sincerely thanked for their substantive contributions to the thinking that is documented here. In no specific order these include Jacquelyn

Lendsey, Sean Milliken, Kelly Campbell, Victor Gelb, William F. Reeder, Vincent Stehle, Audrey Alvarado, Jeanne Anderson, Dianne Russell, Rita Fuerst Adams, Laurie Regelbrugge, Nancy Roob, Yvonne Sparks Strauther, Barbara Dyer, William W. Howard, Brooke W. Mahoney, Richard W. Pogue, Jerr Boschee, Kristen Conte, Richard F. Larkin, Eugene A. Scanlan, Gregg S. Behr, Frank B. Bennett, Jennifer Lantrip, Bob Olsen, Lori Grange, Tom Ralser, Michael Seltzer, Allen Bromberger, Gerald B. Chattman, Andrew Smiles, Terri Lee Freeman, Roland J. Kushner, Herman Art Taylor, Barent L. Fake, Tom McKenna, Robert O. Zdenek, Rick Schoff, Syrinda Page, Rodney Christopher, Mike Burns, and Jason Saul.

Many thanks go to the Morino Institute and the Surdna Foundation for their grants in support of the conference. Special thanks also go to the W. K. Kellogg Foundation, the Rockefeller Brothers Fund, the David and Lucile Packard Foundation, the John C. Whitehead Foundation, and Richard W. Pogue for their general support of NCNE during the period in which this work was carried out. A special thank you is due to Rick Schoff of the Foundation Center for his key role in organizing the book project and moving it to publication. Finally, the present and former staff of NCNE who had a role in this project are also gratefully acknowledged, including Richard Brewster, Sarah Masters, Linda Lumbert, Nicole Lester, Natalija Lovric, Tanya Suphatranand, and Sonu Mulupuru.

Dennis R. Young,
President
National Center on Nonprofit Enterprise

Bernard B. and Eugenia A. Ramsey Professor of Private Enterprise
Andrew Young School of Policy Studies
Georgia State University
Atlanta, GA

March, 2006

Foreword

Mario Morino
Chairman
Venture Philanthropy Partners
Washington, DC

The underlying challenge facing the nonprofit sector today is fiscal sustainability. I come to this conclusion after more than thirteen years creating and supporting nonprofits, driving capital campaigns, and exploring alternate financing sources, and, before that, thirty years building businesses in the private sector. The issue of nonprofit financing, while not new, has taken on greater urgency and garnered increasing attention from nonprofits and funders alike. The reason is the dramatic shift in recent years in the economic, political, and social landscape in which nonprofits operate.

The world of nonprofit finance can best be characterized as uncertain and volatile. The significant growth in the number of nonprofits has increased the competition for funding, in spite of the increases in giving from donors and foundations. Moreover, reductions in public funding are having profound repercussions throughout the nonprofit sector, in fields ranging from education, the arts, health care, and social services. For example, cutbacks have resulted in families losing Medicaid coverage, putting more pressure on nonprofit social service organizations by inadvertently causing an increase in the demand for their services. At the same time, these nonprofits are experiencing funding cuts as well. These factors, combined with increased competition for the donor dollar, create a powerful and challenging multiplier effect for nonprofits.

Even though there is much discussion about business enterprise for nonprofits, capital markets, social investment, venture philanthropy, etc., collectively these sources still represent a very small amount of the funding for nonprofits. Capital—

money to invest in infrastructure to build and grow stronger organizations—remains in acute shortage. And, all this is happening while sea changes reshaping the social sector are under way, whether it is the wave of "new philanthropy" and the thousands of foundations this movement has created, the continuing emergence of social entrepreneurship, or the apparent increased attention to nonprofit accountability.

To survive and thrive in this new, more complex environment nonprofit organizations, especially those addressing our most serious social ills—homelessness, access to education, economic opportunity, and health care—must make profound and often difficult transformations in operations, fund development and financing, and their view of themselves.

Having the proper financial resources year in and year out is the key to enabling nonprofits to continue the vital work they do in our communities and, for those inclined to do so, to grow their efforts over time. Particularly challenging for nonprofit leadership is moving beyond the more traditional view of "fund development"—where bringing in money is mainly the responsibility of the development person or department—toward a more expansive view of a financing strategy that includes multiple revenue sources to fund their organization and move toward fiscal sustainability.

Fiscal sustainability requires long-term financing strategies. It is integral and fundamental to the organization. As such, it must be seen as the responsibility of the lead executive and the board of directors, and cannot and should not be relegated to a fund development person or department.

Nonprofits need to do more to make themselves "attractive to investors" and "fundable," and they need to do so without sacrificing their mission and focus. This includes:

- Demanding solid financial operation and health, with an emphasis on presenting that financial health to donors who may question, or in some cases not trust, the financial integrity or management of nonprofits.

- Operating at a surplus to build up reserves.

- Running a tight financial ship. This requires an understanding of revenues and fully loaded costs (including overhead) at the individual program level in order to know which programs are profitable, which require subsidy, and how aggregated program offerings should be managed.

- Maximizing unrestricted revenues, which most often means investing to build institutional and individual donor development capacity and effectiveness.

- Better "marketing" the value and benefit to prospective donors.

- Building stronger, better-managed organizations with solid boards, good management, clear vision, and focused execution, while at the same time delivering meaningful impact for those they serve.

On the funder side, more effort must come from those who are the sources of capital—individual donors, foundations, and those who advise their giving—to explore new ways to fund the work of nonprofits. Donors and funding organizations must do more to fund entire organizations and not just individual programs. Longer-term commitments should be made by investing in high-performing organizations, sticking with success longer, and resisting the desire to start something new. Similarly, funders should avoid restricting funds to specific uses.

Taking a broader view of the landscape, we must also scrutinize public and tax policies to explore legislation and make changes that could stimulate greater access to capital for nonprofits. Without doubt, the nonprofit sector would benefit from the equivalent of what happened inadvertently in 1986 when pension funds were changed, allowing fund managers to allocate a small percentage of the principal for investments in venture capital. The result was a quantum change in the amount of capital available for venture capital investing. Is there an analog in the nonprofit arena, beyond the current inheritance tax regulations, that could stimulate donors and foundations to provide more capital to high-performing nonprofits?

Donors, nonprofit leaders, foundations, government agencies, business and financial experts, and scholars must engage in a robust dialogue about financial sustainability for nonprofits. *Wise Decision-Making in Uncertain Times: Using Nonprofit Resources Effectively,* and more generally, the work that the National Center on Nonprofit Enterprise (NCNE) has been doing over the years, enriches this critical dialogue by raising important questions and offering meaningful insights into the economics of nonprofit enterprise. This book casts another important stone into the pond, and offers promising potential for a "ripple effect"—specifically, more focus by the academic, business, and nonprofit communities on the critical and fundamental challenge of fiscal sustainability in the nonprofit sector.

Wise Economic Decision-Making for Nonprofits in Uncertain Times: An Overview

Dennis R. Young
Bernard B. and Eugenia A. Ramsey Professor of Private Enterprise
Andrew Young School of Policy Studies
Georgia State University
Atlanta, GA

Introduction

The turn of the millennium was an unnerving and often traumatic time for nonprofit organizations in the United States and around the world. A new political administration in Washington, the events of September 11, 2001, a war on terror and the continuing incidence of terror worldwide, a substantial downturn in the economy followed by a job-stingy recovery, gyrations in the stock market, a war in Iraq, a devastating tsunami in the Indian Ocean, the Gulf Coast hurricanes of 2005, and other developments have rattled and rearranged the political, economic, and social landscapes within which nonprofit organizations do their work and make their critical program, funding, and strategic decisions. Indeed, it is tempting to assert that everything has changed, hence nonprofits need to take a fresh look at all that they do and how they do it.

It is true that much has been altered as a result of recent traumatic events. However, it is also accurate to say that recent developments are part of a much larger picture of continual change, and that such change has three basic parts—long-term trends, short-term volatility, and occasional, unpredictable major shocks. Moreover, nonprofits are regularly subject to all three types of change, and they are best advised to get used to that fact and to find ways of better coping with it. Perhaps the pace of change itself has accelerated; if so, that is all the more reason to prepare nonprofits to cope with change as a matter of course.

In addition, it is important to recognize that nonprofits are not all affected by change in the same way. That is, in addition to understanding the *overall* patterns of the change—the gross trends, the general volatility over time, and the unnerving shocks—nonprofits must determine how their particular environments conform or deviate from these general patterns. For example, a change in government funding over time may reflect an increase for nonprofits in some areas like health care, and a decrease in other areas, such as arts or social services.

Below, we provide an overview of economic, social, and political change and uncertainty as they appear to affect nonprofit organizations in the U.S. in the early twenty-first century. The purpose of this discussion is to provide an appropriate backdrop to considering the contemporary and future challenges of nonprofit economic decision-making as addressed in the remainder of the book. The focus on change and uncertainty highlights some special dimensions of nonprofit economic decision-making; for example, coping with risk and fiscal stress and fostering institutional adaptation and transformation. More broadly, however, acknowledgment of change is arguably required for effective nonprofit economic decision-making across the board; for instance, in raising and investing funds, in determining competitive strategy, in managing human resources, and in measuring and evaluating performance. In this sense, the fact that we live in "interesting times," as the Chinese saying goes, serves merely as a strong incentive for nonprofits to improve the manner in which they make their critical and ongoing resource-related decisions, in all their facets.

The Breezes, Winds, and Storms of Change

It may come as a surprise to many in the nonprofit sector that the economy as a whole has actually been more stable in recent decades than it has been in the past. While the business cycle has not been eliminated by any means, it appears to have been substantially tamed in modern industrialized countries (specifically the so-called G7 countries—Canada, France, Italy, Germany, Japan, the United Kingdom, and the United States). At least this is the general conclusion of distinguished economists writing for a 2003 symposium sponsored by the Federal Reserve Bank of Kansas City. In particular, in the U.S. as measured by variations (standard deviations) from the mean temporal trends, volatility in GDP, nonagricultural employment, inflation, and short-term interest rates have all declined steadily and substantially over the period from 1960 to 2002 (Stock and Watson, 2003). Moreover, the durations of periods of economic recovery have been expanding while those of economic recession have been contracting, while long-term inflation forecasts have been dropping. In other words, the economic environment is more stable now than in the relatively recent past, presumably making it easier to plan for the future. But lest we become too complacent, the economists that offer this analysis also issue a strong cautionary note:

> Whether this shift is permanent or transitory is . . . difficult to know. . . . There is ample reason to suspect that much of the shift is the result of a period of unusually quiescent macroeconomic shocks, such as the absence of major supply disruptions. Under this more cautious view, a reemergence of shocks as large as those of the 1970s could lead to a substantial increase in cyclical volatility and to a reversal of the favorable shift . . . that we have enjoyed for the past twenty years. (Stock and Watson, 2003, pp. 46–47)

It may also be a surprise to many in the nonprofit sector that in several ways social and economic problems of the U.S. population appear to be getting better rather than worse over the long term. Since the 1970s, a preponderance of indicators of health, education, income, crime, urban life, and family life show long-term trends towards improvement, though with lots of variation among subgroups and substantial backing and filling over time (McDonald, 2004). So while the prospect of changes for the worse are most frightening for nonprofit decision-makers, changes for the better often may constitute a more realistic scenario.

Nonetheless, if the economy is indeed less volatile overall, and even if overall indicators of social and economic health are generally rising, this is probably of little solace to contemporary nonprofit sector decision-makers as they struggle with the challenges of making the best economic decisions for their organizations going forward. The reasons for this are severalfold. First, the economy and the society at large are certainly changing in systematic ways that affect nonprofit organizations. These trends need to be understood and appreciated before appropriate choices can be made. Second, economic volatility is a phenomenon that may be modest in the aggregate but more virulent at the local, subsector, or organizational levels. While aggregates such as total national government funding, giving, volunteering, or returns on investment may follow fairly smooth patterns and trends over time, those same variables can gyrate wildly for particular organizations or in specific locations or fields of service. So too, mean social or economic trends, whether positive or negative, may belie substantial local variation. The law of large numbers tends to help out in reducing the variance over large populations compared to smaller samples or subsets. Organizational managers and leaders, therefore, may face greater uncertainty than sector- or economy-level policymakers. Third, there is the question again of external shocks, which can have effects that are more serious in one part of the economy or society than another. For example, a natural disaster that impacts the stock market can have magnified effects on nonprofit institutions that depend more heavily on returns from their endowments. Additionally, parts of the nonprofit sector can be more greatly affected than others. For instance, the attacks of 9/11 led to dislocations in patterns of charitable giving—while overall giving was initially stimulated, some charities not associated with causes connected to relief of victims or other contingencies of 9/11 were hurt as giving shifted to those specifically connected with 9/11. Conversely, some charities, such as the American Red Cross and the Salvation Army, were overwhelmed with new contributions which they were initially unprepared to handle (Greene and Wolverton, 2002). Fortunately, in the tsunami experience of 2004, some of the lessons learned from 9/11 helped to ameliorate some of these problems (Cohen, 2004).

Two of the three dimensions of change—temporal trends and sudden shocks— have been relatively well documented for the nonprofit sector over the last few decades, although obviously the problem of forecasting future shocks is inherently perplexing if not intractable. The issues of both volatility and variations around temporal trend lines have been less well analyzed or documented because they require a second level of analysis—determining not just what is happening on average over time with a particular variable of interest, but also measuring and reporting the variations that exist around the aggregate trends. While technically feasible to calculate in many cases, relatively little volatility data on nonprofit sector-relevant environmental variables are actually available. Certainly, this suggests a fruitful area for future research (see Chapter 14). Geographic and subsectoral variations around trends have been somewhat better documented, though there is much left unattended here as well. With these limitations in mind, the changing economic environment of nonprofit organizations in the U.S. is considered below, in order to identify trends, volatility, variations, and potential shocks that are likely to concern contemporary nonprofit decision-makers.

One clear dynamic is the impressive growth of the nonprofit sector over the past several decades. For instance, from 1977 to 1998, the number of nonprofit organizations in the U.S. increased by approximately 45 percent, while paid employment in the sector increased by 95 percent during the same period (Weitzman et al., 2002). This compares with a growth of approximately 25 percent in the U.S. population as a whole over the period. The implications of this growth are not entirely transparent. However, it is clear that the sector now competes for a larger share of national resources than it did in earlier times, and inevitably there is more competition among nonprofits for those resources. At the same time, nonprofits are more of an economic and political force to be reckoned with. In addition to competing with one another, they now have more opportunities to collaborate with one another to pursue common goals, they have greater potential collective leverage in the marketplace, and through advocacy they have a stronger voice in the public arena. The growth also makes the sector a bigger target for those with public agendas that conflict with nonprofit interests.

Several researchers have paid special attention to the changing character of the economic environment of nonprofit organizations. For example, Weisbrod (1998) and colleagues acknowledged changes in the funding environment of nonprofits in the U.S.; specifically, limitations and changes in philanthropic and governmental support which seem to have encouraged increased commercial activity by these organizations. And in their study of nonprofit organizational change in the Minneapolis-St. Paul metropolitan area, Galaskiewicz and Bielefeld (1998) reviewed both the external shocks and trends that have changed the economic environment of nonprofit organizations in the U.S. since the 1970s, attempting to explain with different strands of theory how nonprofit organizations adapted to these changes in a variety of ways. This study provides a good example of how aggregate trends can mask local volatility and variation. Specifically, while the economy of Minnesota suffered more than most in the recession and subsequent recovery of the 1980s, it also prospered more than most in the economic boom of the 1990s. Galaskiewicz's and Bielefeld's acknowledgment of the shocks experienced by the national nonprofit sector also captures how shocks as well as trends can be magnified or focused on the sector, as compared with the economy as a whole:

> . . . the time frame for this analysis spanned the Reagan revolution, privatization, the New Federalism, two recessions, the AIDS epidemic, church scandals, Aramony and the United Way, a scathing indictment of the sector by the *Philadelphia Inquirer,* a complete reorganization of the health care field, Newt Gingrich, and efforts to rescind property tax exemptions in some states. It certainly has been an exciting period, and it would be foolish not to acknowledge that each of these events impacted the charitable sector in important ways—stimulating demand, raising doubts among donors, burying nonprofit managers in red tape, and giving birth to new nonprofits. (p. ix)

Perhaps the most extensive description of the changing environment of nonprofits is documented by Lester Salamon (2002) and his colleagues in *The State of Nonprofit America.* This project is a comprehensive attempt to capture the important trends and developments affecting the future well-being and effectiveness of nonprofit organizations in the United States, hence various contributions to this study are worth reviewing in some detail in the text below.

While the project is focused on long-term discernible trends, its analyses reveal numerous shocks at various points in time, and substantial instances of volatility and variation. Many of these developments have important implications for economic decision-making at the level of the individual nonprofit organization.

GOVERNMENT FUNDING

One important area of ongoing change for nonprofits is government funding. In the social services, as Smith (2002) points out, the pattern—beginning with federal cutbacks during the Reagan administration—continues to evolve. In general, government funding of nonprofit social services has increased steadily since that time, holding its own as an overall source of support for nonprofit social service organizations as this subsector has grown. However, the composition of that funding has changed and its future continues to be uncertain. Medicaid, as well as several new programs, now play a much greater role in supporting social services as diverse as in-home care, counseling and drug abuse, and long-term care for the disabled and mentally ill. Programmatic emphasis has shifted from traditional social service and welfare, to training, day care, and other services that support the theme of "welfare to work" or which can be logically related to health care. The form of government support also has evolved, from traditional direct funding of services, to intergovernmental grant programs, to insurance programs, to an array of devices including tax credits, loans, and tax-exempt bonds. Many of the latter "consumer-side" financing strategies have shifted the source of uncertainty facing nonprofit organizations from the unpredictability of government funding *per se* to the vagaries of consumer behavior in the marketplace.

Nor is such a complex evolution of government funding of nonprofits limited to the social services. As Wyszomirski (2002) indicates, government funding for the arts has also followed a complicated as well as volatile path in recent decades. Since the 1970s, funding has shifted from the National Endowment for the Arts and the National Endowment for the Humanities to state and local arts agencies, while overall funding has continued to grow. The distribution of arts funding has, however, been very uneven, with some states and localities much more generous than others.

Similar to social services, the field of low-income housing and community development has moved more towards a system of consumer-side subsidies, via Section 8 housing vouchers and low-income housing tax credits. As Vidal (2002) reports:

> . . . demand-side subsidies make life considerably more difficult for nonprofit
> developers. This is so because their developments become more vulnerable finan-
> cially, since they must either attract and serve eligible moderate-income families or
> compete for a very limited supply of low-income certificate-holding households.
> This problem particularly affects nonprofits that work in relatively soft housing
> markets where vacancies in privately owned developments are plentiful. (p. 231)

Governmental funding for nonprofit organizations working in the field of
international assistance (relief and development) exhibits its own special patterns of
change, including longer-term trends, reactions to shocks, and short-term
volatility. As Forman and Stoddard (2002) note, "Official aid funding has not kept
up with national economic growth. . . . [As] a percentage of government
expenditure, overall aid funding . . . by OECD countries peaked in 1992 and then
steadily declined through 1997 . . ." and is predicted to continue its downward
slide (p. 250). The sea change in this field has been a shift to private sector
development which "has NGOs making efforts to forge new partnerships with
corporations . . ." (p. 251). Again, however, the pattern is uneven, with major U.S.
nonprofit relief and development agencies remaining highly dependent on
(federal) government sources of funding. Finally, another important shift is
emerging as a result of 9/11 that has had a dampening effect on private sector
activity while focusing government more heavily on security and military issues:
"NGOs are steeling themselves for uncertain, yet assuredly tough, times ahead, as
aid funding becomes more focused on specific geographic regions, competition
between grantees increases, and organizations attempt to remain distinct from
political-military agendas and operations" (p. 249).

The prominence of government funding for nonprofits continues to raise the
question of whether, over time, this funding exerts a chilling effect on nonprofits'
involvement in advocacy and political activism. If so, nonprofits could face serious
trade offs between seeking government support, either collectively or as individual
organizations, and promoting independent positions on important issues. As
recently as the mid-1990s, members of Congress sought to limit the advocacy
work of nonprofit organizations receiving federal funds (Reid, 1999). However,
evidence that government funding has muted nonprofits' voices in public affairs is
not conclusive (see Chaves, Stephens, and Galaskiewicz, 2004; and Berry and
Arons, 2003). Indeed, there is reason to believe that nonprofits retain their ability
to structure themselves in ways that maintain their flexibility for political activism
(Reid and Kerlin, 2003). In some ways, the latter is also a worrisome trend for
nonprofits. For example, in the 2004 presidential election, nonprofit 527 groups
figured prominently, if indirectly, in campaign fund financing, as vehicles of
partisan politics. Whether such activity is enough to paint the entire sector with a
partisan tone that alienates its contributors remains to be seen. Certainly, the

evolving issue of political activism of nonprofits, and how it is affected by government funding and partisanship politics, is one that is important to monitor, given its potentially broad impacts in the future on both the resource support and the mission effectiveness of nonprofit organizations.

A broader view of the recent changes in government's support of nonprofit organizations is provided by Gronbjerg and Salamon (2002). In the area of government spending, for example, these authors discern several crosscurrents. First, outside of the health field, there has been a substantial retrenchment in federal government support in areas where nonprofit organizations are active. Indeed, by the late 1990s, the real value of federal support in fields such as education, social services, international assistance, and community development were still below 1980 levels. Second, the government has opened fields of nonprofit service to market competition. In a number of areas, such as home health care and HMOs, the government's preference for funding nonprofits has been weakened or eliminated. Third, the forms of government assistance have shifted substantially from producer to consumer subsidies, through voucher, tax credit, loan guarantee, and other programs, creating further competitive pressures on nonprofits. Fourth, new payment systems tied to managed care and performance measurement have been integrated into government funding arrangements, affecting the levels of payments, requiring new management systems, and yielding advantages to for-profit competitors adept at information management and cost control. Fifth, new policies of welfare reform and charitable choice have shifted the market environment substantially for nonprofits, moving resources from traditional income and service support for low-income populations, where nonprofits have traditionally been strong, to work readiness and employment services, where nonprofits' competitive advantage is weaker. Meanwhile, "charitable choice" policies have opened up competition to a new category of faith-based service providers.

In the area of taxation there have also been major shifts affecting the economic welfare of nonprofit organizations. Since 1980, personal income tax rates have been lowered and raised and lowered again, but have generally trended downward. Lower rates, and other changes such as tightened record-keeping requirements, have undercut incentives for charitable giving, while oscillation in rates and in other provisions such as the above-the-line deduction for non-itemizers, has created new uncertainties for nonprofit planners. Meanwhile, other tax developments, such as the reduction of federal estate taxes and restrictions of local property tax exemptions for nonprofits, have undermined charitable giving and threatened to increase costs of nonprofit operation.

Finally, in the regulatory arena, Gronbjerg and Salamon (2002) point out two important trends—the tightening of regulation of charitable solicitation by state attorneys general and, as previously noted, the increased pressure at the federal level to restrict nonprofit advocacy activity. More recently, financial scandals in the corporate sector have resulted in legislation to improve corporate governance, namely the Sarbanes-Oxley Act, which requires chief executives and financial officers of a publicly traded company to sign off on corporate financial statements, restricts insider transactions and conflicts of interest, requires disclosure of various kinds of supporting information, offers whistle-blower protections, and proscribes document destruction (BoardSource and Independent Sector, 2003). While this act does not apply directly to nonprofits, it has led to intensive efforts of sector self-scrutiny in the realization that such legal provisions could easily be extended to cover nonprofits directly. While these kinds of developments have proceeded in fits and starts over the past decade or more, they create considerable uncertainty for nonprofits, and if not successfully addressed, threaten to dampen their ability to attract charitable donations and other resources in the future.

Finally, while the work of Gronbjerg and Salamon (2002) and the others involved in *The State of Nonprofit America* project focuses on basic trends and shifts in government support of nonprofits, there remains a question of whether a basic turning point has been reached in the U.S. government's role in society and its ability to support the social needs of its citizens. A recent analysis by Laurence Kotlikoff (2004), based in part on research originally commissioned by the U.S. Treasury Department, suggests that the "fiscal gap" of the federal government, defined as the difference between the federal government's future expenditures and future receipts, may now have grown, because of various spending and taxation decisions of the Bush administration, to the point where it is beyond remedy without radical future increases in taxation, reductions in programs, or some form of government default on its obligations. Were any combinations of these bleak scenarios to materialize, the nonprofit sector could potentially experience further dislocations.

DEVELOPMENTS IN PHILANTHROPY

While secular trends indicate that charitable giving is becoming a less significant proportion of nonprofit income over time, such revenue promises to remain a critical component of nonprofit support for a number of reasons. First, in absolute terms, philanthropy will continue to grow as the economy grows, constituting a sort of bedrock for nonprofit support, even as its proportional representation may continue to diminish. Second, charitable support reflects a core value of giving that distinguishes nonprofits from other types of enterprises. Third, with government funding constantly under a cloud, philanthropy remains a cushioning source of resources at critical times. Fourth, philanthropy, especially large gifts from foundations, corporations, and major donors, has a leveraging effect, serving as a source of investment capital for nonprofits seeking to build or change programs that ultimately rely on other sources of income. For these reasons, changes in the magnitude or character of philanthropy constitute an important aspect of the nonprofit economic environment.

Smith (2002) points out two important structural changes in philanthropic support in the social services—the relative decline of United Ways as sources of social service funding over the past three decades, and more recently, the propensity of some foundations to adopt a venture capital approach to funding, working more closely with small groups of selected grantees to help ensure their economic viability as well as program effectiveness. Clearly these developments have required nonprofit social service organizations to rethink relationships with their institutional funders. In the arts too, Wyszomirski (2002) observes that many foundations have altered their approaches, putting more emphasis on impacts and outcomes of arts and cultural programming rather than supporting arts for arts sake; hence, they are paying more attention to supporting the infrastructure and viability of arts organizations. Lenkowsky (2002) confirms Smith's observations about United Way, noting that, in general, traditional charity federations have declined or stagnated since the 1980s, in terms of gifts received and their share of overall giving to nonprofits. On the other hand, the number of so-called "alternative funds" that address environmental and other specialized areas, while still relatively small, has been growing quickly. Meanwhile, the United Way movement remains significant, and its recent shifts in strategic focus towards the solution of specific social problems rather than just communitywide fundraising, could ultimately stabilize its role in helping to fund nonprofit human service organizations.

The number and size of grantmaking foundations have also been growing impressively. Assets have quadrupled since 1981. While still providing less than 20 percent of charitable giving, foundation and corporate giving are becoming a more significant part of nonprofits' resource environment over time. Another interesting development, however, is the transformation of one major grantmaking foundation, the Pew Charitable Trusts, from a private foundation into a public charity, signaling a possible constriction and reorientation of its external grantmaking and its position as a potential competitor with other charities for soliciting funds from the public. However, the stated intent of this change is the latitude that the foundation gains in providing the public with information and advancing solutions on important policy issues (Pew Charitable Trusts, 2005).

Nonetheless, if this were to signal a trend on the part of other major foundations, the implications for foundation funding of operating nonprofits could be significant, since most foundation assets and grant dollars are concentrated in the largest two hundred foundations.

More generally, Hodgkinson (2002) summarizes a number of key contemporary trends in giving and volunteering. Overall, giving doubled in real terms between 1971 and 2000. At the same time, it has declined as a share of national wealth and as a share of nonprofit income. There has also been a shift, since 1970, in the objects of giving, towards higher education and the arts, and away from human services, health, and international aid. Obviously these changes have different implications for nonprofits in different fields of service, in addition to generating overall concerns about the reliability of giving as a mainstay of nonprofit finance.

Other trends cited by Hodgkinson affect the cost conditions under which nonprofits operate. In particular, fundraising has become more professionalized and more competitive, requiring nonprofits to spend more to raise charitable dollars. In addition, fundraising has become more complex and more specialized, featuring many new vehicles for giving, including various forms of planned giving. Finally, donor-advised funds have grown in popularity, requiring nonprofits to pay more attention to donor preferences and to devote more resources to donor cultivation and advising, and fund administration. The entry of major for-profit securities firms such as Fidelity and Vanguard into this field poses a particular concern for community foundations and other nonprofits that have traditionally administered such funds.

Certain key demographic and socioeconomic trends also promise to have important effects on philanthropic giving in the future. One development is the growing inequality of income among Americans that, coupled with reduced tax rates for the wealthy, Hodgkinson argues, could erode giving while increasing the intensity of social problems that nonprofit organizations will be asked to address. Another is the large intergenerational transfer of wealth that is anticipated to take place over the next half century in the U.S., which could result in $6 trillion in additional bequests to charity. The manifestation of that windfall, however, is clouded by uncertainty deriving from the phasing out of estate taxes, the difficulty of assessing the philanthropic propensities of the younger generation and future generations, and the alternative demands on the resources of future retirees as they age and as the public and private threads of their safety nets are tested.

The availability of volunteer resources for nonprofit organizations is another economic issue of great importance to nonprofit organizations, and the focus of several important trends and developments (Hodgkinson, 2002). Certain demographic shifts, for example, affect the supply of volunteers. The growing engagement of women in the labor force over the past several decades has diminished their availability for intensive volunteering. The graying of the population promises to magnify the pool of older volunteers, although this is potentially dampened by an increasing tendency to postpone retirement. The growing civic engagement of for-profit corporations has led to an increasing pool of volunteers from the business sector. On the other hand, declining rates of volunteering among college students in the 1980s has led to a number of governmental and nonprofit initiatives to engage youth in volunteer service. Policy initiatives such as the Corporation for National Service and the Points of Light Foundation appear to have positively impacted the levels of volunteering among youth during the 1990s (Hodgkinson, 2002).

Not only are the level and composition of the supply of volunteers changing in various ways, but so are the economic requirements associated with engaging and utilizing volunteers as an effective resource in carrying out the work of nonprofit organizations. In particular, volunteer management is becoming more professionalized and more sophisticated, often requiring paid staff as well as substantial technological sophistication to recruit, train, deploy, oversee, reward, and retain volunteers.

DEMOGRAPHY

As noted in relation to giving and volunteering, shifts in the composition and character of the population over time can have important impacts on the demand and supply of key nonprofit resources. Dighe (2002) identifies several demographic trends with potentially significant implications for nonprofit economic decision-making in the U.S.—increasing population diversity, aging of the population, and changing family structure.

The American population is becoming increasingly ethnically diverse and multiracial. More than 40 percent of young persons are now "minorities" and by mid-century these minorities in aggregate are expected to become the majority. This diversification will inevitably have important economic consequences for nonprofits, although the precise nature of these consequences is difficult to predict. Certainly, marketing strategies and resources will have to become more diversified and more targeted to the needs and tastes of a wider variety of audiences. Similarly, nonprofits will need to devote resources to diversifying, and managing the diversity of, their work forces, volunteers, trustees, and other human resources on which they depend. Indeed, "diversity management" is a new specialty now being taught in some universities. Yet, this is a bigger issue still for the sector as a whole where, historically, minority issues have been important concerns but where minorities themselves have been underrepresented in the establishment and leadership of nonprofit organizations and the choices of social issues addressed. A more diverse population will argue for a more diverse nonprofit sector over time.

So too, the aging of the population will continue to affect not only the volunteer resources available to nonprofits but also the markets for nonprofit services and the priorities for investing and deploying nonprofit resources. An older population will have increased health and social needs, signifying expected growth in some subsectors such as home health and nursing care. Other new markets are emerging as well, such as programs for seniors in colleges and universities. Nonprofits in many different fields will have to consider the implications of aging for both their work forces and audiences. Moreover, as Kotlikoff (2004) points out, the aging of the population in the U.S. implies huge increases in health-related expenditures and social security supported by a diminishing base of working-age tax payers. The implication here is that potential cutbacks in these social supports could magnify the service burdens on nonprofits in the face of constricted government funding.

The changing age and ethnic distributions of the population intersect with another demographic variable of great importance to nonprofit organizations—the religious orientations of U.S. citizens. Since the beginnings of the republic, religion has been a major motivating and organizing force in charitable giving as well as in the development of nonprofit institutions. If the religiosity of future generations differs from that of the current generation, or if faster growing ethnic groups view charitable giving through a different religious lens, the charitable resources available to the sector could be significantly affected. Moreover, religious groups have been growing in influence in the public policy sphere. Evangelical Christian groups, for example, are said to have had an important influence on the 2004 election. Certainly recent initiatives to expand government funding to faith-based institutions in the social services signals the potential impact on the sector of changes in the religious focus of the citizenry. The case of the faith-based initiative is informative on this score. Presently, religious congregations are involved in social service delivery in only a modest way (Chaves, 2002). However, were this to become a major thrust, it could have a number of important implications, including greater competition for traditional social service organizations, and significant challenges to religious organizations themselves, including resource development, public accountability, and staff capacity.

Finally, changing family structures hold potential implications for nonprofit economic decision-making. Growing numbers of single-parent and dual-income families require enhanced support services ranging from day care to social service counseling to information about educational and arts and cultural opportunities. Moreover, the human resource policies of nonprofit organizations will have to accommodate new demands on workers dictated by changing family structures and responsibilities.

TECHNOLOGY

Modern and rapidly improving communications, information, and other technologies continue to transform the economy as a whole in many ways— changing the nature of products and services, the costs of doing business, and the scope and character of markets themselves. The implications for nonprofits have been and will continue to be enormous, though not easily predictable. Nonprofits will continually have to reassess their decisions regarding the technologies and resources they employ to produce services, and how they market and mobilize resources to support those services, how they maintain the technological capacities and information they need to remain competitive, and how they respond to social demands deriving from new technological possibilities. For example, educational institutions face new choices in delivering educational products through the Internet and via modernized electronic classrooms, in collaborating with other institutions or outsourcing certain functions such as library services via electronic networks, in raising funds through electronic solicitation versus conventional means, in governing themselves through electronic versus conventional ways for convening and communicating with boards and advisory committees, in improving productivity decisions with new equipment, networks, or systems and concomitant changes in personnel, in addressing new (global) markets of students made possible through electronic access, and in revamping campuses to accommodate demands for energy conservation, environmental standards, and information infrastructure.

In general, changes in technology are affecting not only how nonprofits develop and deploy their economic resources, but also whom they serve and what they provide. For example, the information overload facing consumers and citizens as a result of the proliferation of new communications technologies may argue for an expanded role of nonprofits as trustworthy "info-mediaries" rather than as conventional service providers (Te'eni and Young, 2003).

Finally, technology is fundamentally affecting the political milieu in which nonprofits operate. Political advocacy and political fundraising now take place on the Internet. To be effective as policy advocates, and indeed to raise funds for their own policy work, nonprofits must now be technically savvy, prepared to adapt the latest communications technologies to their own purposes, and prepared to defend their positions against other technically savvy interest groups.

SEPTEMBER 11TH

In this review of broad trends and developments affecting the economic environment of nonprofit organizations, it is important to return to the events of September 11, 2001. Seen from the perspective of a few years later, there seems no doubt that these were defining events for our era that not only caused immediate tremors and dislocations but which also set in motion long-term shock waves, which the nonprofit sector will be dealing with for many years.

First, it is worth reviewing in further detail some of the short-term disruption caused by 9/11. Clearly certain groups of nonprofit organizations were more affected than others. Certain relief agencies were inundated with contributions as well as demands for assistance, and new organizations were created to address the crisis and its immediate aftermath, while other organizations suffered in the short run from a diversion of charitable and other funds from one set of priorities to another. Certainly nonprofit organizations in lower Manhattan were particularly affected, some having to close up shop or move their operations in the months following the attack, while others tried to help out in whatever way they could (Derryck and Abzug, 2002). In addition, nonprofits in the arts and cultural field, or those in fields such as arts and culture in New York that depended on tourism were strongly impacted by the ensuing contraction of travel and tourism, while local cultural institutions in other places may have gained patronage from the diversion of travel and tourism plans. So too, nonprofits in fields such as higher education and research, which depend highly on international exchange, suffered important losses and disruptions.

Painful as they have been, however, most of these short-term effects have been dissipated or accommodated over time. What really distinguishes 9/11 as a defining event for our era is the set of shock waves that it has set in motion for the long term. The analysis of impacts on New York nonprofits points to one of these waves—a heightened awareness of the need for nonprofits to embed themselves in supportive networks. In particular, Derryck and Abzug (2002) found that those organizations that belonged to a larger supporting infrastructure such as a federation or association were better positioned to absorb the economic shocks of traumatic events such as these, compared to unaffiliated organizations. While the imperatives and tendencies towards greater collaboration were already manifest in the nonprofit sector (Salamon, 2002), the events of September 11th reinforced this movement and highlighted its economic significance.

Certainly, 9/11 also set in motion a long-term change in priorities for the nonprofit sector. Issues of international understanding and cooperation, religious tolerance, and civil liberties have become more significant, as the forces leading to 9/11 and the governmental policies following from it all threaten to undermine these basic democratic values. Particular damage has been done, as well, to Islamic charities, with legitimate ones caught up in the same net as ones allegedly used as fronts to finance terrorism. It is unclear at this writing whether this is a permanent long-term fissure in the American charitable sector or one that will be healed in the near term.

Other kinds of costs resulting from 9/11 have had much broader and longer-term impacts. Security in particular has become a widespread concern for any nonprofit that utilizes major capital facilities such as a school, recreation center, theater, concert hall, hospital, library, research lab, or day care center, as a major part of its operations. Resources once available for program now go for security guards, surveillance systems, reinforced architecture, and training of personnel in security procedures. This security awareness and reorientation has now become ingrained into nonprofit planning and represents a permanent if still evolving allocation of nonprofit resources.

Finally, the events of September 11th appear to have strongly contributed to, and perhaps solidified, a permanent change in the way that the public views nonprofits and their stewardship of resources. While nonprofits were recognized for their magnificent performance under fire during the crisis, their weaknesses and failings were also magnified (Greene and Wolverton, 2002). The Salvation Army illustrated both effects. On the one hand, its relief work at this critical time brought deserved public praise and heightened appreciation for the work of nonprofit organizations in our society. On the other hand, the Salvation Army's promise to help all those in need was beyond its capacity to deliver, leading to severe criticism and organizational crisis until new systems could be installed to handle the overload and clean up the backlog. All this has contributed to a sea change in the public's attitudes towards nonprofits and their management of economic resources. Nonprofits are now more visible and also less likely to have their shortcomings sympathetically evaluated. Performance measurement is now the norm, and the special status of nonprofits as charitable institutions appears to count for less than it did in earlier times. Recent research by Paul Light (2004) indicates that the public views nonprofit organizations as inefficient and unable to steward their economic resources wisely. Accountability for effective deployment and utilization of economic resources, while not a new expectation of nonprofit organizations, has been ratcheted upward as an accelerating force affecting nonprofit economic decision-making, magnified by the aftermath of 9/11.

Uncertainty, Change, and Nonprofit Economic Decision-Making

There are discrete periods in time when the various crosscurrents of change—economic, demographic, technological, political, and so on, converge to cause extraordinary conditions favorable or unfavorable to nonprofit organizations. For example, the period 2001-2002 was described by some as a "perfect storm" where key indicators of the economy, politics, and social unrest all "went south," putting operating nonprofits in a terrible bind, unable to find sufficient support in philanthropy, government funding, investments, or even the marketplace for goods and services (Schram, 2002). While those moments are rare, change itself is certainly not, and nonprofit economic decision-makers always face uncertainty and must continually be prepared to reconsider their key choices. In the remainder of this book, we will provide a wide ranging tour of how this perspective manifests itself in key areas of nonprofit economic decision-making.

We start with an optimistic view, articulated by Reynold Levy, that if nonprofits adopt a suitably entrepreneurial mind set they can best take advantage of the new opportunities created by change. Levy argues that, in the current environment, nonprofits can select from among a variety of market-based strategies to ensure their sustainability and impact. He also cautions that nonprofit organizations ignore market signals at their peril and that they can learn to usefully adapt strategies from the business sector, and from other commercially successful nonprofits.

With Levy's philosophical encouragement, the next three chapters consider three operational imperatives required for nonprofits to successfully manage in the contemporary nonprofit marketplace: the ability to measure performance, the sophistication to manage risk, and the capacity to manage fiscal stress. In Chapter 3, Debra Mesch and Jim McClelland describe the increasing pressures on nonprofits to measure their performance and the special challenges and potential compromises that this may entail. They suggest a variety of ways in which nonprofits can improve their measurement and evaluation practices in order to improve their performance and accountability in a dynamic environment. They also highlight the dilemmas of performance measurement and the trade offs that can emerge between performance and integrity when pressures for performance measurement threaten an organization's ability to stay true to its mission or maintain its basic values.

In Chapter 4, Gene Scanlan and Robin Dillon-Merrill describe the various kinds of risk faced by nonprofit leaders and managers as they address economic decisions in an environment of change and uncertainty. Interestingly, in view of the entrepreneurial mind set encouraged by Levy, Scanlan and Dillon-Merrill argue that nonprofit leaders tend to be inordinately risk averse and that they could often make more effective decisions if they better understood the nature of risk. Hence, they offer improved ways for nonprofit leaders to assess risk, and they describe decision tools that can be applied to making better decisions involving risk.

In Chapter 5, Frederick Lane considers various approaches that nonprofits can take to managing fiscal stress, including programmatic strategies that change the mix of services and clients, financial strategies that seek more revenues or reduced costs, and organizational strategies that look to external relationships and changes in internal structure. He further divides combinations of these strategies into two broad categories—those designed to resist organizational decline through resource acquisition and related initiatives, and those designed to smooth adjustments to economic pressures through cost containment and cutbacks.

The abilities to measure performance, manage risk, and cope with fiscal stress are necessary for nonprofits to survive and prosper month to month and year to year in a changing and uncertain environment. In the longer-term, however, nonprofits need to build their organizational and management capacities in order to best adapt themselves to future environmental circumstances and indeed to shape those circumstances to become more favorable. The next three chapters address these longer-term issues along three lines—investment, institutional collaboration, and public sector support.

In Chapter 6, John Zietlow reviews and critiques current nonprofit investment practices and offers various ways to improve them, based on modern investment principles adapted to the distinct issues facing nonprofits in a dynamic environment. Zietlow gives specific attention to the development of investment policy statements (IPSs) and how such statements can help nonprofits design and manage their investment portfolios in ways that fit their particular circumstances.

In Chapter 7, Steven Rathgeb Smith considers the changing environmental conditions that have led to heightened interest in collaborations and partnerships among nonprofit organizations and between nonprofits, businesses, and government. He reviews current experience on how nonprofits pursue such collaborations and what principles apply to achieving effective collaborations. Acknowledging that nonprofits sometimes need to undergo fundamental structural changes in order to adapt to new circumstances, Smith offers practical advice for achieving successful organizational transformations.

In Chapter 8, Betsy Reid recognizes that government is a major element of the changing environment of many nonprofit organizations. Accordingly, Reid documents the trends that have increased the importance of advocacy activity by nonprofit organizations, including the need to influence governmental resource allocation and public policies affecting service delivery, and to respond to increased public scrutiny. Further, Reid identifies the key challenges, and successful strategies, for nonprofits to become more effective advocates by building their public credibility, their capacity to support advocacy, their ability to shape public debate, and their influence over taxation and regulation policies.

In the next part of the book, we turn our attention to grantmaking foundations, both as key elements in the dynamic environment of operating nonprofit organizations, and as nonprofit institutions which themselves have to cope with change and uncertainty in their own realms of economic decision-making. In Chapter 9, Jim Ferris considers foundation grantmaking in the context of the business cycle, ebbs and flows in the economy at large, and the long-term ability of nonprofits to cope with change. Ferris considers the ability of foundations to conserve and build their own resources, and their role in helping nonprofits to address fiscal stress during difficult economic times. He concludes that foundations are best advised to focus on long-term social investments and to leverage their resources so that nonprofits can build their capacities to sustain themselves over the long term.

In Chapter 10, Greg Cantori considers the continuum of possibilities open to foundations in their grantmaking and investment decisions, as they seek to maximize their effectiveness in a changing environment. These options range from traditional project grants through program-related investments, venture philanthropy, and social venture capital provision. Cantori documents current practices and offers new frameworks, including portfolio (Swiss Army knife) and social investment approaches, for guiding the use of alternative strategies. Overall, Cantori analyzes the challenges of such "holistic grantmaking" from both the funder and recipient organization perspectives, noting that nonprofit grant applicants as well as foundations themselves require assistance in preparing themselves to take advantage of nontraditional forms of support.

The next three chapters of the book recognize that the environment for many nonprofits is also shaped substantially by their relationships with the business sector. In Chapter 11, Arthur Brooks and Alison Louie consider the variety of ways in which businesses and nonprofits are engaged with one another and the importance of these relationships in a changing economy. They further examine how these relationships can be maintained and their benefits maximized. In particular, they ask what healthy and unhealthy nonprofit-business relationships look like, and what guidance can be provided for establishing such relationships and maintaining them over time through investment in communications and other means.

In Chapter 12, Jeff Brudney recognizes that an increasingly important element of business support for nonprofits takes the form of pro bono volunteering by professional workers, such as lawyers and accountants. Brudney asks how pro bono volunteers can be efficiently matched with nonprofit organizations that need their help. He reviews a spectrum of procedures used in practice and offers a framework for evaluating alternative approaches, based on the special nature of pro bono work compared to traditional volunteering.

In Chapter 13, Kevin Kearns addresses more broadly the influences of a changing marketplace on nonprofit economic decision-making. In particular, he surveys the various ways in which nonprofits increasingly compete with one another and with businesses and government, and he reviews the special challenges that such competition creates for nonprofits in different fields and circumstances, identifying key areas of competitive vulnerability for the future. Finally, Kearns offers a set of management concepts and tools to help nonprofits address the challenges posed by such vulnerability.

To conclude, in Chapter 14, this author highlights our considerable areas of remaining ignorance, and suggests a research agenda to continue to build the knowledge base on nonprofit economic decision-making under circumstances of uncertainty and change.

References

Berry, Jeffrey M., with David Arons. 2003. *A Voice for Nonprofits*. Washington, DC: Brookings Institution Press.

BoardSource and Independent Sector. 2003. *The Sarbanes-Oxley Act and Implications for Nonprofit Organizations*. Washington, DC: BoardSource and Independent Sector.

Cohen, Rick. 2004. "The Tsunami Tsunami: The Charitable and Political Response to the Disaster." *The Nonprofit Quarterly*, Winter 2004, pp. 76–78.

Chaves, Mark. 2002. "Religious Congregations." Chapter 8 in Lester M. Salamon (ed.), *The State of Nonprofit America*, Washington, DC: Brookings Institution Press, pp. 275–298.

Chaves, Mark; Laura Stephens, and Joseph Galaskiewicz. 2004. "Does Government Funding Suppress Nonprofits' Political Activity?" *American Sociological Review*, 69:2, April 2004, pp. 292–317.

Derryck, Dennis, and Rikki Abzug. 2002. "Lessons from Crisis: New York City Nonprofits Post-September 11." *The Nonprofit Quarterly,* 9:1, Spring 2002, pp. 6–10.

Dighe, Atul. 2002. "Demographic and Technological Imperatives." Chapter 16 in Lester M. Salamon (ed.), *The State of Nonprofit America,* Washington, DC: Brookings Institution Press, pp. 499–516.

Federal Reserve Bank of Kansas City. 2003. *Monetary Policy and Uncertainty: Adapting to a Changing Economy.* Symposium, Jackson Hole, Wyoming, August 28–30, 2003.

Forman, Shepard, and Abby Stoddard. 2002. "International Assistance," Chapter 7 in Lester M. Salamon (ed.), *The State of Nonprofit America.* Washington, DC: Brookings Institution Press, pp. 240–274.

Galaskiewicz, Joseph, and Wolfgang Bielefeld. 1998. *Nonprofit Organizations in an Age of Uncertainty: A Study of Organizational Change.* New York: Aldine De Gruyter.

Greene, Elizabeth, and Brad Wolverton. 2002. "Learning the Lessons of September 11: Charities Reassess How They Handled Aid." *The Chronicle of Philanthropy,* September 5, 2002.

Gronbjerg, Kirsten A., and Lester M. Salamon. 2002. "Devolution, Marketization, and the Changing Shape of Government-Nonprofit Relations." Chapter 14 in Lester M. Salamon (ed.), *The State of Nonprofit America,* Washington, DC: Brookings Institution Press, pp. 447–470.

Hodgkinson, Virginia A., with Kathryn Nelson and Edward D. Sivak, Jr. 2002. "Individual Giving and Volunteering." Chapter 12 in Lester M. Salamon (ed.), *The State of Nonprofit America,* Washington, DC: Brookings Institution Press, pp. 387–420.

Kotlikoff, Laurence. 2004. "Apres Bush . . . Le Deluge?" *The Milken Institute Review,* Second Quarter 2004, pp. 17–25.

Lenkowsky, Leslie. 2002. "Foundations and Corporate Philanthropy." Chapter 11 in Lester M. Salamon (ed.), *The State of Nonprofit America,* Washington, DC: Brookings Institution Press, 2002, pp. 355–386.

Light, Paul C. 2004. *Sustaining Nonprofit Performance.* Washington, DC: Brookings Institution Press.

McDonald, John F. 2004. "The Glad Game: The Decline of Social and Economic Problems in America." *The Milken Institute Review,* Second Quarter 2004, pp. 46–51.

Pew Charitable Trusts. 2005. *Sustaining the Legacy: A History of the Pew Charitable Trusts,* Philadelphia, PA: available at www.pewtrusts.com, accessed on March 12, 2005.

Reid, Elizabeth J. 1999. "Nonprofit Advocacy and Political Participation." Chapter 9 in Elizabeth T. Boris and C. Eugene Steuerle (eds.), *Nonprofits and Government,* Washington, DC: The Urban Institute Press, pp. 291–325.

Reid, Elizabeth J., and Janelle Kerlin. 2003. "More Than Meets The Eye: Structuring and Financing Nonprofit Advocacy In Complex Organizational Structures." Presented at Annual Meeting of the Association for Research on Nonprofit Organizations and Voluntary Action (ARNOVA), November 20–23, 2003.

Salamon, Lester M. (ed.). 2002. *The State of Nonprofit America.* Washington, DC: Brookings Institution Press.

Schram, Sanford F. 2002. "Social Welfare After September 11." *The Nonprofit Quarterly,* 9:1, Spring 2002, pp. 21–24.

Smith, Steven Rathgeb. 2002. "Social Services." Chapter 4 in Lester M. Salamon (ed.), *The State of Nonprofit America.* Washington, DC: Brookings Institution Press, pp. 149–186.

Stock, James H., and Mark W. Watson. 2003. "Has the Business Cycle Changed? Evidence and Explanations." In Federal Reserve Bank of Kansas City, *Monetary Policy and Uncertainty: Adapting to a Changing Economy.* Symposium, Jackson Hole, Wyoming, August 28–30, 2003, pp. 9–56.

Te'eni, Dov, and Dennis R.Young. 2003. "The Changing Role of Nonprofits in the Network Economy." *Nonprofit and Voluntary Sector Quarterly,* September 2003, pp. 397–414.

Vidal, Avix C. 2002. "Housing and Community Development." Chapter 6 in Lester M. Salamon (ed.), *The State of Nonprofit America.* Washington, DC: Brookings Institution Press, pp. 219–239.

Weisbrod, Burton A. (ed.). 1998. *To Profit or Not to Profit: The Commercial Transformation of the Nonprofit Sector.* New York: Cambridge University Press.

Weitzman, Murray S.; Nadine T. Jalandoni, Linda M. Lampkin, and Thomas H. Pollak. 2002. *The New Nonprofit Almanac and Desk Reference.* San Francisco: Jossey-Bass.

Wyszomirski, Margaret J. 2002. "Arts and Culture." Chapter 5 in Lester M. Salamon (ed.), *The State of Nonprofit America.* Washington, DC: Brookings Institution Press, pp. 187–218.

2

Entrepreneurial Nonprofit Institutions: The Many Roads to Rome

Reynold Levy
President
Lincoln Center for the Performing Arts
New York, NY

It is a propitious moment to hold forth ambitiously about reaching new levels of financial, programmatic, and managerial excellence for nonprofits.

All of a sudden the stars in America's financial sky seem perfectly aligned. Almost everything that should be up is up (Hagerty and Hilsenrath, 2004). The S&P. The Dow. NASDAQ. Employment. Corporate earnings. Take home pay. Consumer confidence. Productivity. And almost everything that should be down is down. Inflation. Inventories. Interest rates. Federal taxes—on individuals and corporations.

To be sure, the twin towering deficits of trade and the federal budget are troublesome, longer-term. And rising state and local taxes and shrinking state and local budgets are problematic.

Still, the best should not be the enemy of the very good in an assessment of the economic environment in which nonprofits currently reside. By and large, it is terrific.

It seems especially appropriate in such a situational setting, to pose the question of what it takes to develop and sustain a nonprofit institution that is entrepreneurial in character.

First and foremost, any institution that aspires to be entrepreneurial must maintain a financially sound base of operations. That means balanced or surplus budgets. It means diversification of revenue sources. No institution should be overly dependent on contributions or on earned income or on governmental sources of support. Indeed, within each of these categories, there should also be diversity.

Everyone is advised by portfolio managers that the diversification of assets is key to prudent personal investment. Why shouldn't the same guiding principle apply to nonprofit budgets and their major revenue sources?

The second prerequisite for developing an entrepreneurial organization is that the nonprofit be driven by its mission and focused on its accomplishment. A well-articulated and understood mission helps to define programmatic choice and helps to guide the allocation of scarce resources.

To be an entrepreneurial organization also necessitates a concentration on results, on performance. When the staff of an organization describes its work by discussing processes, activities, and meetings rather than numbers, metrics, and indicators, it is more than likely that its members do not work for an entrepreneurial organization. As a test, nonprofit executives should stand outside the entrance to their offices. As employees arrive in the morning the executive should pose the question, "No matter what else happens to you today, what is it precisely that you wish to accomplish?" Rare is the employee who is inner directed and purposeful enough to answer that question affirmatively and definitively.

Even for those who know exactly what they are about, in most organizations there is a conspiracy afoot to stop driven professionals from achieving what they wish to accomplish. If employees have no idea of what they want to achieve by the end of a given day or week or month, then they are consigned to answering the phone, responding to their mail, and attending meetings.

Because virtually all nonprofit work is service-oriented and labor-intensive, one of the dominant challenges nonprofit leadership confronts is how to measure and to increase the productivity of their work forces. Aligning individual accomplishment to the overall measurable objectives of a given unit or department is often a key to productivity improvement.

The next precondition to the entrepreneurial organization is a certain brand of leadership. The top of the organization must exhibit an upbeat, can-do attitude. Leaders see opportunities, not problems. They speak of challenges, not troubles. They are optimists, can-do types. They exhibit a sense of humor, a sense of perspective, and a resilience that enables them to face setbacks without seeming defeated. Such leaders are prepared to take calculated risks to accomplish breakthrough gains.

In nonprofit organizations, the continuity and the intelligent memory resides in the board of directors. Good governance practices require approval by the board of informed goal-setting and review by the board of operational execution against those goals. Management needs to give a great deal of thought to the information supplied to the board, the better to improve the quality of advice and guidance it receives.

At the heart of the scandal that allowed Bill Aramony, the former president of United Way of America, to run away with his agency and engage in undetected fraudulent practice and management neglect was the utter failure of governance (Grant, 1992). That on his executive committee sat, among others, the president and CEO of IBM, John Akers, and the chairman and CEO of AT&T, Robert E. Allen, speaks volumes about the utter necessity for trustees to govern. Indeed, the Anglo-Saxon definition of trustee is an individual who holds in trust an institution for service to others (Webster's Revised Unabridged Dictionary, online). In other words, govern is an active verb. The United Way is a classic example of governance passivity.

And that precept leads to the final condition that must be realized if a nonprofit organization is to have the chance to be called entrepreneurial. That requirement is simply stated. The organization must be externally focused. It must be shaped to better serve customers or suppliers or partners. Doing so means that executives within institutions begin to see themselves as others view them. They avoid getting caught in bureaucracy, and in serving one another's needs at the expense of clients who are, after all, to be the beneficiaries of the organization's mission-related efforts.

The following three examples illustrate this condition. At AT&T, sometimes months pass before any senior executive refers to a customer. At the International Rescue Committee, on the other hand, not an hour goes by without a reference to a refugee or displaced person that the organization was formed to serve. And, at Lincoln Center, it is impossible to not immediately detect that everyone in the organization in some fashion is serving artists, audiences, or the general public.

Assuming that these conditions pertain, nonprofits can venture forth more boldly into entrepreneurial behavior than they otherwise could do prudently.

For some that means entering into business undertakings unconnected to the nonprofit mission of the organization, generating what the Internal Revenue Service would call unrelated business income. Bill Shore, the founder of the nonprofit Share Our Strength, writes of entrepreneurial activity in his book *The Cathedral Within* as if it were an article of faith:

> Cathedrals were sustained and maintained because they actually generated their own wealth and support. The main source of funding for their building or renovation was income from accumulated land and property. In this way, cathedrals did not just rely on donations, handouts, or redistributed wealth, but instead created new community wealth. (Shore, 2001, p. 20)

Bill Shore cites Pioneer Human Services as a model job-creating nonprofit because it has launched self-supporting enterprises and programs, annually generating over $50 million in earned revenue by manufacturing and selling high-quality products and services. The founder, Gary Mulhair, has, in effect, run a factory, built a profitable business, and delivered comprehensive social services to a severely challenged population—all at the same time (Shore, 2001, p. 126). To expand to scale and to achieve long-term sustainability requires generating wealth internally or through enduring partnerships as Share Our Strength developed with American Express and with chefs all over the nation. As Shore notes:

> The benefits to them [SOS partners] were so clear and compelling, so directly tied to their own profitability, that they had as strong a vested interest in its continuation and success as we did. It was a partnership that created new wealth. As a result, it was sustainable over time. (Shore, 2001, p. 149)

This notion that only commercial profits plowed back into nonprofit mission-driven activity can create success is dubious. What is incontestable, however, is that earning profits is one entrepreneurial route to scalability and sustainability. The hospital cafeteria and gift shop, the museum store and catalog and sales web site, the university research park, and the research and development contracts of large corporations with nonprofit institutions of higher education all reflect that reality.

But most nonprofits have discovered other roads to Rome. Many nonprofits prefer to stick closer to their knitting, worried about straying from their strategic competencies into for-profit schemes and concerned that, even if successful, these schemes might dwarf the organization's animating purposes.

For example, savvy nonprofits have noticed that whole fields of endeavor that were once their private preserve have now been entered by commercial firms with energy and determination. The charitable are operating side by side with the proprietary, with important consequences to both and telling results for all those served by them.

Consider these ideas.

For-profit institutions represent a sizable portion of the nation's four-year colleges, museums and art galleries, general hospitals, specialized hospitals, family service agencies, theaters, health clinics and nursing homes, day care centers, home health facilities, and vocational education centers.

How can the best of these commercial organizations enter the same fields and often provide the same clients with high-quality services and earn money for their shareowners, while many nonprofit executives engage in comparable work generating deficits for donors to cover? What can nonprofit executives learn about their pricing, marketing, use of technology, and labor policies and practices that can induce greater efficiency and productivity in their work without distorting their institutional mission?

Surely the nation's colleges and universities have something to learn from the country's largest private university, the University of Phoenix, with 96,000 students scattered among 134 satellite locations across twenty-eight states. Instead of tenured faculty, 95 percent of the university's lecturers are working professionals teaching part-time. Rather than having a student demographic of largely eighteen- to twenty-four-year-olds, most University of Phoenix students are thirty and over. As *Business Week* reported in its November 17, 2003 issue:

> In the year ended August 31, earnings of parent Apollo Group, Inc. surged 53% to $247 million as revenues jumped by a third to $1.3 billion. Such stellar performance has given Apollo a market value of $11.4 billion—equal to the endowment of Yale University, the nation's second wealthiest college. (Symonds, 2003, p. 70)

Or, consider Corinthian Colleges which didn't come to market with an initial public offering until 1999. Since then its stock price has moved from $1.13 to $63.03 a share. As James Glassman exclaims in *The Washington Post*:

> Corinthian runs 82 colleges and 15 corporate training centers—in such fields as criminal justice, health care and diesel repair—has boosted its annual revenue in just four years from $133 million to $517 million and its profit from $7 million to $60 million. Earnings in the fiscal year that will end June 30, 2004 are projected to rise 38%, and Value Line expects annual increases averaging more than 30% through 2008. (Glassman, 2003)

Overall, commercial higher education revenues will jump to $13 billion in 2003, up 65 percent since 1999 (Symonds, 2003).

Are nonprofit colleges and universities ignoring the second and third quartile of high school classes and neglecting the community college market?

Are nonprofit colleges failing to target working adults, hungry to acquire not just technical and professional skills but knowledge?

Are nonprofit colleges unwilling to prepare to teach students whose most proficient language is not English on evenings and weekends with largely different faculty than works Monday through Friday from nine to five?

Can nonprofit colleges relate as well to employers, 60 percent of whom provide tuition subsidy to the University of Phoenix, as they have historically to foundations and individual donors (Symonds, 2003)? Outside the area of high-powered executive education courses and graduate school tuitions, very few private schools seek tuition support from the employers of students.

When will the promise of distance learning afforded by twenty-first century technology be redeemed by our leading nonprofit universities? Today, the proprietary sector of higher education is the true leader in this field. Private, nonprofit colleges and universities are the laggards.

Evidence abounds that experimentation by leading universities in exploiting new sources of revenue is hardly being ignored. For example, by turning research into income-producing patents, during a recent year Columbia University earned $155 million or 15 percent of the almost $1 billion in licensing income earned by 222 U.S. and Canadian universities. Indeed, Columbia is joined by the University of California system and by New York University in forming units such as Industrial Liaison/Technology Transfer or Innovation Enterprise (Gershman, 2003). In fact, it is clear that a trend is well developed when a whole new service organization has formed to exploit health, bio-tech, and other research for revenue purposes. It is called the Association of University Technology Managers.

These developments at colleges and universities have their counterparts elsewhere.

At Lincoln Center, executives ask themselves how to more effectively market products to the 3.4 million ticket buyers and the total of 5 million annual visitors to the world's largest performing arts center. Lincoln Center's collective product sales do not reflect the power of the brands of world class arts organizations like the Metropolitan Opera, the New York City Ballet, the Juilliard School, the New York Philharmonic, the Film Society of Lincoln Center, or the New York City Opera.

Simply stated, in 2004 product sales by top-flight performing arts facilities are where America's museums were in the 1950s. Today, the over $65 million of revenue earned by Metropolitan Museum shops and web sites and the over $30 million earned by the Museum of Modern Art are the envy of the commercial retail world (Metropolitan Museum of Art and Museum of Modern Art, 2002). First-rate buying, marketing, and tie-in discounts to museum memberships and exhibitions are all indicators of model merchandising.

Where are the under-explored opportunities for Lincoln Center and how do its executives best exploit them? Locating the major gaps between an institution's promise and performance is the first step to bridging them.

The public hears all the time that the explosion of distribution channels of cable television and the potential of narrowcasting have far outpaced the provision of content. Lincoln Center is only just beginning to move beyond its much admired, over twenty-five-year-old, Emmy-laden, nationwide public television program of the performing arts called "Live from Lincoln Center" to the distribution of other forms of digitized content on commercial stations.

What can Lincoln Center do to convert its product into forms that will earn income beyond its current, collective $565 million base, virtually all derived from live ticket-buying audiences and philanthropic supporters? How can its intellectual property and enviable brand name be converted into a currency that buys more than admiration and applause? By license from the New York City Parks Department, Lincoln Center presides over 16.3 acres of precious open space, a rare, much sought-after asset in a dense, overcrowded city. How can Lincoln Center best take advantage of this precious comparative advantage? By co-investing in a destination restaurant, a coffee bar/sandwich shop, a combination boutique/bookstore, a TKTS-like campuswide facility? All of these alternatives and more are under active consideration.

Every reader of this book is associated with an organization or cause that can be comparably challenged by questions about its potential for future revenue derived from either entirely new products and services or from derivatives of existing lines of business.

And so it can be said of good old-fashioned philanthropy, now at $241 billion and roughly one quarter of total nonprofit income, what of its future (Strom, 2004a)?

Given the veritable explosion of philanthropy and the prospect of an enormous intergenerational wealth transfer in the decades ahead (Steindorf, 2003), why not expand by orders of magnitude the individual, foundation, and corporate gifts that tax-exempt entities are privileged to seek? Indeed, why not seek to significantly enlarge endowment, the income from which can sustain programs and personnel with a great measure of security? Is there a more scalable, more sustainable institution of higher education than Harvard with its $19 billion corpus of assets (Strom, 2004b)?

Far from finding the process of seeking funds from donors beneath the dignity of nonprofits, many regard doing so as the quintessence of competitive, entrepreneurial activity. Persuading others to a cause, selling ideas, moving affluent people from success to consequence, asking others to vote with their funds—these expressions of getting and giving are natural to many true believers who run or govern nonprofits.

Perhaps a special opportunity resides in the relationship of nonprofits to companies. After all the scandals that have washed over Enron, KPMG, PWC, Quest, Citigroup, and the investment and mutual fund industries generally, doesn't it stand to reason that prudent companies need to restore the trust of their customers, shareowners, partners, employees, and communities?

To burnish the brand, to tighten the bond of employee loyalty and shareowner trust, to win the confidence of elected and appointed officials, corporations are willing to consider partnerships that extend well beyond donations. In-kind gifts, voluntarism, use of corporate facilities, advertising and marketing tie-ins, product and service promotional funds—all of these are up for grabs for nonprofits that are fast, agile, and hungry.

And what of plain, traditional earned income?

Are nonprofit institutions pricing their services differently for those who can afford to pay more than for those who cannot? Fifteen years ago, museum admissions were free or a token amount. Today, they are huge sources of income with one night a week still often preserved free of charge and the fee to entry labeled "a voluntary contribution." A decade ago, the opponents of welfare reform predicted disastrous consequences. But as welfare rolls have shrunk, the predicted human casualties go largely undocumented, and not for want of trying. Conventional wisdom, whether liberal or conservative, dies hard in the face of contrary evidence.

All of which is to state that nonprofits' assumptions about affordability of the services they provide have been challenged not only by their own experiences but by the airline and hotel industries' application of "yield management" price-optimization strategies (Kurzweil, 2004), by eBay auctions and Priceline purchasing, and even by reserving seats at movie theaters, for an additional fee, of course.

Consumers who can will pay more for convenience, reliability, and choice and nonprofits have only begun to test their willingness to do so. Between the promise of augmented income through variable pricing and multiplying sales distribution channels and performance of the nonprofit sector, billions of dollars of enduring, incremental earned income await acquisition.

None of these roads to Rome, if pursued to excess or unqualifiedly, is without danger.

Lester Salamon at Johns Hopkins first raised a cautionary flag when in response to domestic budget cuts of the Reagan Administration he detected that social service and recreation agencies were raising prices often beyond the reach of the working poor they were tasked to serve (Salamon, 2003).

Most recently, Derek Bok in his book *Universities in the Marketplace* warns against the perils of commercialization of higher education, pointing to the mission distortions of big-time athletics, of company-sponsored scientific research, and of professors using schools as bases of operation for their real careers in consulting and entrepreneurial activity (Bok, 2003, pp. 6, 10, 35).

More nonprofits run the risks of complacency, lethargy, and tedium more than excessive pursuit of the almighty commercial, entrepreneurial, governmental, or donated dollar. Nonetheless, the warnings of experienced observers should not be ignored. Balance, diversity, and prudence are good guides to departures from conventional practice.

References

Bok, Derek. 2003. *Universities in the Marketplace: The Commercialization of Higher Education.* Princeton, NJ: Princeton University Press, pp. 6, 10, 35.

Gershman, Jacob. 2003. "Columbia Leads Way in Licensing Income Earned." *The New York Sun,* December 19, 2003.

Glassman, James. 2003. "Do the Arithmetic and Go to Schools." *The Washington Post,* December 7, 2003, Final Ed., p. F1.

Grant, Linda. 1992. "Acts of Charity: Furious Donors Blamed a Lax Board After a Funds Scandal Toppled the Lavish-Living Head of the United Way. Now Can the Blue-Chip Agency Regain the Public's Trust?" *The Los Angeles Times,* September 13, 1992, p 39.

Hagerty, James R., and Jon E. Hilsenrath. 2004. "Corporate Profits Increase 29%, Biggest Jump in Almost 20 Years." *The Wall Street Journal,* March 26, 2004, Final Ed., p. A2.

Kurzweil, Ray. 2004. "Breakthrough Ideas for 2004." *Harvard Business Review,* February 1, 2004, p. 13.

Metropolitan Museum of Art and Museum of Modern Art IRS 990 tax forms, 2002.

Salamon, Lester. 2003. *The Resilient Sector, The State of Nonprofit America.* Washington, DC: Brookings Institution Press, p. 16.

Shore, Bill. 2001. *The Cathedral Within: Transforming Your Life by Giving Something Back.* New York: Random House Trade Paperbacks, pp. 20, 126, 149.

Steindorf, Sara. 2003. "Youths Play Old Game of Giving Grants." *Christian Science Monitor,* November 24, 2003, p. 19.

Strom, Stephanie. 2004a. "Charitable Giving Holds Steady, Report Finds." *The New York Times,* June 22, 2004.

———— 2004b. "Harvard Money Managers' Pay Criticized." *The New York Times,* June 4, 2004, Late Ed., p. A18.

Symonds, William C. 2003. "Cash-Cow Universities: For-Profits Are Growing Fast and Making Money. Do Students Get What They Pay For?" *BusinessWeek,* November 17, 2003, p. 70.

3

Managing for Performance and Integrity

Debra J. Mesch
Associate Professor and Director of Public Affairs
Indiana University–Purdue University
Indianapolis, IN

James McClelland
President and Chief Executive Officer
Goodwill Industries of Central Indiana
Indianapolis, IN

Introduction

The nonprofit world is becoming more highly scrutinized and today nonprofit organizations are finding themselves in an environment of increased accountability and oversight. As such, questions as to what constitutes organizational effectiveness have become increasingly important as the public exerts "increased pressure on nonprofit organizations to demonstrate their impact on complex social problems" (Sowa, Selden, and Sandfort, 2004, p. 712). As a result, the nonprofit world is faced with concerns about how to build organizational capacity and achieve greater effectiveness while, at the same time, demonstrating results. Additionally, the nonprofit sector has undergone a dramatic shift in grantmaking where "grants are seen less and less as gifts or contributions than they are as investments" (Easterling, 2000, p. 482). With increased accountability, nonprofits are finding that funders are not as interested in activity-based progress reports (Easterling, 2000), but instead are being challenged by all stakeholders to address the question, "What are the *benefits* or *results* of our programs for customers, clients, or participants and how can we demonstrate our success to our funders?"

We thank Keith Reissaus of Goodwill Industries of Central Indiana for his valuable input into this chapter.

Information on the extent to which programs are achieving their intended outcomes is powerful and useful feedback for programmatic, managerial, and fiscal concerns. As responsibilities for more and more programs are vested in federal, state, and local governments, along with increased contracting with the public sector for services, the need to identify successful programs by looking at outcomes or the measurable results of these programs is even more pressing (Briar and Blythe, 1985). This concern is ubiquitous across the nonprofit sector. The current political and economic climate creates a heightened awareness of the need to weigh the consequences of cuts in human service programs against other investments such as national security and other infrastructure investments.

Performance measurement or outcome measurement is relatively new to most nonprofit organizations. However, research and evaluation efforts of human service agencies that have used outcome measurement have been reported in the literature in such widely diverse areas as drug and alcohol abuse programs (McLellan and Hunkeler, 1998), services to the homeless (Campbell and McCarthy, 2000), rehabilitation of the visually impaired (De L'Aune, Williams, and Welsh, 1999), educational improvement (Henry and Dickey, 1993), and health care (Mihalik, 2001). Additionally, we are finding that "foundations are increasingly investing their evaluation funds to focus on the *outcomes* of the efforts they fund, as opposed to inputs, activities, or outputs" and the importance of these types of activities is increasing (Hendricks, 2002, p. 107).

Traditionally human services programs have been evaluated through such process measures as clients served, number of children attending class, or number of beds occupied. While such measures show how much effort has been generated and for how many individuals, they reveal nothing about the efficacy of the intervention. Outcome measurement shifts the focus from activities to results and from how a program operates to the good it accomplishes for the individuals purported to be served (Plantz, Greenway, and Hendricks, 1997).

This concept sounds very good in theory. Although nonprofits are feeling pressure to respond to increased accountability concerns, performance can be rewarded only if it can be reliably and objectively measured, monitored, and related to the mission and success of the nonprofit. Yet, unlike for-profit firms where pay and performance are more easily measured and matched, useful information on performance in the nonprofit sector is often abstract and not easily obtained (Weisbrod, 1988). There also are costs associated with developing and implementing performance measurement systems—direct operating costs, potential distortions of mission, and potential losses associated with allocating resources to performance measurement activity versus other uses. Furthermore, many nonprofits lack the expertise and skills to proceed, and simply transplanting what we know from the public and for-profit sectors to nonprofits is often inappropriate, if not impracticable.

For several reasons, performance management systems found to be effective in the private sector may not be applicable to the nonprofit sector. First, profitability indicators of performance and progress that are traditionally found in the private sector (such as ROI, ROA, earnings, share price, debt-to-equity ratio) are generally less important or altogether absent in nonprofit organizations—making it particularly difficult to identify, measure, and reward financial performance outcomes. Thus, finding appropriate performance metrics to satisfy stakeholders, as well as determining which performance indicators should be tied to compensation or funding, is much more difficult for nonprofits (Steinberg, 1990). Consequently, nonprofits often rely on more indirect measures of performance, such as activity or process measures, to reward socially desired behavior—measures that are always imperfect (Weisbrod, 1988). Second, nonprofits operate without clear lines of ownership and accountability. While businesses must satisfy their shareholders, nonprofits are in the difficult position of accomplishing their mission while addressing the priorities of multiple stakeholders—donors, clients, board members, staff, and community—none or all of whom may be identified as the key ownership group (Frumkin, 2002). Third, it is often much more difficult to measure performance and to assess meaningful and measurable change in a nonprofit. Although many nonprofits use outcome measurement primarily for program evaluation (Fine, Thayer, and Coghlan, 2000), there is a great deal of subjectivity and overemphasis on process—particularly in the social services area where provider agencies may have "different philosophical beliefs about service delivery, measures of success, and expectations of clients" (Campbell and McCarthy, 2000, p. 343). Fourth, the type of culture, motives, and values of those who choose to work in the nonprofit sector are frequently different from those who choose to work in the for-profit sector. Financial rewards commonly are viewed as secondary to the personal satisfaction of working in a charitable organization (Frumkin, 2002). Finally, the relationship between the CEO and board in a nonprofit tends to go beyond an economic exchange and more towards a relationship based on trust and collaboration (see Miller, 2002). Trust between the CEO and the board in a nonprofit often relaxes the need for clear performance criteria (Gomez-Mejia and Wiseman, 1997). Developing trusting relationships with funders and the board may be viewed as a much more valuable investment of CEO time than time spent on performance management. For the above reasons, the concept of accountability and performance measurement must be defined, evaluated, and considered within the environment and conditions found in the nonprofit sector.

Although it is often more difficult to measure performance in nonprofits, the concept of "integrity" is the same across all sectors. Integrity may be defined as "the quality of possessing and steadfastly adhering to high moral principles or professional standards" (Encarta World English Dictionary, 2003). While the principles and professional standards may vary from one organization to another, efforts to move to an outcomes-based management system should not conflict with values that are central to all organizations in all three sectors (Wholey, 2002). "Results-oriented management is intended to improve the performance of public and nonprofit organizations, not to replace such values" (p. 14). To manage for integrity, it is necessary for organizations to articulate their values, standards, and principles and effectively communicate them to employees. Operating according to those values, standards, and principles must then become an essential part of the organization's culture.

A second definition of "integrity" includes the definition, "wholeness: the state of being sound or undamaged" (Encarta World English Dictionary, 2003). To be "sound" or "whole," an organization must be financially sound. Thus, to have "integrity," organizations must not only possess and adhere to high moral principles and professional standards—they must also be financially viable. When an organization is not financially healthy, there can be a tendency to compromise standards, and mission-related impact is often adversely affected as the organization struggles just to survive. Therefore, nonprofit financial accountability must be considered a crucial component of organizational effectiveness—along with managerial and program performance measures.

Nature of the Challenge

As public and private funding sources diminish and requests for funding grow, competition for scarce resources becomes more intense. Nonprofits that can demonstrate achievement of intended outcomes are the ones more likely to be funded (Briar and Blythe, 1985). Outcome measures can help to identify programs and organizations that are the most successful in helping the clients they serve. Furthermore, these measures also can provide feedback to providers that enable improved management practice, better direction to staff, and, consequently, better services. Therefore, nonprofits need to consider not only program effectiveness, but also management effectiveness in terms of both capacity and outcomes (Sowa, Selden, and Sandfort, 2004). Management refers to organizational management characteristics "that describe an organization and the actions of managers within it"—such as structure and process as well as the outcomes of these management systems and activities (Sowa, Selden, and Sandfort, 2004, p. 714). "Program refers to the specific service or intervention provided by the organization" and also relates to the capacity of the program as well as the outcomes of the intervention (Sowa, Selden, and Sandfort, 2004, p. 714).

There are multiple challenges in managing these systems in the nonprofit sector. We discuss below the most frequently noted challenges addressed in the literature, as well as by nonprofit managers, in developing and implementing performance management systems. These challenges include those in the areas of: 1) developing stakeholder understanding and acceptance, 2) documenting performance and measuring success, 3) allocating resources and obtaining funding, 4) implementing effective reward systems, and 5) reporting and technology issues. Each is briefly discussed in turn.

DEVELOPING STAKEHOLDER UNDERSTANDING AND ACCEPTANCE

Disparities in understanding what is meant by "managing for performance and integrity" can occur amongst nonprofit managers and other stakeholders. Several terms and concepts have been associated with the idea of focusing on results, often leading to confusion and disagreement as to how to operationalize and measure performance. Outcomes-based funding, performance measurement, results-oriented management, and outcome measurement are concepts that focus the energies of key stakeholders on the identification of outcomes, the development of indicators, data analysis, and regular reporting of findings (Morley, Vinson, and Hatry, 2001). However, the concept of managing for results also includes the practice of pay for performance systems, performance-based compensation, and strategic pay—all referring to compensation systems that reward senior managers for organizational performance and where pay is tied to accomplishing the strategic goals of the organization. Further complications arise when considering the differences between capacity (processes and structures) and outcomes (Sowa, Selden, and Sandfort, 2004). "Too often, outcomes alone become the indicators of choice for representing organizational effectiveness. Yet, hidden behind those outcome measurements are complex and diverse dynamics that may vary across and within organizations and programs" (p. 715). The challenge is to reach agreement among important stakeholders as to the key dimensions of results-oriented management, and how these concepts are translated into practice, as well as an understanding of how to tie these results to a strategic framework that emphasizes the customer perspective, measures performance against goals, and uses measurement systems that are tailored to the specific needs of the organization (Poister, 2003). Without this common understanding and acceptance, evaluating programs and managing for performance and integrity will be problematic, if not impossible to achieve.

DOCUMENTING PERFORMANCE AND MEASURING SUCCESS.

Nonprofits often must choose between rewarding what is easily measured (even though this may not reward the desired outcomes), incurring costs by devising better measures, or not rewarding performance at all (Weisbrod, 1988, p. 48). The challenge here is to find a balance by using appropriate and relevant metrics to ensure that results are accurately evaluated and measured without exorbitant costs. Foundations, donors, and government agencies are asking nonprofits to provide answers to questions like, "Where is the money going and what are the outcomes of this funding?" In order to demonstrate what works and what does not, nonprofits need to develop reliable indicators (not those that are simply accessible!) that are tied to the mission of the organization. This may be particularly challenging for nonprofits who have a social or human services mission—where outcomes of programs are elusive or lagging (Easterling, 2000), and where there may be a lack of consensus on what results should be measured and how these measures should be used in determining which performance indicators are tied to compensation. "The more abstract the mission is, the more difficult it is to develop meaningful measures of outcome or mission impact" (Sawhill and Williamson, 2001).

Also included in this challenge is thinking about performance indicators and how to measure performance at different levels of intervention (i.e., programmatic as well as community outcomes) and how to link shorter-term results to longer-term communitywide outcomes. There are multiple dimensions of effectiveness and nonprofits need to consider organizational effectiveness "as more than the mere outcomes of the programs it operates or the services it provides," but the function of its management structures as well (Sowa, Selden, and Sandfort, 2004, p. 715).

ALLOCATING RESOURCES AND OBTAINING FUNDING

Perhaps the greatest barrier in implementing outcome evaluation in nonprofits is a lack of financial support from funders (Taylor and Sumariwalla, 1993). Shifting to a performance management system that involves measuring outcomes requires planning, training, evaluation, development of methodologies for decision-making, as well as data availability and data quality—all of which involve costs. The challenge for nonprofits becomes how to plan for and allocate resources for developing and implementing a performance management system that links program outcomes to mission. Particularly for smaller nonprofits where resources may be more limited, outcome assessment can put undue burden on staff time. Nonprofits increasingly will be challenged about how to manage their valuable resources for developing performance management systems, while at the same time thinking about the trade offs between what is ideal and what is feasible, given the mission of their organization.

IMPLEMENTING EFFECTIVE REWARD SYSTEMS

The challenge in managing for performance and integrity is to balance the importance of identification of outcomes as a way to secure funding with a focus on ensuring that outcome measurement is used to change and improve practice in a way that is consistent with the mission of the organization. If the performance measurement process is seen only as a "hoop" to jump through to secure funding, rather than an opportunity to incorporate performance measurement into an organization's culture, nonprofit leaders will be passing up a valuable opportunity for organizational learning and change. "A learning organization is one that creates, acquires, and communicates information and knowledge, behaves differently because of this, and produces improved organizational results from doing so" (Huber, 2001, p. 88). When organizational members are given access to information and encouraged to "process this information and act on their newly constructed knowledge," organizations will have the opportunity to learn and grow (Minnett, 1999, p. 353). As performance feedback and outcome data become available, the challenge is for nonprofits to use this information to become better performers.

REPORTING AND TECHNOLOGY ISSUES

A challenge often faced by nonprofit managers is overcoming organizational and technical barriers of results-based management (Wholey, 2002). Issues include how to coordinate and support the organization's efforts in making decisions as to how much and how often performance outcomes should be disclosed and to whom this information should be given, how to use logic models to describe how inputs and processes produce intended results, and how to report these data to key stakeholders. Trade offs among cost, validity, reliability, and other statistical issues need to be decided, as well as how much time should be spent in ensuring that performance data are sufficiently complete and accurate (Wholey, 2002).

Maintaining the Integrity of the Mission and the Organization

If all of the challenges outlined above are addressed, "managing for performance" will be irrelevant and lack credibility unless the overarching value and culture of the organization is one of integrity and trust. The culture of the organization must be one in which basic values and principles are followed—this includes respect for people and good stewardship. These values, however, are not inconsistent with taking calculated risks. Action without knowledge is risky. However, an organization can never *always* have full knowledge or information before acting—especially where innovation and continuous improvement are desired organizational traits. If the reward system discourages learning, change, and risk-taking, there is a high probability that any performance management system will fail or, even worse, encourage unethical behavior. Tensions associated with measuring performance in certain ways can inadvertently create incentives that could compromise integrity. The challenge here is ensuring that nonprofit leaders communicate a consistent message of integrity through their reward system, incentive structure, and culture that performance need not be compromised as a result of high ethical standards.

An unintended outcome of a performance measurement system is that nonprofits may be tempted to sacrifice innovation and compromise integrity by: 1) selecting and serving clients who are those most likely to succeed, 2) setting targets that are artificially low to ensure success, 3) distorting performance to reach set targets, or 4) changing indicators to achieve set targets (Hendricks, 2002). When funding is made contingent on measurable results, nonprofits may find themselves in an untenable situation when financial pressure to produce successful outcomes results in excluding the most needy or hard-to-serve citizens, and choosing to serve only those clients who have a good chance of being successful so only positive outcomes can be reported (the practice of "creaming"). Rather than being innovative and creative, nonprofits may focus on tried and true techniques that would guarantee meeting performance expectations and outcomes. Frumkin (2002) refers to this behavior as engaging in strategic gaming. Under these circumstances, risk-taking and innovation may be unintentionally discouraged and integrity compromised.

The challenge for nonprofit leaders is presenting a consistent message of integrity and core values—aligning outcomes that are desired (particularly ethical behavior) with the compensation system and reward structures in place. If a core value is violated, you are gone. A further challenge is to think not only about project-level outcomes over which nonprofits have the most control or for which indicators are most available, but also in setting up positive reward contingencies for organizational change, organizational learning, innovation, and entrepreneurial activities as well as successful achievement of performance outcomes *without sacrificing the integrity of the organization.*

Current Practice

In this section, we describe the ways in which nonprofits are responding to the challenges of increased accountability described in the previous section, as well as the types of decisions that nonprofits need to consider in order to be successful in managing this environment. We use Goodwill Industries of Central Indiana as a case study of an organization that has been successful in addressing many of these challenges.

Nonprofits essentially measure outcomes to increase a program's effectiveness (evaluation) and to communicate a program's value (accountability) and nonprofits today are under pressure to do both (Hendricks, 2002). Today's reality, however, is that nonprofits often engage in performance management processes in response to funding, rather than to improve services or organizational effectiveness. On the other hand, funders need to understand that they cannot rely too heavily on outcome data without also considering important information about inputs, activities, and outputs. This type of information should serve to complement—not replace—outcome data, by going beyond reporting the *level* of outcomes achieved without paying attention to how well programs are managed via those outcomes (Hendricks, 2002).

On the positive side, recent literature in this field attests to the fact that nonprofits are making progress in developing and implementing effective performance management systems (e.g., Campbell, 2002; Hendricks, 2002; Kaplan, 2001; Sawhill and Williamson, 2001). One report found that approximately 83 percent of nonprofits surveyed regularly collected data on some outcomes related to results, although most did not use sophisticated data collection techniques (Morley, Vinson, and Hatry, 2001). United Way of America has taken an early leadership role in the nonprofit sector by requiring outcomes measurement data from the agencies they fund (United Way of America, 1996). In their 1996–2002 strategic plan, United Way called for a review process in which results-based funding was made a larger part of the funding allocation decision-making process (Wholey, 2002). In many United Ways across the country, agencies are required to report current-year program accomplishments in terms of outcomes and to develop program outcome objectives for the next fiscal year (Wholey, 2002). And, United Ways have been successful in aligning the reward system to encourage local agencies to incorporate outcome information into all aspects of decision-making.

What types of outcome information are collected? How do nonprofits determine what is most important to measure? How do nonprofits collect data for measuring performance? Nonprofits must consider these questions about how to collect and use performance information to improve organizational practice and program effectiveness, strengthen accountability, and support policy decision-making (Wholey, 2002). These questions are not easy for a mission-driven nonprofit, where measuring success is far more difficult than in the for-profit sector. Yet, there are many nonprofits that have worked to develop and institute effective mission impact measures (Sawhill and Williamson, 2001).

Sawhill and Williamson (2001) report a case study of The Nature Conservancy that used a model for measuring success that included outcome measures in the areas of impact, activity, and capacity. They asked the questions: "Are we making progress toward fulfilling our mission and meeting our goals? Are our activities achieving our programmatic objectives and implementing our strategies? Do we have the resources—the capacity—to achieve our goals?" (Sawhill and Williamson, 2001, p. 372). The Conservancy spent a year in developing a new measurement system—the product being a list of ninety-eight leading indicators of program performance. They soon realized, however, that when they tried to implement this program, it was far too cumbersome and impractical for staff to understand and process. Their revised measurement system narrowed these indicators down into those that resulted in clear linkages between the organization's mission, vision, goals, strategies, and programs and that were simple, easily collected and communicated, and applicable across all levels of the organization (pp. 374–5). This process resulted in a model of nine broad measures that reinforced these linkages and yet were flexible enough to reflect changes in organizational priorities over time. Based on their survey of senior managers in thirty well-known nonprofits, Sawhill and Williamson conclude, however, that "the nonprofit groups that reported the most success in developing performance measures had all developed specific, actionable, and, most critical, *measurable* goals to bridge the gap between their lofty missions and their near-term operating objectives" (p. 380). Instead of spending effort to measure mission directly, these organizations focused on identifying and achieving goals that moved them in the direction of their mission (e.g., American Cancer Society, Boy Scouts of America).

As the Conservancy case illustrates, an important characteristic of a performance measurement system is that it is ongoing and long term—that outcome information is collected and reported on a regular basis in order to provide early and frequent feedback to clients and other stakeholders, so that adjustments and improvements can be made in a timely manner (Morley, Vinson, and Hatry, 2001). Additionally, an accurate measure of performance requires setting clear and reasonable expectations for measuring outcomes that include provisions for funding, measuring short-term outcomes as well as ultimate results, follow-up, and use of program logic models (Easterling, 2000). It is important that the types of outcome information include not only the consequences or results achieved, but also intermediate outcomes that provide information on perceptions of customer satisfaction or service quality. Organizations seek information on these types of outcomes because they serve as an intermediate step toward an end outcome (Morley, Vinson, and Hatry, 2001). Although effective performance management systems include both types of indicators, it is important that nonprofits include indicators that reflect improvement in the condition of the clients they serve and not only the intermediate outcomes (Morley, Vinson, and Hatry, 2001).

As previously discussed, financial accountability must be considered a crucial part of any performance management system. Although it may be more difficult for nonprofits to measure financial performance, as is commonly done in the for-profit sector, recent research indicates that financial outcomes are not as elusive as once thought. (For examples of research on nonprofit financial measures, see Chang and Tuckman, 1991; Keating, 1979; Keating and Frumkin, 2003; and Ritchie and Kolodinsky, 2003.) Ritchie and Kolodinsky (2003), for example, examined financial performance data from IRS Forms 990 and, based on factor analysis, categorized performance factors of university foundations into: 1) fundraising efficiency (total dollars raised relative to monies spent on fundraising activities), 2) public support (ability to generate revenue), and 3) fiscal performance (total revenues to total expenses). Chang and Tuckman (1991) also explored dimensions of performance in nonprofits using measures of financial vulnerability and attrition (as a measure of the inability of nonprofits to survive). The results of these and other studies provide support for the distinctiveness of financial performance measures in the nonprofit sector and provide managers with "a parsimonious number of financial performance measures enabling relatively easy assessment of three important performance-related dimensions" (Ritchie and Kolodinsky, 2003, p. 376).

"Outcome data are meaningless if they are not used" (Morley, Vinson, and Hatry, 2001, p. 43). Other recent studies of human service nonprofits suggest that the majority of outcome information is used for purposes of program improvement or evaluation (i.e., Fine, Thayer, and Coghlan, 2000; Hoefer, 2000). Fine, Thayer, and Coghlan (2000) found that more than half of the nonprofits they surveyed indicated that their purpose for conducting an evaluation was to measure program outcomes, and that the evaluations were designed primarily to measure outcomes. In fact, 43 percent of respondents indicated that they measured outcomes because of a funding requirement, while only 15 percent reported doing so for the purpose of program planning. They also reported that although outcome information is reported to numerous stakeholders, the majority of nonprofits report evaluation data to current funders (69%) followed by program staff (61%). In a survey in

Dallas, Hoefer (2000) found similar results: over four-fifths of their respondents reported conducting an outcome-type evaluation, three-fourths of respondents use results to verify program outcomes, and over half report they use results to advocate for more resources from funders. Morely, Vinson, and Hatry (2001) found that almost half of the organizations they surveyed reported using outcome data primarily for program improvement.

Goodwill Industries of Central Indiana: A Case Study

We use Goodwill Industries of Central Indiana as an exemplar to demonstrate how one organization has responded to the challenges of managing for performance and integrity in developing and implementing an outcomes measurement system.

The primary mission of Goodwill Industries is to help people with barriers to employment prepare for and find jobs. The main goal of the Twenty-First Century Initiative of Goodwill Industries International, Inc. is "to help 20 million individuals and members of their families increase their economic self-sufficiency through work by 2020." For decades, Goodwill Industries has tracked the number of people served (an activity metric) and the number of persons placed in jobs (an outcome metric). Both, however, are imperfect measures. The former provides an indicator of the organization's reach, but not its effectiveness; and the latter is an indicator of mission-related impact, but gives no information on how successful the job placements were or how much they helped increase an individual's "economic self-sufficiency."

Goodwill Industries of Central Indiana, Inc. (GICI), based in Indianapolis, is one of the largest Goodwill entities in North America. GICI strongly believes it must do a good job in both its business and financial operations *and* in its mission-related services. It defines its overall objective as maximizing mission-related impact while maintaining a financial position that enhances the organization's long-term viability. As the organization and its planning processes have evolved, so have the key metrics it uses.

In 1997, GICI staff began looking at the balanced scorecard approach described in the work of Kaplan and Norton (1996). In 1999, Goodwill formed a cross-functional team to develop a balanced scorecard for the organization. The balanced scorecard is a performance measurement management system used in the private sector that has been adapted to nonprofits (Kaplan, 2001). This approach elevates the role of customer and recognizes "that nonprofits should be accountable for how well they meet a need in society rather than how well they raise funds or control expenses," by bridging the gap between mission and strategy and day-to-day operations (Kaplan 2001, p. 369). The balanced scorecard concept looks at performance from four perspectives: financial, customer/client, internal process, and learning and growth. It looks not just at historical data, but also at leading indicators. In other words, are you doing the things you must do today if you are to be successful tomorrow?

It took the team at GICI a full year to come up with its first corporate scorecard. Because GICI is a multidivisional organization, each division had to develop its own scorecard that would be aligned with and feed into the corporate scorecard. From the outset, GICI viewed this effort as a work in progress, and the scorecard has been revised in efforts to make it more meaningful and useful. Similar to the experience in The Nature Conservancy described above, the early versions of the GICI scorecard included too many metrics, and there was a growing recognition that in this case, at least, "less is more."

The adoption of a new strategic plan in 2003 provided another opportunity to improve the product. In the development and subsequent use of the strategic plan, there has been great emphasis on ensuring that everything is well-aligned— mission, values, basic principles, vision, strategy, structure, operations, primary metrics, and reward systems. The primary metrics in the plan fall into four categories: financial, mission-related impact, stewardship, and customer/employee satisfaction. Specific key metrics that are included in the corporate scorecard include: 1) number of people placed in jobs, 2) one-year retention rate of people placed in jobs, 3) increase in earnings of people placed in jobs, 4) total revenue, 5) net income, and 6) employee retention rates. Other important metrics are included in the divisional scorecards, and the quarterly strategic plan implementation reviews also include qualitative evaluations. Qualitative evaluations (i.e., perceptual measures) from clients, customers, and the community, along with objective outcome measures, are needed to fully capture the dimensions of organizational effectiveness (Sowa, Selden, and Sandfort, 2004).

The plan also includes eight major strategic directions, each of which has one or more specific goals. All major decisions—including those related to proposals for new initiatives; major additions to, deletions from, or other changes in existing programs; changes in organizational structure, etc.—are considered in relation to their "fit" with the strategic plan, its major strategic directions, and the anticipated effect on the primary metrics identified in the plan. A Strategic Plan Implementation Group that included key leaders from all parts of the organization was formed to review and make recommendations on some of the proposed actions related to implementation of the plan. That group did not replace the normal decision-making process, but served a useful purpose by providing a forum for discussion and consideration of points of view that might otherwise have been overlooked. Eighteen months after the strategic plan was adopted, the Strategic Plan Implementation Group was replaced by an expanded executive staff that continues to perform the same functions. To ensure that the strategic plan remains dynamic and relevant, a quarterly review is conducted by senior staff, and the results are reported to the board of directors, which also offers its comments and suggestions. The quarterly review includes identification of any major changes— internal or external—that might warrant additions to, deletions from, or other modifications to the strategic plan.

While solid data is available for most metrics, it is difficult to track the success of the people GICI has placed in jobs with other firms. The organization, in conjunction with its partners, has placed over 8,000 people a year during each of the last several years, and it is virtually impossible to stay in touch with all of them. Consequently, it is necessary to use statistical techniques to provide a reasonably valid and reliable indicator of one-year retention rates and increase in earnings (which is used as a proxy for increase in economic self-sufficiency).

GICI has implemented continuous improvement processes in every part of the organization, and information from the scorecard is used in efforts to improve performance. Aligning reward systems—especially compensation—with key metrics is more difficult, however. In any type of organization, there can be frightening unintended consequences of basing compensation solely on "hitting a number." While GICI has a "lack of merit" principle that eliminates or defers compensation increases for employees whose performance has been deemed unsatisfactory, the organization has yet to develop a means of directly linking a portion of compensation to progress toward specific strategic objectives. A critical part of any such system is ensuring the integrity of the data used, and great care must be taken to ensure that the incentive system drives the desired performance and behavior.

As the organization continues to evolve, new programs and services are created and others are eliminated. GICI is providing services for a growing number of young people, and some of those services do not have job placement as a primary goal. For example, charter high schools developed by GICI focus on the year-to-year change in standardized test scores of each individual student, four-year graduation rates, and post-secondary participation rates. Other youth-oriented and adult services focus on increasing basic literacy (as measured by standardized tests), improving English language proficiency of those who have a native language other than English, and earning industry-recognized certifications. All of these are important indicators of the effectiveness of individual programs and services and are used internally to evaluate and improve effectiveness. Of course, outcomes are also reported to various funding and regulatory bodies, as well as other stakeholder groups.

In summary, GICI has addressed many of the challenges described earlier. First, in order to garner support and buy-in for the balanced scorecard approach, management and staff participated in cross-functional teams in developing the indicators or outcomes. This resulted not only in increased stakeholder acceptance of the performance management system from staff, but also demonstrated commitment and buy-in from their management team. Any new administrative practice requires commitment from top management—especially because the first response to introducing outcome measurement into a nonprofit is often one of fear, dread, and resistance—particularly if this is initiated by the funder (Easterling, 2000). Wholey (2002) discusses the importance of developing management and staff commitment and support for efforts to engage in activities required in implementing performance management systems and for achieving results as a necessary *first* step so that staff do not see this as an "add-on" to their current responsibilities. Additionally, support must be obtained from key stakeholders outside of the organization to ensure that these entities will support efforts to achieve specific results—which also may require cooperative interagency efforts.

Second, the performance measurement system GICI developed is mission-driven, yet tangible, practical, and flexible enough to be understood and used by staff on a daily basis. Although these indicators are relevant to GICI today, they also were developed with thinking about success in the future in mind. Additionally, the metrics selected were derived from the strategic plan—ensuring that the strategy, outcomes, and reward systems were aligned, congruent, and consistent with the mission of the organization. GICI's strategic plan includes the mission statement, historic values, and basic principles, all of which serve as constant points of reference for day-to-day decision-making.

Third, GICI considers both internal organizational factors as well as external factors in developing criteria for organizational effectiveness—as well as a consideration of the relationship between program effectiveness and management capacity. Performance management systems cannot be considered without first considering such factors as revenue generation, fundraising, cost-sharing, and other measures of financial health. Does the organization possess sufficient resources to conduct its major operations and be true to its mission? GICI relies on their strategic plan, human resource systems, and reporting technologies as critical components of their performance management system. Only by having these in place can a nonprofit measure the degree to which a program will achieve its purpose. (Sowa, Selden, and Sandfort, 2004).

Fourth, and of utmost importance, the performance measurement system at GICI has been integrated into the culture of the organization. The true test of any performance management system is in its ability to foster cultural change without sacrificing the integrity of the organization. Is the organization functioning more effectively as a result of the data provided to its decision-makers? Have the decision-makers used the information to engage in data-based decision-making—allowing for organizational growth, change, and learning? GICI has been able to stay true to its mission and maintain its core values, even in the face of cultural change. They have accomplished this through basic principles of continuous improvement and informed decision-making throughout their work. They view performance outcomes always as a work in progress within the culture of a learning environment where taking calculated risks is encouraged.

New Ways of Thinking

Recently, nonprofits have begun to address many of the challenges in managing for performance and integrity. In this section, we highlight several themes that have been highlighted in this chapter and identify ways in which organizations can become more innovative and creative in addressing these challenges of improving performance and accountability.

Ultimately, "success in nonprofits should be measured by how effectively and efficiently they meet the needs of their constituencies" (Kaplan, 2001, p. 353). The definitive measure of performance should be how one serves their clients, customers, donors, and users of their services or products. That is—what do your clients say about you? This is easier to do for some nonprofits. Those that have a more focused, measurable mission—such as Goodwill Industries—are able to collect more detailed indicators that relate directly to their mission. Other nonprofits may have more indeterminate or abstract missions that are more difficult to measure. All nonprofits, however, need to think about ways to measure mission in a practical way, where measuring mission depends on measurable goals (Sawhill and Williamson, 2001)—even for those nonprofits that may have a more ambiguous mission.

It has been suggested that one way to accomplish this is to measure shorter-term outcomes that serve as proxies for *longer-term* results. That is, measure short-term outcomes such as increases in knowledge or avoiding unhealthy behavior, rather than measure the "hard" effects that occur over the long term, such as graduation from high school or maintaining healthy behaviors (Easterling, 2000). We are not suggesting here that we lose sight of the *longer-term* outcomes, but using proxies may be a means to link project-level results with community-level outcomes. Although this may be difficult, nonprofits have been and can be successful in developing and measuring indicators that serve to play a constructive role in community planning and evaluation. (See Campbell [2002] for findings from their research project conducted in collaboration with economic development organizations in California.) The downside of starting at project-level outcomes, of course, is that the organization can lose sight of the "big picture"—its mission and strategy—resulting in mission-creep.

We also foresee that nonprofit organizations will become more successful in the future in measuring financial performance along with other measures of success. Little empirical research has been conducted in this area (for exceptions, see Chang and Tuckman, 1991; Keating, 1979; Keating and Frumkin, 2003; Tuckman and Chang, 1991), but recent literature suggests that nonprofits will need to think about this as well—especially nonprofits that receive funding or contracts from public/governmental agencies. Although we do not have data from GICI at this time, we feel that there exists a strong correlation between financial strength and mission-related outcomes as measured by job placements. Thus, managing for performance and integrity is enhanced by a reasonably strong financial position.

Nonprofits also need to think about ways in which to build evaluation capacity through changing the culture of the organization and by becoming learning organizations. The process of managing for performance and integrity should lead to organizational learning and change by teaching organizational members to think empirically and to make data-based decisions (Minnett, 1999). Nonprofits need to think of performance measurement as a tool for continuous improvement and organizational learning. Agency culture is a key factor in outcome evaluation and staff need to believe that performance measurement and evaluation are of value to the organization (Poole et al., 2001). Nonprofit leaders need to help staff think about ways in which their organization can grow and benefit (i.e., develop new skills and knowledge) as a result of the process they undertake in developing and implementing a performance management system that focuses on outcomes. They need to think carefully about how to build capacity for outcome measurement into the organization—by assigning staff responsibilities and by allowing time and resources for data collection and reporting requirements. Those in leadership roles need to help staff to not see this as an "add on" in job tasks—but, instead, as an activity that is part of their essential job duties and part of the core responsibility of the organization. This requires managerial support for staff in the form of training and technical assistance to allow their agency to make the transition into a learning organization.

"Any results-based accountability system depends on working governance mechanisms and effective leadership" (Campbell, 2002, p. 254). The board of directors is key here. It is critical that the board be in sync with the CEO and other key stakeholders in delivering a consistent message that they trust the leadership of the organization in managing for performance and integrity—trust and delegation is at the heart of integrity and performance. Performance measurement is not worth doing if the data are not used. The management team needs to feel comfortable in bringing performance data to the board with the understanding that the CEO will be allowed to take calculated risks in exploring different options as a result of the data presented. The CEO may not necessarily be rewarded for taking risks—but certainly the message should be that he or she will not be punished for doing so. The message should be that the culture of the organization will allow for this—and the board is critical in getting this message across. Agency CEOs also can communicate this message. For example, managers can ensure that outcome evaluation practices are an essential and integral part of the organization's practice by aligning the performance appraisal process and reward system with accomplishment of outcomes and by using decentralized decision-making to encourage risk-taking and creativity—allowing for innovation and change (Poole et al., 2001).

Future Directions and Conclusions

Although the topic of this chapter speaks to the issue of managing for performance and integrity, and more specifically, using outcome measures to respond to an environment of increasing accountability—it is important to keep this topic in perspective. Outcome measurement is only one of many tools available to nonprofit leaders. Nonprofit leadership involves governance, management, and vision. It is only within this larger framework that any performance management system will be successful.

Rewards dictate the behavior of its organizational members. As such, it is critical that funders and leaders of nonprofits think about the ways in which their reward systems are structured, so that the organization is rewarded through increases in funding (or at least no decreases) for innovation, risk-taking, and continuous improvement. Funders, too, need to think about big-picture issues concerning organizational capacity and performance.

Nonprofits need to make sure that what they are measuring is meaningful for *their* organization and for *their* mission. As such, it is critical that the performance measurement system be tailored to the specific needs of the organization. As Dennis Young points out in Chapter 1, the nonprofit sector is not monolithic— "nonprofits are not all affected by change in the same way." Here, too, there is no cookie-cutter formula for developing and implementing a performance management system that is generic across the sector.

Finally, nonprofits need to consider their mission and use their strategic plan in their day-to-day decision-making as a blueprint in implementing a performance management system. Without this, it is questionable that any performance management system will result in meaningful information.

In terms of future research, there are two major issues that need to be addressed. First, methodologically—different types of research methodologies need to be employed to better capture the interrelationships between the dimensions of organizational effectiveness. Sowa, Selden, and Sandfort (2004) make a case for the need for multilevel hierarchical modeling that allows for examination of variation at different organizational levels—rather than a focus on a single level of analysis (i.e., either organization or program). This type of rigorous design requires that data be collected from different units of analysis within the organizational structure. In addition, pilot studies and case studies on local nonprofits need to be conducted in order to add to the body of literature in this field—especially in nonprofits with more abstract missions and difficult to track clients. These types of in-depth case studies, in combination with studies involving a more rigorous research design using random assignment of clients, should address how shorter-term outcomes lead to *longer-term* results, as well as providing us with the "bigger picture" in capturing the complexities of organizational life.

Second, more work is required for understanding the relationship between incentives and outcomes in tying pay to performance indicators. Recent literature on managerial compensation practices in nonprofits suggests that nonprofits tend to pursue goals other than performance outcomes or efficiency; they focus on outputs that are more easily measured rather than the critical performance indicators important to organizational success (e.g., Roomkin and Weisbrod, 1999). Research needs to be conducted on the practice of nonprofits when more objective measures of performance are available and how nonprofits use these measures in rewarding top management and staff.

References

Briar, S., and B. J. Blythe. 1985. "Agency Support for Evaluating the Outcomes of Social Work Services. *Administration in Social Work,* 9, pp. 25–36.

Campbell, D. 2002. "Outcomes Assessment and the Paradox of Nonprofit Accountability." *Nonprofit Management and Leadership,* 12, pp. 243–259.

Campbell, G. J., and E. McCarthy. 2000. "Outcome Measurement: Services to the Homeless in New York City." *Policy Studies Journal,* 28, pp. 338–353.

Chang, C. F., and H. P. Tuckman. 1991. "Financial Vulnerability and Attrition as Measures of Nonprofit Performance." *Annals of Public and Cooperative Economics,* 62, pp. 655–672.

De L'Aune, W. R.; M. D. Williams, and R. L. Welsh. 1999. "Outcome Assessment of the Rehabilitation of the Visually Impaired." *Journal of Rehabilitation Research and Development,* 36, pp. 273–294.

Easterling, D. 2000. "Using Outcome Evaluation to Guide Grantmaking: Theory, Reality, and Possibilities." *Nonprofit and Voluntary Sector Quarterly,* 29, pp. 482–486.

Encarta World English Dictionary. 2003. North American Edition.

Fine, A. H.; C. E. Thayer, and A. T. Coghlan. 2000. "Program Evaluation Practice in the Nonprofit Sector." *Nonprofit Management and Leadership,* 10, pp. 331–339.

Frumkin, P. 2002. *On Being Nonprofit: A Conceptual and Policy Primer.* Cambridge, MA: Harvard University Press.

Gomez-Mejia, L. R., and R. M. Wiseman. 1997. "Reframing Executive Compensation: An Assessment and Outlook." *Journal of Management,* 23, pp. 291–374.

Hendricks, M. 2002. "Outcome Measurement in the Nonprofit Sector: Recent Developments, Incentives and Challenges." In K. Newcomer, E.T. Jennings, C. Broom, and A. Lomax (eds.), *Meeting the Challenges of Performance-Oriented Government.* American Society for Public Administration: Washington DC, pp. 99–123.

Henry, G. T., and K. C. Dickey. 1993. "Implementing Performance Monitoring: A Research and Development Approach." *Public Administration Review,* 53, pp. 203–212.

Hoefer, R. 2000. "Accountability in Action? Program Evaluation in Nonprofit Human Service Agencies. *Nonprofit Management and Leadership,* 11, pp. 167–177.

Huber, G. P. 2001. "Organizational Learning: The Contributing Processes and the Literature." *Organizational Science,* 2, pp. 88–115.

Kaplan, R. S. 2001. "Strategic Performance Measurement and Management in Nonprofit Organizations." *Nonprofit Management and Leadership,* 11, pp. 353–370.

Kaplan, R. S., and D. P. Norton. 1996. *The Balanced Scorecard: Translating Strategy into Action.* Cambridge, MA: Harvard Business School Press.

Keating, B. P. 1979. "Prescriptions for Efficiency in Nonprofit Firms." *Applied Economics,* 11, pp. 321–332.

Keating, E. K., and P. Frumkin. 2003. "Reengineering Nonprofit Financial Accountability: Toward a More Reliable Foundation for Regulation." *Public Administration Review,* 63, pp. 3–15.

McLellan, A. T., and E. Hunkeler. 1998. "Patient Satisfaction and Outcomes in Alcohol and Drug Abuse Treatment." *Psychiatric Services,* 49, pp. 573–575.

Mihalik, G. J. 2001. "Integrating Performance Measurement: Two More Approaches from the Accreditors." *Behavioral Health Accreditation and Accountability,* 6, pp. 3–5.

Miller, J. L. 2002. "The Board as a Monitor of Organizational Activity: The Applicability of Agency Theory to Nonprofit Boards." *Nonprofit Management and Leadership,* 12, pp. 429–450.

Minnett, A. M. 1999. "Internal Evaluation in a Self-Reflective Organization: One Nonprofit Agency's Model." *Valuation and Program Planning,* 22, pp. 353–362.

Morley, E.; E. Vinson, and H. P. Hatry. 2001. *Outcome Measurement in Nonprofit Organizations: Current Practices and Recommendations.* Washington DC: Independent Sector.

Plantz, M. C.; M. T. Greenway, and M. Hendricks. 1997. "Outcome Measurement: Showing Results in the Nonprofit Sector." *New Directions for Evaluation,* 75, pp. 15–30.

Poister, T. H. 2003. *Measuring Performance in Public and Nonprofit Organizations.* San Francisco: Jossey-Bass.

Poole, D. L.; J. K. Davis, J. Reisman, and J. E. Nelson. 2001. "Improving the Quality of Outcome Evaluation Plans." *Nonprofit Management and Leadership,* 11, pp. 405–421.

Ritchie, W. J., and R. W. Kolodinsky. 2003. "Nonprofit Organization Financial Performance Measurement: An Evaluation of New and Existing Financial Performance Measures." *Nonprofit Management and Leadership,* 13, pp. 367–381.

Roomkin, M. J., and B. S. Weisbrod. 1999. "Managerial Compensation and Incentives in For-Profit and Nonprofit Hospitals." *The Journal of Law, Economics and Organization,* 15, pp. 750–781.

Sawhill, J., and D. Williamson. 2001. "Mission Impossible? Measuring Success in Nonprofit Organizations." *Nonprofit Management and Leadership,* 11, pp. 371–386.

Sowa, J. E.; S. C. Selden, and J. R. Sandfort. 2004. "No Longer Unmeasurable? A Multidimensaional Integrated Model of Nonprofit Organizational Effectiveness. *Nonprofit and Voluntary Sector Quarterly,* 33, pp. 711–728.

Spiegel, R. A. 1999. *Accountable Good: Program Evaluation in the Nonprofit Sector.* Washington, DC: The Advisory Board Foundation.

Steinberg, R. 1990. "Profits and Incentive Compensation in Nonprofit Firms." *Nonprofit Management and Leadership,* 1, pp. 137–151.

Taylor, M. E., and R. D. Sumariwalla. 1993. "Evaluating Nonprofit Effectiveness: Overcoming the Barriers." In D. R. Young, R. M. Hollister, V. A. Hodgkinson, and Associates (eds.), *Governing, Leading, and Managing Nonprofit Organizations.* San Francisco: Jossey-Bass.

Tuckman, H. P., and C. F. Chang. 1991. "A Methodology for Measuring Charitable Nonprofit Organization Financial Vulnerability." *Nonprofit and Voluntary Sector Quarterly,* 20, pp. 343–358.

United Way of America. 1996. *Measuring Program Outcomes: A Practical Approach.* Washington D.C.: United Way of America.

Wholey, J. S. 2002. "Making Results Count in Public and Nonprofit Organizations: Balancing Performance with Other Values." In K. Newcomer, E. T. Jennings, C. Broom, and A. Lamax (eds.), *Meeting the Challenges of Performance-Oriented Government.* American Society for Public Administration: Washington DC, pp. 13–35.

Wiesbrod, B. A. 1988. *The Nonprofit Economy.* Cambridge, MA: Harvard University Press.

4

Risky Business: Understanding and Managing Risk in the Nonprofit Sector

Eugene A. Scanlan
President
eScanlan Company
Bethesda, MD

Robin Dillon-Merrill, Ph.D.
McDonough School of Business
Georgetown University
Washington, DC

Introduction

This chapter provides an overview of risk and decision-making in the nonprofit sector with examples and a thought exercise on general and specific ways to examine and manage risk in an organization. According to the *Dictionary of Word Origins* (Ayto, 1990, p. 446), the origins of the word "risk" are obscure. The English word came from a French word, which, in turn, may have been derived from an Italian verb meaning "run into danger." The word may also be linked to the phrase "to sail dangerously close to the rocks" from the Greek word for cliff. Even in its origins, the word risk includes action, although of a negative nature. Some might argue that the only way to truly avoid risk is to not take action. But in the rapidly changing world of the nonprofit sector, not to take action may in itself involve risk. This chapter will explore the risks faced by nonprofit organizations and will provide some guidelines for managing these risks.

Nature of the Challenge

Many nonprofit organizations seem to make decisions based upon risk aversion (see also Chouinard, 2000.) The goal of this chapter is to move decision-makers from being risk averse to approaching risks realistically based on understanding the actual risks, possible outcomes, and future decisions that will need to be made. In the highly competitive nonprofit environment those organizations that can effectively make major decisions under risk will be the ones to survive and prosper.

Current Practice

If a person or an organization is primarily motivated by behavior that attempts to avoid risk, that person or organization is often described as "risk averse." They are more often driven by fear of negative outcomes or consequences rather than a desire for change. What are some signs of risk-averse behavior? A partial list might include:

- Postponing or not making major decisions;

- Focusing only on less important decisions and believing these will suffice;

- Hoping passively that others will make decisions;

- Delegating actively the process to others who can be held accountable;

- Continually wanting more information before committing to a decision;

- Avoiding a situation where a decision has to be made; and

- Pretending the situation requiring a decision does not exist.

Based upon the experiences of the authors, nonprofit leaders often exhibit one or more signs of risk-averse behavior. The paradox is that nonprofits must change in order to survive—it can no longer be business as usual, regardless of whether the organization is small and struggling or large and established. Change is not only in the air, it is in the ground in which the nonprofit sector is rooted. Here are only a few of the many challenges nonprofits face in the current environment:

- There are more than 1 million nonprofits, forcing greater competition for volunteers, funding, and other resources;

- There have been and probably will continue to be major cutbacks in federal and state funds available for the sector;

- Recently an extended downturn in the economy has placed increasing pressure on many nonprofits to deliver their services to growing numbers of people;

- Many nonprofits report greater difficulty in recruiting volunteer leadership, as two-career families and single parents face major decisions about time commitments to job, family, and other obligations;

- Recent scandals, media coverage, and general public perceptions of the sector have made it more difficult to present a positive image; and

- There is growing consensus among government leaders for the need for more federal and state regulation and oversight of nonprofits.

These trends mean that managing risk and making key decisions must become more important to nonprofit decision-makers. Despite the urgent need to change, many nonprofit boards and staff continue to operate in an environment where key decisions are not made, and therefore needed changes do not occur. The pervasive attitude is often driven by risk aversion, resulting in not taking on the "major decisions" that will affect the future of the organization. Too often discussions within an organization focus on the reasons something should not be done, possible negative consequences of making a decision, frequent postponement of decision-making, or even not putting major decisions on the table.

When legal and/or financial issues need to be resolved, the risk factors are often very clear. But in other areas, risk factors are not objectively analyzed and the true consequences of various decision options are not understood before the decisions are made. Moreover, the chain of subsequent decision points resulting from a single major decision are almost never addressed, especially prior to making that major decision.

Here are a few examples of risk-averse behavior of nonprofits:

- A nonprofit organization has a feasibility study carried out to determine if funds can be raised for a much-needed new facility. The study indicates there is about a fifty-fifty chance of the campaign succeeding. Despite the need for the new facility, the nonprofit elects not to undertake the campaign because they fear it will not be successful. The primary reason they cite is "competition from other campaigns in the area."

- A nonprofit has undertaken a lengthy strategic planning process. The final strategic plan would involve a number of major changes in the organization's operations. The organization decides not to move forward with the plan as the changes will be "too difficult" to make.

- An organization has identified a potential major donor. After considerable internal discussion, it is decided not to approach this person for a substantial gift, because the board member who is the contact with her "feels she might be offended if she is asked to give."

In the business world risk-taking is expected, and successful (or unsuccessful) risk-taking is usually reflected in the bottom line. Market surveys, focus groups, test marketing, and other methods are used all the time to evaluate the risk and the benefits of new products. Even where the risks are high, where the critics and competition say "it can't be done" or "it won't succeed," corporate leaders often push forward. The success of Apple's iPod, despite criticism that there were already a number of digital music players on the market and that the price was too high, is one example where the risk was high, but the benefits were even greater. The other side of the story was the "New Coca-Cola," which, despite being thoroughly tested, was a popular failure.

Risk factors in the nonprofit world and their impacts are often not as clear cut. Because most nonprofits do not have the resources to use the many risk evaluation techniques available to the for-profit sector, estimation of risk becomes more of an implicit process, and nonprofit executives must be highly sensitive to their many publics (people served, funders, and board members).

Volunteer leaders (board members) of many nonprofits often come from corporate backgrounds where they are used to high-risk decision-making. Highly entrepreneurial types are not driven by risk aversion but by a willingness to move ahead despite the risks. Yet put these same types on a nonprofit board and the "entrepreneurial switch" may be turned to "off"—they often become suddenly risk averse. If they continue to be high-risk takers, they may become increasingly frustrated with the board's aversion to risk and may leave.

While risk aversion can be a powerful deterrent to effective and necessary decision-making in the nonprofit sector, risk and risk aversion are topics rarely explored in the nonprofit sector, except in such areas as investments or insurance. Nonprofit leaders and managers tend to read in their own field and have failed to move into the rich resources that are just beyond the edge of the sector but which can provide valuable information and insights.

Moreover, there is a general failure on the part of nonprofit leadership to explore and understand risk and risk aversion and the major impacts they have on decision-making. Risk factors are not systematically incorporated into decision-making processes, nor is there an analysis of the alternative possible outcomes of various decisions. When decisions are made:

- Factual, statistical, experiential, and probability information are often not considered in making critical decisions;

- Analytical tools frequently used in the for-profit sector to ensure accounting for risk factors and effective decision-making are not understood; and,

- Human factors in effecting change are not maximized.

Underlying these behaviors is a more basic failure to understand the differences between perceived risk and actual risk. Perceived risk is what the individual or organization believes is the probable outcome of certain actions: "If I do this, than that result is likely to happen." Actual risk is the statistical or analytical likelihood of specific outcomes from certain actions. Nonprofits reflect the typical patterns of many people in society because they operate based upon risk aversion because of perceived—not actual—risks. According to Bernstein writing in *Against the Gods: The Remarkable Story of Risk:*

> We have trouble recognizing how much information is enough and how much is too much. We pay excessive attention to low-probability events accompanied by high drama and overlook events that happen in routine fashion. (Bernstein, 1998, p. 272)

Here are some examples that might highlight the differences between perceived and actual risk:

- Common examples of people operating based upon perceived risk are those who avoid flying, especially after 9/11. Yet statistically, as the airlines keep reminding us, you are much safer flying than you are driving.

- Based upon perceived risk, people are often highly fearful of shark attacks. But in actuality these vicious killers of the deep are much less dangerous than coconuts, which, according to George Burgess, the director of the University of Florida's International Shark Attack File, are fifteen times as likely to kill you as sharks. (Cited in UNISCI Daily University Science News online.)

- And finally, according to some recent studies, you are about twice as likely to die from bad medical decision-making as you are to die in a car accident. (Harvard Medical Practice Study, as cited by Migdail and Murray)

In each of the above cases, the perceived risk and the actual risk are at odds with each other. Here is an example experienced by one of the authors where risk aversion caused an interesting misperception of the dangers in a situation:

> A former highly decorated combat-proven Marine (in Vietnam, including some of the worst fighting in the war), who had held senior rank with the Marine Corps, retired, and became president of a large international nonprofit organization. The decision was made to hire outside counsel to plan a major fundraising campaign. At the end of the first meeting with counsel, the former Marine pulled one of the consultants aside and plaintively asked, "I'm not going to have to ask people for money, am I?" Here was a person who had been in extremely high-risk, life-threatening situations, but was fearful of the perceived risk and possible outcomes of asking others for money. The consultant reassured him that it was unlikely he would find himself in a gun battle with potential donors, but it took a long time for the perceived risk to diminish.

A simple diagram might assist one's thinking about perceived versus actual risk.

FIGURE 1. PERCEIVED RISK VS. ACTUAL RISK

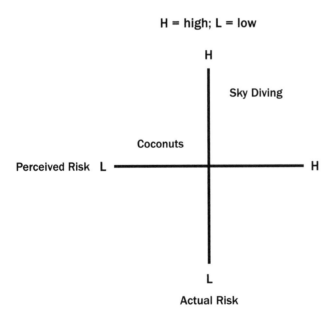

What does this simple diagram tell us about perceived and actual risk? It demonstrates that in various situations the perceived and actual risks may have a variety of relations. For example, for many the perceived risk of injury or death from skydiving is very high. According to many insurance policies, in actuality this is the case. Using the above diagram, skydiving would fall somewhere near the outer edge of the upper right quadrant. But using our coconut example, at least as compared to sharks, death by coconut attack would probably fall in the upper left quadrant—very low perceived risk, but (again as compared to sharks) much higher actual risk.

Another concept related to perceived and actual risk is presented by Nassim Nicholas Taleb in *Fooled by Randomness.* Taleb discusses and characterizes what is "out there" that may influence our decisions:

- "Noise" only represents true randomness—it cannot serve as a basis for effective decision-making.

- "Information" is usually what we use to make our decisions, but Taleb holds that information is "toxic." Often there is so much information available that it is difficult to choose on what basis to make a decision. One need only look at the current debate over what is a good diet to see that this can be true.

- "Meaning" is Taleb's third category. For him meaning is " . . . a precisely intended message," and is the only valid basis for making decisions. (Taleb, 2001, pp. 2, 51–53, 56–59)

Applying Taleb's categories to perceived and actual risk, one could conclude that perceived risk is usually based on "noise" or possibly "information," while actual risk is based upon "meaning."

The nonprofit sector must begin to use the same approaches, techniques, and tools used in other sectors in order to ensure that effective decision-making is not hindered by inaccurately perceived risks and the resulting risk aversion.

New Ways of Thinking

Nonprofit organizations can be very slow to change. The process of change for a nonprofit organization has been described by one of the authors as similar to "moving the elephant." How do you move an elephant? One step at a time.

How can nonprofits move beyond operating in an environment where risk aversion drives decision-making, or the lack of effective decision-making? How can nonprofit leadership create a better understanding of the actual risk involved in any possible decisions, as opposed to operating based upon perceived risk? What tools, techniques, and ideas are available to help nonprofit organizations ride the waves of change? The remainder of this chapter will present some examples of ways that positive change can be accomplished in nonprofit organizations, including ways to improve perception of risk and move the organization to a less risk-averse basis for decision-making. Detailed examples will be provided of the use of one tool—decision trees—common to the government and corporate sectors, but little used in the nonprofit sector.

Each of the techniques and tools presented can, if used properly, help:

- Improve accuracy of perceived risk;

- Create a better understanding of actual risk and the consequences of decision-making;

- Provide more objective ways to anticipate the outcomes of various possible decisions, and anticipate what might go wrong before it happens; and,

- Creatively use people to bring about change more rapidly.

CREATING SUCCESSES

At times, the risks of taking some action may be perceived as high (having a high likelihood of negative consequences and a low likelihood of achieving the desired outcome), while the actual risk is low (having a high likelihood of achieving the desired outcome and a low likelihood of negative consequences). If one is aware of the actual or most likely outcomes of a particular action, while others perceive it as high risk, this information can be used to create a success.

Example: Consider a nonprofit sector fundraising situation where a feasibility study has identified, through an interview process, the most likely lead donors to a campaign. While the consultants cannot directly reveal to the organization who indicated their willingness to make lead gifts, they can use this information to create successes. Board members are often reluctant to ask for gifts, based in part on their perceptions of risk and outcomes, including possible failure (rejection), offending friends, etc. If the consultant can help ensure that the most reluctant board member(s) make(s) the first few gift calls on those the study revealed are ready to make a commitment, the board member(s) will probably dismiss their earlier feelings of fear of asking and will now perceive that the risk involved with the gift solicitation process is much lower than originally thought.

USING INFLUENCERS

Malcolm Gladwell's popular book *The Tipping Point* extensively discusses how three basic types of "influencers" can be used to create a "social epidemic"—rapid, nonlinear, and widespread societal or organizational change (Gladwell, 2002, pp. 30–88). These three types are:

- "Connectors"—These are the people who know "everybody"—the "people people." Because they are widely connected and respected as sources for meaningful information, they can ensure the rapid spread of ideas, facts, etc. Gladwell sites the example of Paul Revere's midnight ride as compared to the midnight ride of William Dawes, which occurred at the same time and under the same circumstances. Revere was a connector—he was widely known and respected in the Boston area and apparently knew many of the people living in the towns through which he rode. Dawes was not well known and likely did not know most of the people in the towns through which he rode. Revere is still famous for spreading the message "the British are coming"; Dawes has largely disappeared from history.

- "Mavens"—These are the people who are virtual encyclopedias of information on particular topics or areas. They don't usually provide specific recommendations, but, for example, if you want suggestions for several possible restaurants to take an out-of-town guest to, the maven has them. The maven can list the pluses and minuses of each restaurant and provide various alternatives for food to order. Mavens may not know "everybody," unlike the connectors, but when people know who they are, they are consulted for new information.

- "Salesmen"—As the term indicates, salesmen are those people who are very convincing about what you should do or get—they're the persuaders. Salesmen are probably not the formal salesmen associated with retail outlets, telemarketing, etc., but people you already know whom you rely on for their specific recommendations on what to do when a decision has to be made. Unlike mavens, they are not sources for a wide range of information. They may not be connectors. But when you need to know what type of paint to buy for your house, if you like the appearance of his house, you might well consult with your next-door neighbor and take his recommendation.

Gladwell argues that it takes all three types to create a social epidemic—rapid change.

Example: As you examine your nonprofit board, you may well be able to identify people who fit each of the three types characterized by Gladwell. You may have a "salesman" who seems to be able to convince the other board members to do something. You may also have a connector who knows most or all of the board members and can effectively relate to them. And you may have a maven who can lay out in great detail a series of options and alternatives for action. If you can effectively use each of these people and each person's unique abilities, you may be able to move the board away from risk aversion-based decision-making to a point where needed decisions are made.

CHANGING THE RULES

Wars are often fought to defend or acquire territory. Thus the emphasis is on major population centers, production/industrial centers, military bases, etc. One of the messages President Abraham Lincoln tried to get across to each of his commanding generals, and the lesson that General Grant took to heart, was not to seek to conquer geographic areas, but to conquer Lee's army. Essentially, Lincoln and Grant changed the rules of the Civil War. The opposing side now was forced to respond in different ways and had to make different decisions, as did Grant's army.

Sometimes changing the rules can help change the attitude of nonprofit leadership about the need to make major decisions. The old "rules" might be that the organization should continue on its current path and therefore no major decisions need to be made. But the basic rules might get changed by outside events, such as a major cutback of public funding, new or emerging needs, or another unforeseen event. It can no longer be "business as usual" for organizations facing these situations. Or sometimes the rules actively are changed by internal factors or people, again forcing a change in thinking.

Example: A new executive director arrives at an organization and sees that board meetings consist primarily of a series of committee and staff reports. There are rarely any action items on the agenda, except for some procedural matters. The executive director decides to have staff and committee reports submitted in writing at least one week prior to each meeting, so that all board members will have had time to read them before the meeting. This enables most of the meeting time to be devoted to discussions and action on a number of major items the executive director wants to undertake to move the organization forward.

USING SIMULATION AND ROLE-PLAYING TECHNIQUES

Using simulations and role-playing techniques can help change people's perceptions of the risks involved in making decisions and taking action, as well as have them "rehearse" the process and the steps necessary to reach a goal. A well-designed simulation or role-playing scenario can make people feel more comfortable when they confront the real situation. In a simulation or role play, possible steps, outcomes, and consequences can be explored in a relatively "safe" environment. The end result of an effective simulation or role play should be, when in the real situation, "I've been through this before and I know what to do."

Example: Board members are often reluctant to ask for gifts and support for the organization. Each board member is given an information kit on the organization and other solicitation materials, including a fictional profile of the donor prospect he or she will be calling. Each board member is assigned to have a simulated gift solicitation meeting with another board member, with the remainder of the board observing each meeting. After the "meeting," the prospect is first asked to comment on how the meeting went, followed by comments by the solicitor, and then comments from the other observers. The facilitator then points out observed strong and weak points and gives some general principles for making an effective solicitation call.

Risk analysis tools can be used in these simulations to explore what can go wrong, how likely it is to happen, and the consequences of various decision options before actual decisions are made. The next section details how such tools can be used.

USING DECISION TOOLS TO STRUCTURE COMPLEX DECISIONS

Often what makes a decision difficult is its complexity. Trying to simultaneously think about all the constituent parts is simply too hard. Many methodological (especially graphical) tools exist to help decision-makers think about organizing their decisions, and we will focus on decision trees here. Decision trees (Lindley, 1985; Clemen, 1996) allow us to separate the uncertainties from the certain events, the payoffs from the probabilities, and the ancillary decisions from the main decisions.

In our previous discussions, we focused on decision-makers' thinking about risks as the possibilities of losses. In structuring complex decisions, we need to think about all kinds of uncertainties, not only losses. Therefore, in structuring a decision tree, uncertainties are important outcomes that are not known at the time of the decision.

The Basics of Decision Trees

Decision trees are useful graphical tools to structure complex decisions, especially when the larger problem can be broken down into a sequence of problems. Decision trees typically begin with a decision node (represented in Figures 2, 3, and 4 below by a square). Branches off the decision node correspond to the alternatives available to the decision-maker. The first decision node can be followed by either subsequent decision nodes or by uncertainty nodes. (Uncertainty nodes are represented in later figures by circles.) At an uncertainty node, the decision-maker has no control over which branch is selected, and instead the possible paths are modeled based on the decision-maker's best beliefs about the probabilities of the events occurring. A typical decision tree therefore consists of a series of branches comprised of both decision and uncertainty nodes.

The third component of the decision tree is the outcomes. Once the decision-maker has structured the possible paths, each path through the tree has a corresponding value or outcome. A useful outcome measure could be the money in dollars associated with that scenario, but other measures can be used (e.g., time to complete the project, overall satisfaction of visitors/donors, etc.). Figure 2 shows a simple decision—to invest or not in a stock—with one uncertainty node; the stock price increases or decreases.

A complete decision tree includes the relevant decision alternatives, the relevant uncertainties with probabilities associated with each branch, and the outcome values associated with each path through the tree. If all of these data are specified, the decision tree can be "solved." A decision tree is solved starting at the ends of the tree and working backwards to the base. At each uncertainty node, the expected value of the possible emanating branches is calculated. (For example, if the stock in Figure 2 has a 50 percent chance of increasing in price to $100 and a 50 percent chance of decreasing in price to $12, the expected value of the stock price is $0.5 \times 100 + 0.5 \times 12 = \$56$.)

FIGURE 2. SIMPLE DECISION TREE EXAMPLE

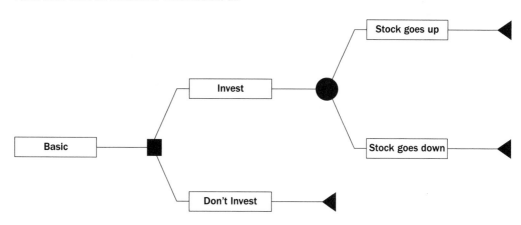

At each decision node, the branch that maximizes the expected value is chosen. By taking the expected values at the uncertainty nodes and maximizing at the decision nodes, the best decisions and their expected values are determined. Consider the stock example again, if the current stock price is $75, the decision is to keep the $75 or invest in the stock with an expected value of $56. In this case, the optimal decision is to not invest.

In the two examples that follow, we use decision trees to structure the thought process. In the first example, we do not fully specify all the possible paths, uncertainties, and outcomes. In the second example, we provide example estimates for probabilities and outcomes. The probability estimates and outcome values should be based on any historical data that might be available, but in reality most analyses will have to rely on the subjective probability assessments of the decision-makers. Relying on expert assessments is acceptable and encouraged because those data are the data that would be used to make the decision without the analysis; completing the decision tree simply provides clarity and explicitness to a formerly implicit process. (For more on the mathematical computations associated with decision trees, see Lindley, 1985, and Clemen, 1996.)

In the first example, we wish to demonstrate how creating the scenario is an important step even if quantifiable data are not available. We believe that it is a useful task just thinking about: What can go wrong? How likely is it to happen? If it happens, what consequences are expected? And then: What can be done? What are the trade offs among the various policy options? What are the impacts of current decisions on future options? The second example includes the numerical calculations. The two examples that follow are: 1) deciding whether to announce a capital fundraising campaign (and if so what will be the goal), and 2) should a nonprofit participate in an activity that has the potential to earn unrelated business income.

Case: Capital Campaign Example

Decision: Should we announce a capital fundraising campaign and if so what will be the goal?

Uncertainties/Risks:

- If you announce a campaign and then fail to meet the goal it reflects poorly on the organizers and the organization and reduces future opportunities.

- If senior management, particularly the president, leaves during the campaign, success will be jeopardized.

- An organization can only have a campaign every several years. If you delay you are also delaying future opportunities.

- If you set a goal that is too low you may succeed at the campaign but not generate the resources that you truly need and could have gotten.

- If you announce a campaign at the same time as similar nonprofits, you will significantly reduce your donor pool.

- If you ask for funding for the wrong purposes and you are turned down, it is difficult to go back with other needs.

- If internal leadership (primarily trustees) won't provide significant leadership gifts it will be difficult to attract external support (particularly foundations).

Figure 3 shows the decision tree that we structured for this problem. The decision-maker has two initial decisions: whether or not to announce a new capital campaign, and if he/she decides to announce, how much to set as the campaign's goal. The first square in the figure represents the first decision: announce the launch or delay the announcement. If the decision is to delay the announcement, at this time there are no other events associated with that branch of the decision tree. If he/she decides to announce a new campaign, we included three possible fundraising goals in the second decision: $500,000, $1 million, or $5 million. The three major uncertainties that we included are shown following the $5 million branch. (These same uncertainties would apply for the other goals also, but for simplicity in the diagram we did not reproduce them in the figure.) The uncertainties considered most important in terms of reaching our campaign goals are: whether or not our organization's leadership leaves during the campaign, whether or not other peer organizations announce a campaign simultaneously, and whether or not we have the support of our trustees. The thought process of thinking about the major uncertainties and how likely each event is to occur can contribute significantly to supporting decision-making. To fully complete the tree, we would need to consider the uncertain events for each goal and each prior event, i.e., what is the probability of having trustee support given our leadership staying versus our leadership leaving. Once the uncertainties are fully expanded, then we would need to consider the financial outcomes of each scenario to complete the entire tree.

FIGURE 3. DECISION TREE FOR CAPITAL CAMPAIGN EXAMPLE

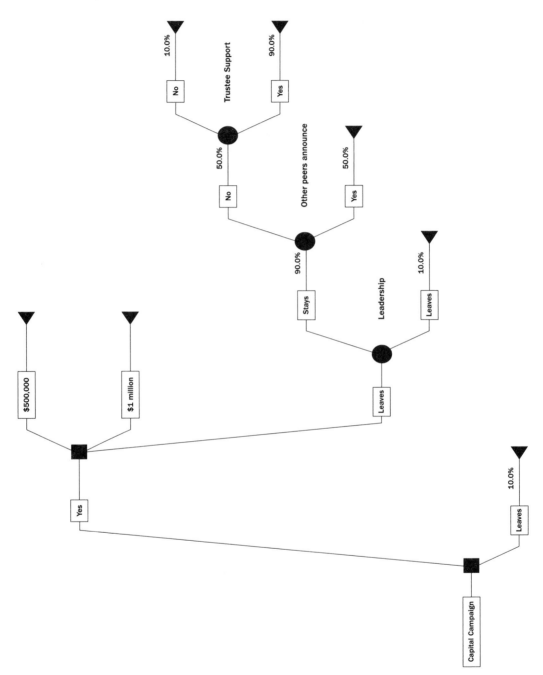

Case: Entrepreneurial Activities—Earning Unrelated Business Income

Decision: Should we participate in an activity that has the potential to earn unrelated business income?

Uncertainties/Risks:

- Do we have the resources and expertise to manage the entrepreneurial venture? We could underestimate the complexity of competing in the venture and/or it could take too many resources away from our primary mission.

- We could alienate the community. Donors may feel that we have strayed from our mission or businesses may feel that we are using our not-for-profit status unfairly for competitive advantage.

- The community could develop the perception that we are using our status unfairly, in which case we will incur the costs of defending ourselves. We could be materially affecting other businesses, in which case we need to consider the costs of exiting or altering the venture.

- There could be unforeseen catastrophic consequences that have associated financial liabilities not covered by our traditional insurance policies. For example, we have a venture that involves food sales but due to violations in health codes someone gets sick and dies.

Similar to Figure 3, Figure 4 shows the decision tree that we structured for this example. We focus on the first decision, whether or not to participate in the venture, and consider two major uncertainties: whether or not we can manage the activity well, and whether or not there are any actual or perceived impacts on our stakeholders and the community. For each scenario, we included revenue expectations. In the best scenario (activity managed well and no impacts to the community), we estimate that the revenues from the venture will be $100,000; however, the probability of this scenario is about 1 in 4 (60% × 40% = 24%). There is a greater probability (40%) that we will not manage the venture well and will only be able to produce $20,000 in revenue. Managing the venture well but having an actual or perceived impact on the community also limits our revenues (24% chance of $60,000 if perceived impacts and 12% chance of $50,000 if actual impacts). For all scenarios, the expected revenue returned from the venture is $52,400. Therefore, if $52,400 exceeds the costs of participating in the venture, this "risky" decision would be acceptable to most corporate decision-makers.

FIGURE 4. DECISION TREE FOR ENTREPRENEURIAL VENTURE

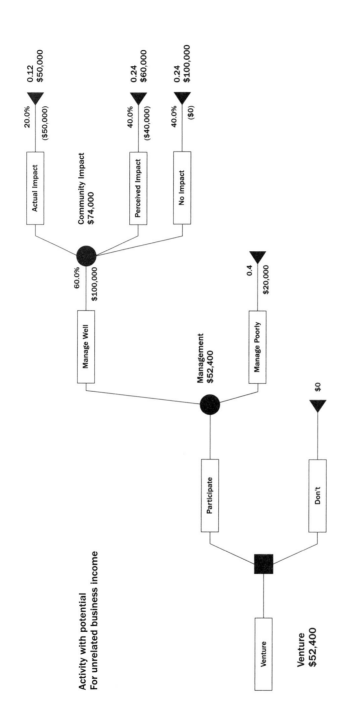

Activity with potential
For unrelated business income

Future Directions

Risk, risk-taking, and risk aversion are topics that are rarely examined in terms of their impacts on nonprofit organizations and especially their board and staff leadership. Often research on risk and decision-making is carried out in the for-profit and government sectors, but results may have little applicability to the nonprofit sector. Research specific to the sector is needed to better understand these factors and their implications. Additionally, human factors in decision-making are beginning to be better understood, but there have been few attempts to apply this information to the sector or to carry out more nonprofit-oriented research. Finally, analytical tools and methodologies that are common in the for-profit and other sectors need to be applied more frequently to ensure effective, change-positive decision-making by nonprofit leadership.

References

Ayto, John. 1990. *Dictionary of Word Origins.* New York: Arcade Publishing.

Bernstein, Peter L. 1998. *Against the Gods: The Remarkable Story of Risk.* New York: John Wiley and Sons.

Burgess, George. Online citation in UNISCI Daily University Science News, at www.unisci.com/stories/20022/0523024.

Chouinard, Claudia. 2000. "Seven Habits of Highly Effective Nonprofits." *Grantmakers in the Arts Reader,* Volume 11, No.1.

Clemen, Robert T. 1996. *Making Hard Decisions.* Pacific Grove: Duxbury Press.

Gladwell, Malcolm. 2002. *The Tipping Point.* Boston: Little, Brown and Company.

Lindley, D. V. 1985. *Making Decisions.* London: John Wiley and Sons.

Migdail, Karen, and Kevin Murray. Online citation, including discussion of the Harvard Medical Practice Study in the Agency for Healthcare Research and Quality at www.ahcpr.gov/research/errors.htm

Taleb, Nassim Nicholas. 2001. *Fooled By Randomness.* New York: Texere.

5

Managing Fiscal Stress

Frederick S. Lane
Professor
School of Public Affairs
Baruch College
The City University of New York
New York, NY

Introduction

Friday, February 4, 2005, was a bad day for the nonprofit sector in Poughkeepsie, New York. Two important local nonprofit institutions closed on the same day.

Poughkeepsie is a city of 30,000 inhabitants on the Hudson River, halfway between New York City and Albany, the state capital. It is the county seat of Dutchess County, with a population of 300,000, a median family income well above and an unemployment rate well below the national average.

The two nonprofit organizations that closed their doors that day were the Youth Resource Development Corporation (YRDC) and the YWCA of Dutchess County. Each served several hundred clients annually. YRDC was a twenty-year-old, youth-focused, job and life skills training nonprofit. A year before, it had thirty-two staff; on February 4, 2005, all nine remaining staff members were laid off. The loss of state and federal contracts apparently was the immediate source of YRDC's fiscal problems (Valkys, 2005).

This chapter originated in a panel at the second NCNE national conference in January 2004. In addition, The Nonprofit Group of the School of Public Affairs, Baruch College, City University of New York, has twice convened invitational panels to discuss managing nonprofits under conditions of fiscal stress. These were held April 23, 2003, and June 9, 2004. Special thanks to the participants, especially Joe Cruickshank and Jack Krauskopf.

Over one hundred years old, the Dutchess YWCA's closure was seemingly prompted by an inability to pay for liability insurance and some of its payroll, which in turn forced the County Youth Bureau to cut funding for teen and family services. The Y's pool also had major structural problems and leaked, and the Y apparently owed the IRS a year of back payroll taxes as well as debts to some vendors.

The Y consisted of a brick building and other facilities on nine acres of land; it employed about seventy-five, mostly part-time staff. Some in the community were aware of the Y's fiscal problems from October, 2003, when it failed to meet its payroll on time. The next sixteen months brought attempts at cost-cutting and the turnover of the longtime executive director as well as outside technical assistance regarding its finances. The closure appeared rather sudden to many clients, especially those using the YWCA for day care services (Lee, 2005).

These two nonprofits were hardly, however, the only ones encountering fiscal stress in this time period, but the stories vary greatly. For example:

- The National Warplane Museum, in Horseheads, New York, near Elmira, closed in September 2001, "undermined by budget battles in Albany (New York State government) and then thrust aside by last week's terrorist attacks" (*Newsday*, 2001). But, it reopened nearly a year later as Wings of Eagles, still nonprofit, with some new and some old board members.

- Ocean Journey, the $93 million accredited aquarium in Denver, with annual attendance in the hundreds of thousands, shut down in 2002 when it could not find donors to rescue it from debt (*New York Times*, 2002); subsequently, the aquarium was taken over by a corporation and renamed.

- Founded in 1969, the American Association for Higher Education (AAHE), a membership organization, announced just after its annual meeting that it was shutting down in March 2005, although there had been no public discussion of the closure at that meeting. A voice for innovation and change in higher education, AAHE indicated it would close rather than compromise on the quality of its programming. AAHE's membership, conference fees, and foundation grants had apparently declined (Lovett, 2005).

- Founded in 1977, the Management Center in San Francisco managed itself out of business in May 2004. It had been an important technical assistance provider to nonprofits in northern California. As part of its planned termination, the Management Center sold its three principal programmatic assets: its nonprofit jobs web site, OpportunityKnocks, to the Georgia

Center for Nonprofits in Atlanta; and its annual wage and benefit survey as well as its well-known training program, Executive Director 101, jointly to the Los Angeles-based Center for Nonprofit Management and San Francisco-based CompassPoint Nonprofit Services. (Management Center, 2004)

For our purposes we use "fiscal stress" to mean an imbalance between revenues and expenses in any given time period that threatens a nonprofit's effectiveness in attaining its goals or even the organization's survival. For many nonprofits, fiscal stress means going from financial "black" to "red"—gradually or, sometimes, quickly and even dramatically. While researchers in this area have similarly defined financial distress as an overall decline in program expenses or a significant (say, 20 percent) decrease in net assets over a three-year period (Keating et al., 2005), these attempts to refine the meaning of fiscal stress still seem inadequate in trying to explain the wide range of circumstances, time frames, and impacts actually encountered by nonprofit organizations over the last five years.

One of the complicating factors in the effective management of fiscal stress is the "mentality of growth." Widely held, the idea is that bigger and broader are better—financially, strategically, even psychologically (Tichy, 1999; Deans and Kroeger, 2005). On the contrary, this chapter contends that fiscal stress is as common, as recurring, and as natural in the nonprofit organizational life cycle as is growth. Moreover, if fiscal stress is well managed, nonprofits can return renewed, even if sometimes reinvented.

Resource Dependence and the Nature of Nonprofit Organizations

Nonprofit organizations are similar to businesses in terms of their financial bottom line; they can and do go out of business. Yet, nonprofits are also similar to government agencies in their public purpose, the resulting difficulties in measuring their effectiveness, and just how politicized their functioning can be. However, nonprofits are also unique in that they rely on voluntarism—voluntary contributions of money and time. These characteristics make nonprofit organizations very difficult to manage, and when fiscal stress occurs, all of these characteristics are relevant.

Financial turbulence can come in many forms, and is problematic for organizations in all three societal sectors—business, government, and nonprofit— but managing fiscal stress seems especially difficult for nonprofit organizations. *It is a function of the perennial mismatch between the compelling mission of most nonprofits and the need to raise sufficient funding in order to achieve that mission.*

This resource dependence is fundamental to understanding the management of nonprofit organizations (Pfeffer and Salancik, 1978). Nonprofits attempt to acquire the financial resources they need, and if they can, without creating too great a dependency on any one resource provider.

FIGURE 1. STRATEGY AND FISCAL STRESS: MISSION AND REVENUES

	High Contribution to Mission	Low Contribution to Mission
Positive Impact on Revenues		
Negative Impact on Revenues		

See Sharon M. Oster, "Product Portfolio Map: Waverly Community House," in *Strategic Management for Nonprofit Organizations: Theory and Cases* (New York: Oxford University Press, 1995), p. 93, and Cheryl Dahle, "We've Got Two Bottom Lines—The Money and the Mission," *Fast Company* (April, 2000), pp. 172-184. This type of analysis originated with the Boston Consulting Group.

Paraphrasing a presidential campaign slogan of some years ago, a recent *Guidestar Newsletter* said, "It's the money, stupid." Forty-six percent of newsletter readers who responded to the March, 2005, "Question of the Month" indicated that "finding the money to accomplish our mission" was their organization's greatest challenge. "All other challenges pale in comparison to the need to keep our doors open and accomplish our mission," commented Roshani Shay, executive director of the Hawaii Wellness Institute. The executive director of the SPCA of Central Florida, Barbara Wetzler, concurred, telling Guidestar, "We never lack for vision, ideas, or enthusiasm. The challenge is always finding sufficient funds today to safeguard the agency's financial vitality while working toward a progressive and stable future." No other single response totaled above 17 percent (Coffman, 2005).

Further evidence of this can be found in a 2001 study of over 1,000 executive directors of nonprofits of a wide range of types and sizes. A research team sorted out the most significant challenges for executives. Anxiety about organizational finances and fundraising went along with high stress, long hours, and managing people (Peters and Wolford, 2001).

Figure 1 depicts the relationships of organizational strategies according to two dimensions: contribution to mission and contribution to revenues. Sometimes a nonprofit might operate a program that is underfunded but is a good fit with its mission. Other times, a nonprofit might operate a program that is not especially central to its core mission but contributes significantly to its revenue stream. However, with the possibility of fiscal stress in mind, nonprofit leaders are reminded of both bottom lines: strategies that yield a high contribution to mission *and* a positive impact on revenues.

The Case of 9/11 and Nonprofits in the New York Metropolitan Area

The years 2001 through 2005 were not easy for American nonprofit organizations. An economic recession, weak philanthropic climate, and declines in government funding produced significant fiscal stress among nonprofits with a wide range of missions.

Furthermore, the period was defined by three cataclysmic events: the terrorist attacks in New York, Washington, and western Pennsylvania on September 11, 2001; a devastating tsunami in the Indian Ocean on December 26, 2004; and hurricane Katrina's catastrophic impact on New Orleans and the Gulf Coast on August 29, 2005. All of these events resulted in an unprecedented philanthropic outpouring by the American public, but also, at least in the short run, diverted attention and some charitable contributions away from many U.S. charities.

The New York region contains 21 million residents and some 76,000 nonprofit organizations. In some ways, 9/11 represented "the perfect storm" for many New York metropolitan area nonprofits. It is also instructive as to how a confluence of events can magnify daily awareness of resource dependence into full-fledged fiscal stress, although each nonprofit encountered its external setting in its own unique way.

The problems for nonprofits actually started before 9/11, even if most nonprofits did not recognize the changing environment. The local economy weakened throughout 2001. After 9/11, the local economy almost immediately entered into a recession. State and local government revenues went into a free fall, thereby providing fewer dollars for grants and especially contracts. Federal actions over the next several years made the financial picture even more difficult for many nonprofits. Even without Hurricane Katrina, federal policies projected through fiscal year 2010 have raised concerns in the nonprofit sector (Abramson and Salamon, 2005).

Business was in trouble, especially high-tech firms, and so corporate giving was reduced. The stock market weakened, and foundation grants tapered off.

Less disposable income and a less optimistic psychological environment resulted in less individual giving. The attack on the Twin Towers of the World Trade Center occurred just as end-of-the-year fundraising was beginning and as forms for those who donate through payroll deduction were beginning to circulate in corporations and other large organizations in New York. After 9/11, crisis charities raised unprecedented amounts of money quickly; some of this giving was "add-on," but some apparently was diverted from previous patterns of giving to local nonprofits.

In addition, local, national, and international concerns about safety, and to a lesser extent, affordability, had an impact on participation in some nonprofit services, such as hospitals and museums. In the six weeks after 9/11, New York City hospitals lost an estimated $367 million due to the decline in admissions of new patients, many of whom come from all over the country and the world. For the month after 9/11, attendance at the Museum of Natural History was down 50 percent over the same period a year earlier.

Other conditions also had their impact on nonprofits. Unemployment increased dramatically. The emergency food network in New York City was already operating at its capacity. Mental health professionals reported increased demand. And welfare reform really started in December 2001, with the end of the five-year, lifetime-maximum period for some beneficiaries. Finally, hundreds of nonprofits were displaced from their offices in lower Manhattan.

By November 2001, the leaders of New York's nonprofit sector understood the conditions promoting fiscal stress. Four years later, most nonprofit organizations in the metropolitan area seemed to still be suffering from fiscal stress.

Causes of Fiscal Stress

As it turns out, there are a wide range of causes of fiscal stress in nonprofit organizations. Many are external to the agency, while internal problems sometimes contribute as well. Two examples of external forces—insufficient governmental and community support, especially unrestricted support, and over-dependence on one or just a few major funders—have already been mentioned. Attractiveness of competing organizations and a tarnished organizational image also fit here (Hager, 2001).

Nonprofits can be thrown into fiscal stress for many reasons, and one relates to clients. Either too many *or* too few might induce fiscal stress. The number and needs of more clients can overwhelm the budgeted resources for a nonprofit's services. Too few clients for a nonprofit's capacity might mean less reimbursement, and hence a budget shortfall.

But internal factors also can play a role. These include: the small size of many nonprofits, making them more vulnerable; the newness of some nonprofits, not sufficiently networked in their communities; over-expansion, especially when encouraged by project start-up grants from foundations and donors; insufficient cash reserves or access to equity; organizational instability due to board or staff turnover; poor planning and leadership failure by the board and top management; and failure to follow legal and regulatory rules (Galaskiewicz, 2004; Wilder Foundation, 1987).

The warning signs of fiscal stress are many and varied. Each organization needs to construct its own key indicators, but timely and strategic information is essential. Has your nonprofit:

- lost a significant percentage of its financial support?

- fallen behind in its financial obligations?

- consistently been behind in meeting financial and service delivery projections?

- aggressively sought a wide range of available funding regardless of your organization's core mission? (Wilder Foundation, 1987)

Perhaps more fundamentally:

- Does your nonprofit have a varied portfolio of revenues, balancing commercial enterprises (for example, fees for services rendered, dues, and revenue-producing ventures) with government contracts and philanthropic donations?

- Is your organization's liquidity (the ratio of cash and cash equivalents to average daily expenses) sufficient? That is, does your organization have enough cash available to meet expenses?

- Has your nonprofit grown to sufficient size and built sufficient assets (such as endowment and operating reserves) to assist it in adapting to shortfalls in the acquisition of resources?

- Is your organization tenacious about cost reduction, especially related to administrative expenditures?

The Need to Respond

In November 2001, California-based CompassPoint Nonprofit Services surveyed 198 participants in its workshops and at a conference on finance. It found that 78 percent of the nonprofits represented thought that 2002 would be a much more difficult year than 2001. Besides, 73 percent had already experienced difficulties in the form of greater number of clients, decreased attendance at special events, or decline in foundation, corporate, and major individual gifts. Despite this emerging awareness of fiscal stress in their organizations, only 59 percent had taken one or more steps in response, like actively scaling back expenses, instituting a hiring freeze, or changing their fundraising strategy. Thus, nearly half of all nonprofits surveyed were either unaware of forthcoming problems or were taking a wait-and-see approach (CompassPoint Nonprofit Services, 2001).

By January 2004, the Johns Hopkins University Center for Civil Society Studies reported on a nationwide sample of nonprofit organizations from its Listening Post Project. It reported that nonprofits were experiencing significant fiscal stress but were coping with it. Over 85 percent of organizations surveyed reported "some level of fiscal stress," with a majority reporting "severe or very severe stress." While three-quarters of the organizations judged their coping with fiscal stress over that year to have been very or somewhat successful, nearly one in five saw their coping strategies as very or somewhat unsuccessful (Salamon and O'Sullivan, 2004).

In general, nonprofit organizations are not especially well managed nor are they poorly managed. Rather, they are undermanaged. Part of this is the tradition of program professionals becoming executive directors, as well as the absence of appropriate, widespread management preparation for executives in this sector. As for fiscal stress, financial deficits are not uncommon for nonprofit organizations, even some of the largest ones. In 2003, thirty of the nation's one hundred largest nonprofits showed operating deficits ranging from $500,000 to over $300 million (Jones, 2004).

Most nonprofits need "early warning systems," *and need to face reality and react quickly when indicators turn downward.* However, the question of indicators of fiscal stress turns out to be a difficult one, and there is only limited research in this area (Keating et al., 2005).

Strategies for Coping with Fiscal Stress

When the leadership of a nonprofit organization determines that change is indeed coming, no matter how distasteful it may be, it is important that the organization "pivot"—make the decisions and adjustments that are necessary—and implement the strategies selected. As it turns out, managing fiscal stress requires a good understanding of the entire organization, beyond just its budget.

In the terms of strategic planning, there are three basic sets of organizational strategies in which nonprofits engage: program, financial, and organizational. First, programmatic strategies involve the mix of services and clients. Second, financial strategies typically include seeking more revenues and cutting costs. Third, organizational strategies stress external relationships and internal structure. To illustrate, when encountering fiscal stress, a nonprofit might emphasize core programs (program strategy), cut costs and seek to raise more money, especially unrestricted funding (financial strategies), and collaborate more with similar nonprofits (organizational strategy).

FIGURE 2. THE TWIN FOCUS IN MANAGING CHANGE: LONG-TERM VISION AND SHORT-TERM RESULTS

Long-Term Vision

		Strong	**Weak**
Short-Term Results	**High**	Sustainable success	Unsustainable success
	Low	Aborted vision	Stagnation

Adapted from: John P. Kotter. "Winning at Change," *Leader to Leader,* No. 10 (Fall, 1998).

In the uncertainty of fiscal stress, nonprofits often focus on a short-term route to stability. While this is important, thinking short-term only is also quite limiting. In terms of change, Harvard Business School scholar John Kotter emphasizes the importance of considering short-term *and* long-term perspectives together. As shown in Figure 2, Kotter indicates that *both* short-term results and long-term vision are necessary for sustainable organizational success.

While undergoing fiscal stress, the organizational process is quite important: the need to focus leadership, make decisions—often quickly—and communicate well with stakeholders. Maintaining a positive organizational climate during this difficult period is also a key to success. More powerful stakeholders (say, the board chair and the executive committee as well as the executive director) often visibly dominate at this time, in ways that may not be true during other time periods.

In a recent example, Tulane University's leadership was criticized for its December 2005, plan to resurrect the university following hurricane Katrina without an adequate pattern of participation, particularly by faculty. The Tulane plan called for a refocused mission, restructuring, and extensive layoffs (Tulane University, 2005).

In general, strategies to deal with fiscal stress can be put in two categories: those that resist and those that smooth the decline. "Resistance" normally centers on resource acquisition activities. These include protecting the organization's resource base, more successful fundraising, and revenue enhancement from all sources including government, increased fees, and revenue diversification.

"Smoothing" stresses cost containment and cutbacks. These focus on three interrelated organizational components:

- staffing—hiring freezes, attrition, early retirement schemes, retrenchment of paid staff, and reduced compensation;

- program—curtailment of specific services based on centrality to mission, client demand, and program effectiveness; protection of basic services; increased collaboration with similar agencies; transfer of programs to other organizations and curtailing the start-up of new programs; greater productivity;

- spending—across-the-board cuts, targeted budget cuts, one-time deep cuts, repeated small cuts; better cash management; securing a line of bank credit and perhaps borrowing; reduced or delayed purchasing, including capital assets; restructured or consolidated debt to reduce monthly payments; renegotiated leases or other obligations; and the use of financial reserves.

There are any number of special problems associated with cutback management. Should budget cuts be targeted or across-the-board? Should cuts be made up of a series of incremental cuts or a one-time deep gouge? How are program and nonprogrammatic cuts balanced?

In the end, strategies proposed for managing fiscal stress have to be tested for their potential impact on the organization. First, strategies have to respond to the short-term financial and long-term strategic issues facing the nonprofit. This includes likely impact on mission, vision, and programs. There is important evidence that coping with fiscal stress can lead to the erosion in the quantity and quality of services provided by nonprofits (Atkins et al., 2004). Second, the impact on revenues and expenditures has to be calculated with great care. It is the imbalance in these two that caused the fiscal stress to begin with. Third, impact on key stakeholders must be assessed. Major resource providers—individual and institutional—along with board, paid staff, volunteers, clients, and organizational partners, just to name a few, play an important role in the future of any nonprofit. Finally, impact on organizational performance is central. If cost containment and other measures severely hamper the nonprofit's performance or endanger its neediest clients, other strategies should be revisited.

Crisis Management and Retrenchment

Fiscal stress can vary in its severity and in the time frame over which it occurs. Figure 3 illustrates this, with an emphasis on difficult, short-term situations and the importance of immediate and direct responses. Crisis management and, almost inevitably, retrenchment become the focus. Leadership during a fiscal crisis—good or bad—often becomes part of an organization's lore.

FIGURE 3. DIMENSIONS OF FISCAL STRESS

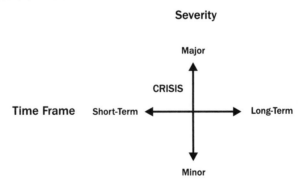

Continuing the saga of nonprofit organizations in New York in the years following 9/11, a survey of executive directors in early 2005 found that fiscal stress had resulted in some important decisions: over 40 percent had laid off staff and nearly 40 percent had closed programs. In addition, one in four had closed service delivery sites or offices, one in five had reduced the number of clients served or cut back on program hours, and one in ten had reduced the geographic area of service (Baruch College, 2005).

It is too easy to advise a nonprofit to detect and contain the financial problem as rapidly as possible, or to act fast and smart in a financial squeeze, or to think only about cutting at the margin. Fiscal stress presents itself in a variety of ways to nonprofit organizations, and no simple, single strategy can solve all of these conditions.

Many managers have a good sense of objectives but an imprecise notion of exactly how to achieve them. Robert Behn refers to this as management by "groping along" (Behn, 1991). Part past experience, part hunch, even part theory, managers tend to experiment as they devise solutions to new challenges. This suggests that problem-solving under conditions of fiscal stress might result in a behavior of small steps or partial solutions or a short-term focus. At the same time, fiscal stress often demands better planning and more comprehensive solutions.

Cost-cutting in a crisis often seems especially difficult in nonprofit organizations, and layoffs are quite painful, even under extreme conditions. Most nonprofits would do almost anything to avoid layoffs. Management consultant David Maddox (1999) warns, "Assume that everyone is looking for the answer to one question—will I lose my job?" Successful layoffs mean special attention to employees who are terminated, but also special attention to the psychologically wounded employees who are retained. Even the vague threat of agency closure, a "death watch," can damage morale and stifle individual creativity and organizational vitality.

In a crisis situation, best practice focuses on the process by which the cuts are made as well as which cuts are selected. In many ways, these are not so different from standard management practice, but fiscal stress makes things much more difficult (Behn, 1996). Some of this advice starts before a crisis.

Step 1. Know the nonprofit well, and be familiar with evaluation reports. Also know what things cost in its operations.

Step 2. Leaders need to face and explain the reality affecting the organization. Rapid change requires new vehicles for participation. A group process is important symbolically, but participation—especially with imperfect information and under rapidly changing conditions—can also help improve decision making too. Both inside and outside the organization, fiscal stress often mandates more effective communication. With layoffs likely, morale is a serious issue. Even under these conditions, work hard to retain the best staff.

Step 3. If possible, seek a certain level of stability, at least for a limited amount of time, and determine the planning process that will be used in this situation. Also assess if outside assistance is needed.

Step 4. With the appropriate information and analysis, decide what is necessary to cut (Behn, 1996) and be prepared to explain these choices. Remember to focus on both bottom lines: program and finances. While stressing the short-term, also remember to look at long-term implications. Because a fiscal crisis almost invariably requires asking the "big" questions—about mission and vision—fiscal stress can also be a time of organizational innovation. Treat those being laid off with respect, and provide appropriate assistance. Remember that continuing staff will judge how you will treat them based on how you treat these newly downsized employees.

Step 5. Maintain the organization's image and rally key stakeholders to support the nonprofit (Behn, 1996).

Step 6. Adapt to the new normalcy as quickly as possible, and encourage creative thinking about the tasks that have to be done.

In managing fiscal stress, it is useful to tell the story of A Contemporary Theatre (ACT), a highly regarded thirty-eight-year-old nonprofit in Seattle. In February 2003, just three months short of starting its new season, ACT found itself $2.7 million in debt, essentially insolvent, and unable to begin its new season. A million dollars of next season's subscription fees had been used to pay last season's bills. There was a half-million dollars in accounts payable, a $1 million line-of-credit already used, and only $3,000 in the bank (Trapnell and Janeway, 2004; Berson, 2003).

Apparently there had been warning signs and high staff turnover, but these were largely ignored. ACT's annual budget approached $6 million. A changing market and a breakdown in board-staff communication were parts of the problem (Trapnell and Janeway, 2004; Downey, 2003).

In response, a new board chair, soon joined by a cochair, exerted herself. The cochair was a bankruptcy attorney and assumed responsibility for managing the short-term payment priorities and legal issues. She also could explain clearly to others the day-to-day financial situation.

A plan was developed to postpone the beginning of the next season and reduce the annual budget to $3.8 million. The board was asked to pay the bills during the next ten weeks. Some key staff continued, but on a volunteer basis; hundreds of others in the community stepped up to help. All departments were reduced in size. Special efforts were made to communicate with external and internal stakeholders. A board-staff team was developed, and in time a recovery plan for the next two years was formulated. This allowed fundraising to begin again, and many in the community remembered just how much they valued the ACT Theatre (Trapnell and Janeway, 2004).

On July 17, 2003, Seattle's mayor declared "ACT Theatre Day," and the new season opened. That year the board and finance division were strengthened, and revenues exceeded the budgeted expenditures (Berson, 2004). By fiscal year 2005, ACT had a legitimately balanced budget for the first time in nine years (Trapnell, 2005).

Summary

In their organizational life cycle, most nonprofit organizations regularly encounter conditions that induce fiscal stress. These conditions are typically external to the agency, but are sometimes internal as well. Fiscal stress can often be traced to the dependency of nonprofits on resource providers in order to accomplish their missions.

The onset of fiscal stress requires organizational attention as quickly as possible. An appropriate organizational process is necessary for legitimacy, as are careful choices among the wide range of strategies designed to both resist and smooth the decline. Prolonged fiscal stress suggests a mismatch between the important mission of a nonprofit organization and its ability to acquire the resources required to implement its mission. The result can be a "hollow" nonprofit that promises much but in the end is unable to deliver.

The most difficult actions are those required when the severity of financial difficulties is great and the time frame is short. Crisis management imposes special requirements, and can be a tipping point in the organization's evolution.

The unique characteristics of nonprofit organizations make managing fiscal stress especially difficult. If fiscal stress is well managed, however, revitalized nonprofits can emerge.

References

Abramson, Alan, and Lester M. Salamon. 2005. *The Nonprofit Sector and the Federal Budget: Fiscal Year 2006 and Beyond.* Washington, DC: Nonprofit Sector Research Fund of The Aspen Institute.

Atkins, Patricia; Mallory Barg, Joseph Cordes, and Martha Ross. 2004. *Thin the Soup or Shorten the Line: Washington Area Nonprofits Adapt to Uncertain Times.* Washington DC: Brookings Institution and the George Washington University.

Baruch College, City University of New York, School of Public Affairs, The Nonprofit Group and Survey Research Unit. 2005. "New York City Nonprofit Executive Outlook: Clients Up, Dollars Down." Spring.

Behn, Robert D. 1991. *Leadership Counts: Lessons for Public Managers.* Cambridge, MA: Harvard University Press. Chapter 5.

Behn, Robert D. 1996. "Cutback Management: Six Basic Tasks." *Governing.* March.

Berson, Misha. 2003. "Is It Curtains for ACT Theatre?" *The Seattle Times.* February 15.

Berson, Misha. 2004. "ACT Back on Track: Seattle Theatre Eyes Future with Hope, Caution." *The Seattle Times.* April 4.

Coffman, Suzanne E. 2005. "Nonprofits' Three Greatest Challenges." *Guidestar Newsletter.* April.

CompassPoint Nonprofit Services. 2001. FlashPoint Research Report. San Francisco: CompassPoint Nonprofit Services, November 2001.

Deans, Graeme K., and Fritz Kroeger. 2005. *Stretch!: How Great Companies Grow in Good Times and Bad.* San Francisco: Jossey-Bass.

Downey, Roger. 2003. "Stage Elegy—Dream Weavers: ACT's Crash Reflects a Seattle Arts Culture of Big Talk and Board Stiffs." *Seattle Weekly.* February 26–March 4.

Galaskiewicz, Joseph. 2004. "What Went Wrong: A Study of Nonprofit Mortality." Washington, DC: Nonprofit Sector Research Fund of the Aspen Institute.

Hager, Mark A. 2001. "Financial Vulnerability among Arts Organizations: A Test of the Tuckman-Chang Measures." *Nonprofit and Voluntary Sector Quarterly,* vol. 30. June.

Jones, Jeff. 2004. "Several NPT 100 Groups Posted Operating Deficits." *The NonProfit Times.* November 1.

Keating, Elizabeth K.; Mary Fischer, Teresa P. Gordon, and Janet Greenlee. 2005. "Assessing Financial Vulnerability in the Nonprofit Sector." Faculty Research Working Paper RWP05–002, John F. Kennedy School of Government, Harvard University. January.

Lee, Michelle J. 2005. "Cash Problems Shut County YWCA." *Poughkeepsie Journal.* February 6.

Lovett, Clara M. 2005. "Letter from the President." American Association for Higher Education. March 24.

Maddox, David. 1999. "Strategic Budget Cutting." *The Grantsmanship Center Magazine.* Fall.

Management Center. 2004. "Management Center Transfers Programs, Closes Doors." Press Release. March 18.

Newsday. 2001. "Warplane Museum, Hurt by Albany Budget Battle, Shuts Down." September 19.

New York Times. 2002. "Debt Is Closing Denver's 3-Year-Old Aquarium." March 24.

Pfeffer, Jeffrey, and Gerald R. Salancik. 1978. *The External Control of Organizations: A Resource Dependency Perspective.* New York: Harper and Row.

Peters, Jeanne; Timothy Wolfred, and Associates. 2001. *Daring to Lead: Nonprofit Executive Directors and Their Work Experience.* San Francisco: CompassPoint Nonprofit Services, August.

Salamon, Lester M., and Richard O'Sullivan. 2004. "Stressed but Coping: Nonprofit Organizations and the Current Fiscal Crisis." *Listening Post Project Communique No. 2.* January 19.

Tichy, Noel. 1999. "The Growth Imperative." *Leader to Leader.* No. 14. Fall.

Trapnell, Susan. 2005. Telephone interview with author. September 30.

Trapnell, Susan, with Kate Janeway. 2004. "A Year of Disaster and Grace: ACT Theatre Survives Its Near Demise." *Centerpiece.* March.

Tulane University. 2005. "Tulane University Announces Bold Renewal Plan: University Will Be Academically Stronger, More Focused and Financially Secure." Press Release. December 8.

Valkys, Michael. 2005. "City Agency Facing Cash Crunch to Shut." *Poughkeepsie Journal.* February 5.

Wilder Foundation, Amherst H., Management Support Services.1987. *Nonprofit Decline and Dissolution Project Report.* Saint Paul, MN: Amherst H. Wilder Foundation.

Additional Reading

American Association of Museums, Accreditation Commission. 2003. "Considerations for AAM Accredited Museums Facing Retrenchment or Downsizing." August 28.

Angelica, Emil, and Vincent Hyman. 1997. *Coping with Cutbacks: The Nonprofit Guide to Success When Times Are Tight.* Saint Paul, MN: Fieldstone Alliance.

Hirschhorn, Larry, and Associates. 1983. *Cutting Back: Retrenchment and Redevelopment in Human and Community Services.* San Francisco: Jossey-Bass.

Klein, Kim. 2004. *Fundraising in Times of Crisis.* San Francisco: Jossey-Bass.

Young, Dennis R. 2002. "Lessons from the Sinking of the Vasa." *The NonProfit Times.* June 15.

6

Investment Strategies

John Zietlow
Professor of Finance
Malone College
Canton, OH

Introduction

Managers of nonprofits are becoming more aware of the potential for improving their organization's financial position through strategic investing. They have avoided the fraudulent schemes such as New Era Philanthropy (Stecklow, 1995) and the high-risk strategies exemplified by Orange County (*Economist,* 1995) to navigate their organizations into commendable risk-return profiles. Proficient organizations have led the way by seizing investment opportunities, determining the appropriate level of cash reserves, defining the investment management process, developing an investment policy statement and a board investment committee, determining the role (if any) of an endowment fund, outsourcing most of the investment decision-making, and procuring accurate and timely investment performance evaluations. This chapter demonstrates how well-managed organizations accomplish those milestones.

What Gives Rise to Investment Opportunities?

The issue here is what provides an organization with investable funds? We find seven possible sources, some of which apply to most nonprofit organizations.

First, an organization may be profitable—meaning simply that it generates net revenue on an ongoing basis.

Second, an organization may experience seasonality of cash flows. For example, many charities receive large cash inflows coming from donations in the

November/December period. Less commonly, an organization may experience early receipt of funds via grants/contracts (prior to the disbursement required). Having the funds in hand prior to disbursing them for expenses or loan repayments gives rise to a short-term investment opportunity. Organizations that invest at no other time of the year may yet have sizable funds to invest during these short periods. Leaving those funds in a non-interest-bearing account or negotiable order of withdrawal (NOW) account making less than one percent interest per year is poor stewardship.

Savings for anticipated future outflows is a third source of investable funds. Many nonprofits, following an unwritten financial policy, prefund their upcoming capital expenditures through annual operating surpluses. They may do this due to difficulty in tapping the capital markets (nonprofits may not issue stock and may be turned down by underwriters of bonds or by banks), or a philosophical reluctance to taking on non-mortgage debt (Hankin, Seidner, and Zietlow, 1998). Others conduct a capital campaign to raise these funds, and a significant portion of the funds may remain invested until eventual disbursement for materials or contractors. Traditional pension plans and the recently proposed guaranteed account pension plans represent another investment challenge. Endowments represent a final category of investments, with the anticipation that an income stream from those endowments will provide a steady revenue source for years to come. For example, the top five symphony orchestras in the U.S. have a combined endowment level of $800 million. We will return to the endowment issue later in this chapter.

A nonprofit organization may be investing for a fourth reason: savings for unanticipated dips in future revenues or unpredictable upward spikes in future outflows. This fits the "money for a rainy day" purpose—but could be for a variety of one-time events. This set-aside of reserves may be money to hedge against uncertain revenue or anticipated expense volatility.

A fifth occasion for having funds to invest arises from windfalls, for example, the donation influx received by the Red Cross and Salvation Army post-9/11, as profiled in Chapter 1. It may arise from a major vendor deciding to donate, rather than charge for, supplies bought from it over a certain time frame. Undesignated wills or bequests also fit this category, although the way in which these funds should be invested will obviously differ.

Proceeds of a bond issue or other debt, not ready to be deployed, constitute a sixth source of investable funds. This may be similar to the prefunding of capital expenditures described earlier, or it may be other debt that is issued to generate funds for working capital—receivables, inventories, and the like.

The proceeds from the maturing of another investment represent our final source of investment funds. An organization that has followed a strategy of "rolling over" one-year certificates of deposit (CDs) periodically faces a reinvestment decision.

In all, nonprofit organizations face multiple opportunities to utilize investments to enhance their financial strength and organizational stability. As they face the increasingly difficult competitive and economic environment addressed throughout this book, investments fill a critical place in their funding streams.

The Role of Short-Term Investments: What is the "Right Level" of Cash Reserves?

This is the fundamental question underlying a nonprofit organization's short-term investment amounts and strategy. Three issues drive the answer to this question: the degree to which the organization's cash inflows and outflows occur at the same time and in the same amounts, the variability of cash flows over time—including the business cycle and stock market bull and bear markets, and the degree to which cash flows are predictable. Let's consider these in turn, from the standpoint of how each might cause an organization to set policy to hold larger levels of cash reserves and short-term investments.

Issue 1. Cash flows are unsynchronized. Wouldn't it be wonderful if donations, dues, grants, or contracts came at just the right moments and in the right amounts to make payroll and pay suppliers? Many organizations, in reality, have a few periods within the year—such as November and December—when cash receipts exceed cash expenditures, but more periods when cash expenditures outstrip cash receipts.

Issue 2. Cash flows are uneven. For example, revenues may rise and crest as the business cycle upswings, but drop off markedly during a recession. Sometimes an organization will see an upward trend in revenues, and stable expenses; other times, it will experience an upward trend in expenses, and be stable in revenues. For example, many nonprofits are now absorbing large and growing health care expenses in their employee benefit category of expense. Or, an organization may be in a growth phase, closely linked to prefunding of capital expenditures or linked to new program rollouts.

Issue 3. Cash flows are unpredictable. Negatively, this may imply unforeseen cash outflows: lawsuits (wrongful termination suits represent a major risk for many charities, and are the single largest type of lawsuits against religious organizations), damage or injury to property or persons, and the like. These risks are particularly significant for those who self-insure, and apply especially to organizations in health-related and early childhood fields of service. Positively, great opportunities that may arise in the future are also unpredictable, giving rise to the "speculative demand for cash" that must be addressed with the organization's investment portfolio, borrowing, or a grant from a foundation, or friendly major donor.

Implications for Cash Reserves and Short-Term Investments

For known and possible transactions needs, an organization should have between three and six months of cash, relative to expenses, in operating reserves; this amount must be kept very liquid (e.g., a small demand deposit amount, and the remainder in overnight or up to three-month securities).

To the degree an organization prefunds capital expenditures or new program expansion, the target for these additional needs might range from twelve to twenty-four months of cash. Recognize that it is artificial to relate this target to expenses, since capital expenditures may have little relationship to one year's expenses. In some cases, this investment amount may be in one- and two-year securities—but the cash forecast drives both the maturity structure and the amounts by maturity.

Possibly an organization may find itself with more funds to invest if: 1) some of the factors we mentioned in the previous section have resulted in a build-up of funds for investment; or 2) special factors lead to growth of investment funds, such as building an endowment (permanent or quasi-endowment) or very large capital expenditures. Again, the cash forecast and the long-term financial forecast jointly determine the investment portfolio's maturity structure. We shall provide more guidance on eligible instruments later in the chapter.

Now that we have an understanding of why an organization will invest, and the amounts it may be investing for short-term and long-term purposes, we now turn our attention to the two phases of the investment asset allocation process: creating a written investment policy statement (IPS) and investment management. First, we consider the all-important investment policy statement. A carefully crafted investment policy statement should make the investment management process, the management of endowments, and performance evaluation run more smoothly and professionally for an organization. We will shift our focus to those topics after gaining an understanding of the investment policy statement.

The Investment Policy Statement (IPS)

A surprising number of nonprofits have not yet created a written IPS, the first phase in the investment allocation process. Others have a basic IPS, with no specifics on short-term cash reserve investments—despite the fact that all nonprofits will have invested for the short term from time to time. See Figure 1 for an example of a short-term investment policy proposed by Hankin, Seidner, and Zietlow (1998). Figure 2 provides a long-term investment policy from that same source, one that is representative of how permanent investment funds might be invested. Funds from bequests or trusts, and in endowments or foundations, are invested based on this type of policy, which is customized to the objectives, needs, and constraints an organization faces.

FIGURE 1. SHORT-TERM INVESTMENT POLICY EXAMPLE

This example may be best suited for a large organization and may be compared and used in the development of organizational policies.

Investment Committee

Within the spectrum of activities of this organization, it is necessary to provide a framework for the regular and continuous management of investment funds. Because there is currently no formal Investment Committee, the Directors will assume this responsibility.

Investment Policy

The policy shall be to invest excess cash in short-term and intermediate-term fixed-income instruments, earning a market rate of interest without assuming undue risk to principal. The primary objectives of such investments in order of importance shall be preservation of capital, maintenance of liquidity, and yield.

Investment Responsibility

Investments are the responsibility of the Vice President of Finance. This responsibility includes the authority to select an investment adviser, open three accounts with brokers, establish safekeeping accounts or other arrangements for the custody of securities, and execute such documents as necessary.

Those authorized to execute transactions include: (1) Vice President of Finance, (2) Director of Accounting, and (3) cash manager. The Vice President of Finance shall ensure that one qualified individual is always available to execute the organization's investments.

Reporting

The Treasurer shall be responsible for reporting the status of investments to the Directors on a quarterly basis. Those reports should include a complete listing of securities held, verified (audited) by parties either inside or outside this organization who have no connection with the investment activities.

FIGURE 1. (CONTINUED)

Investments

A. Obligations of the U.S. Government or Its Agencies

Specifically, these refer to the U.S. Treasury, Federal Home Loan Bank, Federal Home Loan Mortgage Corporation, Federal National Mortgage Association, Federal Farm Credit Bank, Student Loan Marketing Association, and Government National Mortgage Association. Note: When-issued items must be paid for *before* they may be sold.

B. Banks—Domestic

The organization may invest in negotiable CDs (including Eurodollar denominated deposits), Eurodollar time deposits (with branches domiciled in Cayman, Nassau, or London), and BAs of the 50 largest U.S. banks ranked by deposit size. Thrift institutions whose parent has long-term debt rated A by Moody's or Standard & Poor's are acceptable. Exceptions may be local banks or thrift institutions that have lent the corporation money or that would be appropriate to use for some other reason. (These banks and institutions should be listed, along with the maximum dollar amount of exposure allowable for each.)

C. Banks—Foreign

The organization may invest in negotiable CDs (including Eurodollar denominated deposits), Eurodollar time deposits (with branches domiciled in Cayman, Nassau, or London), and BAs of the 50 largest foreign banks ranked by deposit size. However, the issuing institution's parent must have a Moody's or Standard & Poor's rating of at least A.

Limitations

(1) The organization's aggregate investments with foreign entities shall not exceed 50 percent of total investments, and

(2) No more than 10 percent of total investments shall be exposed to any one foreign country's obligations, or $X million per country, whichever is greater.

D. Commercial Paper

All commercial paper must be prime quality by both Standard & Poor's and Moody's standards (i.e., A- by Standard & Poor's and P1 by Moody's).

FIGURE 1. (CONTINUED)

E. Corporate Notes and Bonds

Instruments of this type are acceptable if rated at least A by both Moody's and Standard & Poor's credit rating services.

F. Municipal

Municipal or tax-exempt instruments (suitable only if your organization pays federal income tax). Only tax-exempt notes with a Moody's Investment Grade One rating, or bonds that are rated by both Moody's Investor Service, Inc., and Standard & Poor's as A, may be purchased. Not more than 15 percent of the total issue size should be purchased, and issues of at least $20 million in total size must be selected.

G. Repurchase Agreements

Repurchase agreements (repos) are acceptable, using any of the securities listed above, as long as such instruments are negotiable/marketable and do not exceed other limitations as to exposure per issuer. The firm with whom the repo is executed must be a credit-acceptable bank or a primary dealer (reporting to the Federal Reserve). Collateral must equal 102 percent of the dollars invested, and the collateral must be delivered to the organization's safekeeping bank and priced to market weekly (to ensure correct collateral value coverage) if the repo has longer than a seven-day maturity.

H. Money Market Funds

Acceptable funds are those whose asset size place them among the 30 largest cording to the Morning Star Report and that are in the TUP rating or Standard & Poor's Corporation.

I. Safekeeping Accounts

Securities purchased should be delivered against or held in a custodian safekeeping account at the organization's safekeeping bank. An exception shall be: (1) repos made with approved (see above) banks or dealers for one week or less, and (2) Eurodollar time deposits, for which no instruments are created. This safekeeping account will be audited quarterly by an entity that is not related to the investment function of this organization and the results of that audit shall be provided to the Vice President of Finance.

FIGURE 1. (CONTINUED)

J. Denomination

All investments shall be in U. S. dollars.

K. Diversification of Investments

In no case shall more than 15 percent of the total portfolio be invested in obligations of any particular issuer except the U.S. Treasury.

Maturity Limitations

Overall, maximum weighted average maturity shall be three years. However, on "put" instruments, which may be redeemed (or put) at par, the put date shall be the maturity date.

Review and/or Modification

The Vice President of Finance shall be responsible for reviewing and modifying investment guidelines as conditions warrant, subject to approval by the Directors at least on an annual basis. However, the Vice President of Finance may at any time further restrict the items approved for purchase when appropriate.

FIGURE 2. LONG-TERM INVESTMENT POLICY EXAMPLE

The purpose of the ABC Foundation's endowment is to support the educational mission of the ABC University by providing a reliable source of funds for current and future use. Investment of the endowment is the responsibility of the Investment Committee (Committee). The Committee establishes investment objectives, defines policies, sets asset allocation, selects managers, and monitors the implementation and performance of the Foundation's investment program. The Committee is supported by the office of the Vice President—Finance, which analyzes investment policies and management strategies, makes recommendations to the Investment Committee, and supervises day-to-day operations and investment activities.

I. Statement of Investment Objectives

The endowment will seek to maximize long-term total returns consistent with prudent levels of risk. Investment returns are expected to preserve or enhance the real value of the endowment to provide adequate funds to sufficiently support designated University activities. The endowment's portfolio is expected to generate a total annualized rate of return, net of fees, 5 percent greater than the rate of inflation over a rolling 5-year period.

The Foundation's spending policy governs the rate at which funds are released to fund-holders for their current spending. The Foundation's spending policy will be based on a target rate set as a percentage of market value. This rate will be reviewed annually by the Investment Committee. The spending target rate is 5 percent for Fiscal Year 1995–1996.

II. Asset Allocation

To ensure real returns sufficient to meet the investment objectives, the endowment portfolio will be invested with the following target allocations in either domestic or global securities:

	Minimum (%)	Target (%)	Maximum (%)
Fixed-income	30	35	40
Equities	60	65	70

FIGURE 2. (CONTINUED)

The Investment Committee may appoint equity and fixed-income managers, or select pooled investments, when appropriate. It is the overall objective to be 100 percent invested in equities and fixed income. If at any time the equity manager determines it is prudent to be invested at less than 80 percent, the Committee shall be notified. Equity managers may invest cash positions in marketable, fixed-income securities with maturities not to exceed one year. Quality rating should be prime or investment grade, as rated by Standard & Poor's and Moody's for commercial paper, and for certificates of deposit, a B/C rating by Thompson Bank Watch Services. The managers are expected to reasonably diversify holdings consistent with prudent levels of risk.

At the discretion of the Committee, the endowment portfolio will be rebalanced annually to target allocations as opportunities permit.

III. Guidelines for the Selection of Fixed-Income Securities

A. Diversification

Except for the U.S. government, its agencies or instrumentalities, no more than 5 percent of the fixed-income portfolio at cost, or 8 percent at market value, shall be invested in any one single guarantor, issuer, or pool of assets. In addition, managers are expected to exercise prudence in diversifying by sector or industry.

B. Quality

All bonds must be rated investment grade (BBB/Baa or better) by at least one of the following rating services: Standard & Poor's or Moody's, except that bonds not receiving a rating may be purchased under the following circumstances:

- The issue is guaranteed by the U.S. government, its agencies or instrumentalities.

- Other comparable debt of the issuer is rated investment grade by Standard & Poor's or Moody's.

The average quality rating of the total fixed-income portfolio must be AA or better. Securities downgraded in credit-quality rating subsequent to purchase, resulting in the violation of the policy guidelines, may be held at the manager's discretion. This is subject to immediate notification to the Investment Committee of such a change in rating.

FIGURE 2. (CONTINUED)

C. Duration

At the time of purchase, the average duration of the bond pool should be no longer than the average duration of the current Merrill Lynch 3–5 Year Treasury Index plus one year.

IV. Guidelines for Selection of Equities

A. Diversification for Each Manager

No more than 5 percent at cost, and 10 percent at market value, shall be invested in any one company. In addition, managers are expected to exercise prudence in diversifying by sector or industry.

V. Performance

Performance of the endowment and its component asset classes will be measured against benchmark returns of comparable portfolios as follows:

Total Endowment	SEI Balanced Median Plan Median Plan, Merrill Lynch Balanced Universe
Domestic Equities	S&P 500 Index; Russell 2000 Index Top third of the Merrill Lynch Equity Specialty Universe
Global Equities	MSCI World Index
Fixed-Income	Merrill Lynch 3–5 Year Treasury Index

At least annually, the Investment Committee will conduct performance evaluations at the total endowment, asset class, and individual manager levels. At the total endowment level, the Committee will analyze results relative to the objectives, the real rate of return and composite indices. Further, investment results will be reviewed relative to the effects of policy decisions and the impact of deviations from policy allocations.

On the asset class and individual manager levels, results will be evaluated relative to benchmarks assigned to investment managers or pooled investments selected. These benchmarks are a vital element in the evaluation of individual and aggregate manager performance within each asset class.

The Committee may utilize the services of performance measurement consultants to evaluate investment results,

FIGURE 2. (CONTINUED)

examine performance attribution relative to target asset classes, and other functions as it deems necessary.

VI. Permissible and Nonpermissible Assets

All assets selected for the endowment must have a readily ascertainable market value and must be readily marketable. The following types of assets are permitted:

Equities	Fixed-Income
Common stocks	U.S. Treasury and agency obligations
Convertible securities	Mortgage-backed securities of U.S. government
Preferred stocks	Money-market funds
Index funds	Short-term investment fund accounts
Warrants	Certificates of deposit
Rights (corporate action)	Bankers acceptances
Rule 144a stock	Commercial paper
American depository	Repurchase agreements
Receipts (ADRs)	Asset-backed securities/ Collateralized bond obligations
Corporate securities	
Collateralized mortgage obligations	
ABC Shared Appreciation Mortgage Program	
First trust deeds of gift properties	
Index funds	

Within the mortgage-backed securities and collateralized mortgage obligations sector, investments in CMO tranches with reasonably predictable average lives are permitted, provided at time of purchase the security does not exceed

FIGURE 2. (CONTINUED)

the average duration of the current Merrill Lynch 3–5 Treasury Index plus one year. Interest-only and principal-only (PO) securities—or other derivatives based on them—are prohibited, as are securities with very limited liquidity.

Emerging market investments are permitted within the global equity manager's portfolio, subject to a maximum of 10 percent. Likewise, currency hedging as a defensive strategy is permitted in the global portfolio.

The following types of assets or transactions are expressly prohibited without prior written approval from the Investment Committee:

Equities	Fixed-Income
Commodities	Unregistered securities, except rule futures 144-A securities
Margin purchases	Tax-exempt securities
Short selling	Any asset not specifically permitted
Put and call options	
Direct oil and gas participations	
Direct investments in real estate	

VII. Selection of Investment Managers

The Investment Committee may choose to select and appoint managers for a specific investment style or strategy, provided that the overall objectives of the endowment are satisfied.

VIII. Responsibilities of the Investment Manager

A. Adherence to Statement of Investment Objectives and Policy Guidelines

1. The manager is expected to observe the specific limitations, guidelines, and philosophies stated herein or as expressed in any written amendments or instructions.

2. The manager's acceptance of the responsibility of managing these funds will constitute a ratification of this statement, affirming his or her be-

FIGURE 2. (CONTINUED)

> lief that it is realistically capable of achieving the endowment's investment objectives within the guidelines and limitations stated herein.
>
> B. Discretionary Authority
>
> The Manager will be responsible for making all investment decisions for all assets placed under its management and will be held accountable for achieving the investment objectives stated herein. Such "discretion" includes decisions to buy, hold, and sell securities (including cash and equivalents) in amounts and proportions that are reflective of the manager's current investment strategy and that are compatible with the endowment's investment guidelines.

To craft its first investment policy, or revise it, an organization should work through these three steps:

1. Specify the organization's present and anticipated financial position, constraints, and risk-return preferences.

2. View historical market data in order to compose reasonable expectations, and consider various investment styles and methodologies, culminating in a refined profile of the organization's risk-return preferences.

3. Write an IPS listing the organization's investment objectives and what policies and constraints will be used in managing the organization's funds.

(Based on material contained in Chapter 13 of Francis and Ibbotson, 2002.)

Consider each of these steps in turn. An investment policy is not created in a vacuum. The nonprofit's present and anticipated financial position is especially important for determining which funds belong in the short-term portfolio—much of which is invested in maturities ranging from overnight to three months—and what portion may be invested in the two-year and beyond maturity range. The organization's liquidity and financial plans are an integrated part of this evaluation. For example, a large capital expenditure for a building renovation planned for two years from now implies a significant investment in two-year securities. The number of months of cash reserves being held (relative to annual operating expenses) is another key component here: the larger the number, the longer the allowable maturity within the short-term portfolio.

Constraints include legal, regulatory, and donor restrictions on which securities may be held or for what time periods. Fry (1998) points out that nonprofits are largely accountable for following the "prudent investor rule," and that the wide range of allowable types of investments gives boards and investment committees great latitude in their investing. The biggest mistake most nonprofits make is limiting their investments to ultra-safe securities such as Treasury bills and insured bank certificates of deposit (CDs)—even within their long-term portfolios. By focusing almost solely on one type of risk, default risk (the risk of issuer nonpayment of interest or principal), the investor is overlooking reinvestment risk (changes in the rates at which interest and principal are to be reinvested) and purchasing power risk (the loss of purchasing power due to upswings in the inflation rate).

The investor's time horizon is another essential concern. Donation-dependent nonprofits, especially, tend to self-fund anticipated expenditures, and will invest based on the expenditure date. When foundations and endowments are not generating an income stream sufficient to provide for the funding purpose (or to provide the 5 percent payout), the policy must anticipate that securities will have to be liquidated. Pension plans represent another horizon-linked investment situation. A good example of a nonprofit policy showing how investment purpose might translate into time horizon is the following breakdown from the Institute of Electrical and Electronics Engineers (IEEE, 2003). The investment policy is based on the following investment time horizons:

- Long-Term Investment Fund: 10 years

- Intermediate-Term Investment Fund: 5 years

- Operational Cash Fund: less than one year

Tax laws and legal constraints represent another fundamental issue bearing on the investment policy. Trusts may stipulate whether the nonprofit has latitude to sell donated investments. Many nonprofits have a policy of selling donated securities, if the donor does not specify otherwise, due to the lack of investment expertise and time on the part of the organization's officers and directors to oversee individual investments. In most states, delegation of authority regarding investment decision-making is permissible (see below).

Finally, the organization's tolerance for risk and openness to taking on more significant risks in order to earn more significant returns must be factored into the IPS. One may present the board with some realistic scenarios, and then poll the board members to ascertain their comfort levels with the associated risks. To illustrate, the U.S. stock market gained 26.38 percent in 2003, but suffered a -23.37 percent total return decline in 2002, based on the Standard and Poor's 500 Index™. From September 2002 through March 2003, that same barometer of U.S. stocks declined 42 percent. Could the organization's managers and board (and other stakeholders) accept these losses? If not, a 100 percent allocation to a representative group of U.S. stocks will not be an appropriate investment strategy, and the IPS must include carefully worded constraints.

The second step a nonprofit organization must take preparatory to crafting the IPS is to develop reasonable investment performance expectations based on historical data. The nonprofit's board and officers should know what is achievable, so as not to overrely on investment returns to fill large gaps in the organization's funding stream. Studies of investor expectations show large knowledge gaps: While 68 percent of Americans age 25 or older are either "very" or "somewhat" confident they will have adequate retirement savings, only 58 percent of the respondents are currently saving for retirement (surely they do not think Social Security will provide all they need!), and 45 percent of the respondents have household assets (excluding their home) of less than $25,000 (TIAA-CREF, 2004). Nonprofit officers and directors may be similarly over-optimistic. They may be too averse to risk, giving up the opportunity to earn the investment returns necessary to meet obligations or reach organizational targets. Decision-makers should understand that investment markets in the U.S. and in developed countries abroad are efficient, and higher returns come by taking on more risk. Portfolio managers may brag about their ability to time the market, but hard data shows almost none of them can do so consistently over bull and bear markets. One study found that caution is warranted, because more than one in ten stock mutual funds are likely to beat the performance of the average stock fund for three years in a row merely as a matter of chance (DeBondt and Thaler, 1985). Claims that a portfolio manager "beat the market" or "beat the peers" several years in a row neither assure special skill nor that this performance will continue into the future.

The third step in the investment allocation process, and the culmination of Phase 1, is the creation of the IPS. This statement includes who is responsible for the investment program, who does the investing, the organization's investment objectives, investment constraints, what risk and performance measurement policies will be used in managing the organization's funds, and who will be responsible for policy review and modifications (Francis and Ibbotson, 2002, p. 367). Recognize that specific investments cannot (or at least should not) be made until this IPS has been formulated, reviewed, and approved by the board.

Let's illustrate the investment objectives for the short-term portfolio:

> It shall be the policy of this organization to invest its temporary surplus cash in short-term and intermediate-term fixed-income instruments to earn a market rate of interest without assuming undue risk to principal. The primary objectives of making such investments shall be, in their order of importance, preservation of capital, maintenance of liquidity, and yield. (Hankin, Seidner, and Zietlow, 1998, p. 369)

This objectives statement embodies the "SLY" approach to short-term investment selection popularized by William Donoghue: safety first, then liquidity, then yield. Nonprofits often park short-term monies in money market mutual funds because these instruments follow a safety-first philosophy and preserve the price ("net asset value") of the fund's shares at $1.00. (For guidance on longer-term investing, refer back to Figure 2 for sample objectives for a long-term endowment pool.)

The board is ultimately responsible for the investment program, but the conduct of the program is normally assigned to a person or committee. Often, an investment committee is charged with all aspects of investment program management. This committee normally includes one or more of the organization's senior financial and administrative managers, one or more board representatives, and possibly one or more other individuals possessing financial expertise. This committee often drafts the IPS for board approval. The committee's responsibility typically includes the following: 1) set policy on how investments should be managed; 2) make decisions on asset allocation (see below) and determine a spending policy for an endowment fund, if any; 3) select the investment manager(s); 4) conduct investment performance reviews, including comparisons to benchmarks and any available peer organization investment performance data; and 5) provide performance reports to the board. Typically, corporate resolutions approved by the board will be provided to banks and securities dealers, indicating the scope of authority of each authorized person. A nonprofit example of asset allocation targets as well as the range the investment manager must maintain when values swing up or down, and the benchmark against which performance will be compared, is given in Figure 3.

FIGURE 3. EXAMPLE OF ASSET ALLOCATION TARGETS AND RANGES

Asset Class	Benchmark	Target	Rebalance Max.	Rebalance Min.
U.S. Domestic Equity	Russell 3000 Index	47.0%	50.0%	44.0%
Developed Int'l Equity	MSCI EAFE Index	15.0%	17.5%	12.5%
Emerging Int'l Equity	MSCI EMF Index	3.0%	4.5%	2.5%
Fixed Income	Lehman U.S. Universal Bond Index	35.0%	38.0%	32.0%

Source: Investment Strategy Statement, General Board of Pension and Health Benefits of The United Methodist Church. (www.gbophb.org/invest/pdf/invpol.pdf; www.gbophb.org/invest/pdf/invpol.pdf). Accessed: September 4, 2004.

Not only should the policy detail the asset classes an organization will invest in—including a range for what percent may be invested in each—but it should also include a statement to the effect that "unless specifically permitted under the guidelines, all other investment instruments are prohibited" (Hankin, Seidner, and Zietlow, 1998, p. 373). The investment committee's periodic review of this constraint statement will give consideration to new asset subclasses (such as small company growth stocks) that should be made allowable. Other constraints will address diversification guidelines to keep the portfolio from being overly concentrated in any particular asset class, market, sector, geographic region, industry, company, or individual security.

We close this section with a picture of what an organization may strive for in setting its investment policy and asset allocation strategy. The YMCA's retirement fund investment policy provides an example of a long-term investment asset allocation framework (YMCA, 2004). In Figure 4 we see the framework, along with allowable deviations from the target allocation and the benchmark against which each asset class and asset subclass will be monitored.

FIGURE 4. YMCA RETIREMENT PLAN ASSET ALLOCATION AND BENCHMARKS

Target Policy Porfolio (effective July 1, 2003)

Asset Class	Target Allocation		Maximum Deviation	Performance Benchmark
Stocks		55.5%		
US Large Cap Equities	28.0%		+/-3.0%	Russell 1000
US Small Cap Equities	11.5%		+/-2.0%	Russell 2000
International Equities	16.0%		+/-2.0%	MSCI ACWI Free ex-US
Alternative Assets		5.5%		
Private Equity	1.5%		+/-1.0%	Cambridge Vintage Year
Absolute Return	3.0%		+/-1.0%	90 Day Treasury Bills +5%
Real Estate	1.0%		+/-1.0%	NCREIF/NAREIT
Bonds		38.0%	+/-5.0%	Lehman Aggregate Index
Cash		1.0%	+/-0.5%	90 Day Treasury Bills
Total Porfolio		100.0%		

Source: YMCA Retirement Fund Statement of Investment Policy, Investment Guidelines, of Investment Functions (2003) pg. 2: www.yretirement.org/ymcarf/pdf/invest_policy.pdf. Used by permission of YMCA Retirement Fund, New York, NY.

The YMCA's alternative investments include buyout and venture capital funds; real estate investments (perhaps REITs, which are like mutual funds and invest in real estate or loans backed by real estate); when market conditions favor them, investments in distressed debt (debt of troubled companies, in which the value has fallen to 80 cents or less per $1 of face value); subordinated debt (such as bonds that are not paid on unless and until other, "senior" bondholders get paid); and emerging market debt (relatively high-yield bonds issued by nations whose economies are considered to be developing, typically including most of Africa, Eastern Europe, Latin America, Russia, the Middle East, and Asia outside of Japan). Bear in mind that this is a retirement fund investment policy, so it is geared to long-horizon investing and holding periods. Also, compared to most nonprofit policies, this one would qualify as an advanced and sophisticated policy.

The Investment Management Process

There are four steps in Phase 2 of investment management, as follows. These four steps are:

1. Prepare estimates about future asset class investment returns based on a study of current conditions.

2. Allocate the investment funds to allowable asset classes, based on targets and permissible ranges specified in the IPS. Be sure to identify and adhere to any constraints specified by donors to endowments and foundations. Any requirement to pursue "socially responsible investing" (SRI) should also be spelled out, such as avoiding alcohol, gambling, tobacco, or defense industry stocks.

3. Issue and execute investment orders.

4. Conduct periodic performance evaluation, issue reports, gain feedback, and make any necessary revisions to investment goals and policies. (Francis and Ibbotson, 2002, p. 367)

Much of this analysis and decision-making may be done by outside investment managers. A full discussion of these steps is beyond our scope. However, two points need to be made about Step 2. First, the portfolio manager must be sure to identify and adhere to any constraints specified by donors to endowments and foundations. Second, the Uniform Management of Investment Funds Act of 1972 (for charities' ongoing investments and for their endowments) and the Prudent Investor Act of 1997 (for trusts) govern investment activities for many nonprofits in many states, and provide sound guidance for all nonprofits wherever they may reside. The notion of "prudent investing" is attributed to Judge Samuel Putnam, who stated in *Harvard v. Armory* (1830): "Those with responsibility to invest money for others should act with prudence, discretion, intelligence, and regard for the safety of capital as well as income."

Two key laws largely govern the practice of prudent investing for nonprofits in the U.S. The Uniform Management of Institutional Funds Act (UMIFA), enacted in 1972, has been adopted in some form by all states except Alaska, Pennsylvania, and South Dakota (for the full text and comments, see University of Pennsylvania Law School, n.d.). The Uniform Prudent Investor Act (UPIA), enacted in 1994, has been adopted by thirty-eight states up to the present time. (University of Pennsylvania Law School, n.d.; do not confuse this Act with the Uniform Principal and Income Act of 1997, or as revised in 2001, which deals with apportioning funds between interest and principal and ensuring that the trust creator's intentions are honored). Many analysts believe that the charity investor is expected to follow a diversification strategy in order to be deemed "prudent." Even then, one should exercise care in not being over-optimistic regarding what annual rate of return such a portfolio will bring: the expected rate of return for a diversified portfolio of stocks should be based on more than mere extrapolation of postwar average stock performance (Steuerle, 2004a). Implementing a diversification strategy, in turn, implies an understanding of and adherence to the tenets of Modern Portfolio Theory (MPT; see Bodie, Kane, and Marcus, 2004). Think of diversification as the opposite to "putting all of one's eggs in one basket." Undiversified or under-diversified portfolios are not only unwise—they neither provide the greatest rate of return for a given amount of risk nor do they provide the smallest amount of risk for a given rate of return—but they raise the possibility that an organization may not be investing its long-term investment assets in a prudent fashion.

The one area in which corporate and nonprofit institutional investors may deviate from portfolio theory is in investing more in bonds than capital market theory would suggest. Empirical justification for buying bonds, especially inflation-indexed bonds, has recently been developed by academic researchers (Campbell and Viceira, 2002, Chapter 3). In addition to underscoring the importance of diversification, UMIFA and UPIA as well as ensuing case law permit nonprofits to: 1) sell off some investments ("invade principal") to supplement income to provide for the organization's (or, for a foundation, grantees') needs, and 2) delegate investment decision-making and not be held to be in violation of their fiduciary duty (Fry, 1998). A further discussion of the legal environment is available in Fremont-Smith (2004). However, legal counsel should of course be sought to ensure that the organization adheres to the ground rules in its particular state.

The Role of Endowments

If an organization is small and still raising funds to get its facilities built and programs launched, the thought of an endowment may seem like some distant mirage. However, as the organization grows, it will soon get to the point where an endowment is an important item for the board's agenda. As we found in the earlier section on cash reserves, monies that are invested provide a revenue stream that may become an important and dependable component of the overall funding picture.

Fry (1998, pp. 183–185) suggests four reasons for having an endowment. First, an endowment represents saving, not hoarding. He uses the analogy of owning a building within which to conduct an organization's operations—since we do not think of this as hoarding, neither should we look askance at holding large amounts of financial assets that provide an income stream that represents a significant and dependable portion of the annual operating budget. The resulting smoothing effect on the organization's cash flows may be deemed good stewardship. Second, when the organization cannot raise funds for a certain program or outreach, the endowment earnings can fill the funding gap. Third, when the organization grows and must maintain and operate new and larger facilities, the endowment earnings may come from an additional portion of the endowment, which may be thought of as an "endowment for maintenance" that keeps core programs funded without their being impaired due to diversion of (normal operating) funds to building maintenance and operation. Finally, some donors do not wish to give to current operations, but will give to endowment funds. They may also think of large one-time gifts from wealth differently than annual campaign gifts. Accordingly, endowment fundraising is not necessarily "taking from Peter to pay Paul," and the organization ends up with additional funds. This assumes, however, that the organization has an endowment that can receive such gifts.

The payout percentage from the endowment or foundation portfolio is a subject of controversy (NCNE, 2004; Cordes and Rooney, 2004). UMIFA and UPIA, mentioned earlier, allow the organization and portfolio managers acting on its behalf to manage on a total return basis (as opposed to focusing mostly on income from bonds and dividend-paying stocks). This gives the organization the ability to maintain its 5 percent (or other) payout policy by selling certain securities when the income stream from investments is not ample to provide the funds for this payout.

Again, "socially responsible investing" (SRI) constraints may need to be applied to endowment or foundation investment selection. Givers are more and more concerned about the destination of their funds, especially avoiding investment in objectionable stocks or bonds. During some market periods SRI stocks do relatively well compared to the overall market indexes, and in other periods they may perform under market averages.

Finally, a nonprofit organization may also consider a quasi-endowment. These are not permanent endowment funds having donor restrictions, but board-designated reserves. The board may determine at a future date to release the funds from the "endowment" in this case. Two cautions regarding these funds are to let any donor to such a fund know the terms and conditions upon which the board can tap these funds, and also to provide such information in the organization's marketing materials that refer to this fund's existence (Fry, 1998, p. 186). A sample quasi-endowment resolution is provided in Fry (1998, Appendix F–1).

Investment Performance Evaluation

Nonprofit organizations are beginning to benchmark their investment portfolios' returns against widely available market indexes or benchmark securities' yields. The stock portfolio might be compared to the S&P 500™, and the cash reserves income return compared to the three-month Treasury bill yield for that period. However, best practice in the business sector has shifted to customized indexes that match more exactly the asset sub-class (e.g., small company growth stocks) or manager style (e.g., value investing). To illustrate, businesses wishing to benchmark both their very short-term cash reserves portfolio and their short-term portfolio now may compare these portfolios' returns to customized benchmarks data developed by Decision Analytics (San Francisco) for the Association for Financial Professionals (www.decisionanalytics.com). Nonprofits are urged to shift to this new customized benchmark paradigm, providing a better and fairer "par" for the portfolio manager.

As noted earlier, the benchmark against which each category of investments is to be compared should be spelled out in the IPS. This further motivates a periodic revisit to the IPS by the investment committee, since new and better yardsticks are emerging over time. Refer to Figure 4 to see the interesting benchmarks utilized by the YMCA retirement plan.

Finally, if an organization is comparing actual investment results to an expected return established at the beginning of the investment period, it may be surprised by the "underperformance." However, the benchmark return, or "par," might be set too high or too low. Steuerle (2004b) notes that some analysts promote calculating expected returns without any reflection on the relative level of the initial stock price-to-earnings ratio (assuming it is properly measured) and the initial interest rate on bonds. As a result, he notes, a charity investing in a mixed stock and bond portfolio should have expected a fairly high return in the early-to-mid 1980s, and should be expecting a very moderate return today.

We have only scratched the surface of performance evaluation, but we note in closing that this is a very important part of the fiduciary duty of the investment committee and/or the board of directors. It is an activity that must be done well. Consult Fry (1998) and Hankin, Seidner, and Zietlow (1998) for more on this topic.

Conclusion

Strategic investing allows an organization to advance from a "tin cup" begging and less-than-professional mentality to an "empowered agency" model, in which it proactively and professionally sizes up and takes advantage of reasonable return-risk investing opportunities. We have seen how they may do this by seizing investment opportunities, determining the appropriate level of cash reserves, defining the investment management process, developing an investment policy statement and a board investment committee, determining the role (if any) of an endowment fund, outsourcing most of the investment decision-making, and procuring accurate and timely investment performance evaluations. By following this protocol, the empowered nonprofit organization secures investment income as one of the most valued revenue sources supporting its mission.

References

Bodie, Zvi; Alex Kane, and Alan J. Marcus. 2004. *Essentials of Investments,* 5th edition. Boston: McGraw Hill Irwin. Chapters 5–7.

Campbell, John Y., and Luis M. Viceira. 2002. *Strategic Asset Allocation—Portfolio Choice for Long-Term Investors.* London: Oxford University Press.

Cordes, Joseph J., and Patrick M. Rooney. 2004. "Fundraising Costs." Chapter 5 in Dennis R. Young, ed., *Effective Economic Decision-Making by Nonprofit Organizations.* New York: The Foundation Center.

DeBondt, Werner F. M., and Richard Thaler. 1985. "Does The Stock Market Overreact?" *Journal of Finance,* 40(3), pp. 793–805.

———— 1995. "Financial Decision-Making in Markets and Firms." In R. A. Jarrow, V. Maksimovic, and W. T. Ziemba (eds.), *Handbooks in Operations Research and Management Science, Volume 9: Finance.* Amsterdam: Elsevier.

The Economist. 1995. "Agent Orange." *The Economist,* April 15, 1995, pp. 19–21.

Francis, Jack, and Roger Ibbotson. 2002. *Investments: A Global Perspective.* Upper Saddle River, NJ: Prentice Hall.

Fremont-Smith, Marion R. 2004. "Investment and Expenditure Strategies." Chapter 6 in Dennis R. Young, ed., *Effective Economic Decision-Making by Nonprofit Organizations.* New York: The Foundation Center.

Fry, Jr., Robert P. 1998. *Nonprofit Investment Policies: Practical Steps for Growing Charitable Funds.* New York: John Wiley and Sons.

Hankin, Jo Ann; Alan Seidner, and John Zietlow. 1998. *Financial Management for Nonprofit Organizations.* New York: John Wiley and Sons.

IEEE. 2003. *IEEE Investment Operations Manual (IOM).* September 16. (accessed online Jan. 17, 2001). www.ieee.org/portal/cms_docs/about/whatis/policies/investopsmanual.pdf

National Center on Nonprofit Enterprise. 2004. Comments made at NCNE Conference.

Stecklow, Steve. 1995. "False Profit: How New Era's Boss Led Rich and Gullible into a Web of Deceit," *The Wall Street Journal,* May 19, pg. A1.

Steuerle, Eugene. 2004a. Comments made at NCNE Conference.

———— 2004b. Personal communication. August 21.

TIAA-CREF. 2004. "Survey: Americans Need to Save More for Retirement," *TIAA-CREF Advance,* Summer, pg. 6.

University of Pennsylvania Law School. n.d. Uniform Management of Institutional Funds Act. Accessed online Jan. 17, 2005 at: www.law.upenn.edu/bll/ulc/fnact99/1970s/umifa72.pdf.

———— n.d. Uniform Prudent Investor Act. Accessed online Jan 17, 2005 at: www.law.upenn.edu/bll/ulc/fnact99/1990s/upia94.pdf.

YMCA. 2004. The YMCA Retirement Fund: Statement of Investment Policy, Investment Guidelines, Delegation of Investment Functions. July 1. Accessed online Jan. 17, 2005 at: www.yretirement.org/ymcarf/pdf/invest_policy.pdf.

7

Institutional Collaborations and Transformations

Steven Rathgeb Smith
Director
Nancy Bell Evans Center for Nonprofit and Philanthropy
Daniel J. Evans School of Public Affairs
University of Washington
Seattle, WA

Collaboration and cooperation are central concerns in contemporary nonprofit management. Public and private funders increasingly expect nonprofits to engage in collaborative relationships with nonprofit and public sector organizations, especially as it pertains to new programmatic initiatives. Collaborations between nonprofits and businesses have also gained increasing salience (Austin, 2000), particularly given the competition for public contracts and private donations and grants.

But collaboration between nonprofit organizations and other agencies and groups can be complicated. It presents nonprofit staff and volunteers with a host of management challenges, particularly since many nonprofit agencies tend to be focused on growing and building their own organization rather than developing cooperative relationships with external organizations. Collaboration with other organizations may also present complicated management and programmatic trade offs. Collaboration can be time-consuming and may lead to staff and volunteer frustration and attrition unless it is successful. Consequently, the potentially considerable transaction costs of collaboration suggest the need for nonprofit staff and volunteers to weigh very carefully the circumstances under which they engage in collaborative relationships.

This chapter is based in part on a presentation at a panel entitled, "Institutional Collaborations and Transformations" at the biennial conference of the National Center for Nonprofit Enterprise (NCNE), Washington, DC, January 2004. The author is indebted to Melissa Stone, Stephen Wernet, Dennis Young, and Robert Zdenak for comments on earlier versions of this chapter.

This chapter focuses on the management challenges, trade offs, and strategic concerns pertaining to collaborations involving nonprofits. In the next section, an overview of the "collaboration" movement is presented, followed by a discussion of the distinctive challenges faced by nonprofit agencies as they strive to forge collaborative relationships with various nonprofit, public, and for-profit agencies. The subsequent section details important components of successful and sustainable collaborations as well as specific strategies for nonprofit organizations to consider when undertaking collaborative initiatives. The chapter concludes with an examination of the implication of current trends in funding and management on nonprofit collaborations and partnerships.

The Collaboration Movement

Prior to the 1960s, the universe of nonprofit organizations in any given community was quite modest, and except for large urban areas such as Boston and New York City, restricted to a relative handful of different service categories in social welfare, health, education, and the arts. Growth in the number of nonprofits tended to be incremental. Further, most nonprofit agencies in these local communities faced little direct competition from other agencies and tended to occupy a distinctive market niche. And, most nonprofits were relatively small (except for the larger universities, hospitals, and cultural institutions). In the social welfare arena, the predecessor organization of the United Way, the Community Chest, helped ensure that the existing nonprofit agencies received a predictable, steady stream of revenues. Most nonprofits depended upon fees and modest cash and in-kind donations. Few agencies received significant public funding (Smith and Lipsky, 1993).

In this context, nonprofit agencies faced little financial or political incentive to collaborate. This situation began to change in the 1960s and 1970s with the big growth in federal funding of nonprofit organizations. Through a variety of major federal initiatives, nonprofit organizations in almost every category—from the arts to health to social welfare—were the beneficiaries of a sharp increase in federal aid. Initially, many of the established nonprofit organizations resisted accepting federal funding, but eventually most agencies agreed to accept the new money. Over time, federal funding led to a rapid increase in the number of new nonprofit organizations, especially in service categories newly targeted by federal funds, such as community mental health, alcohol and drug treatment, youth rehabilitation, and workforce training.

While federal funding has experienced many ups and downs since the 1970s, the overall trend has been upward, especially in social welfare and health. Private giving by individuals, foundations, and corporations has risen in absolute terms. Due in part to this increase in public and private funding, the number of 501(c)(3) agencies has more than tripled in the last twenty-five years (Smith, 2002; Independent Sector, 2003). But recently, public funding has been declining, albeit unevenly depending upon the jurisdiction and the service area. And private giving has been flat, when inflation is considered. The result is much greater competition for public and private funds, placing pressure on nonprofit agencies to think creatively about ways in which collaboration might usefully lower their costs or bring in new revenue.

The proliferation of nonprofit organizations has also tended to fragment the organizational universe, with many agencies occupying the same market niche and sometimes sharing this niche with for-profit and public organizations (Smith and Lipsky, 1993; Sosin, 1990). For instance, Robert Egger, the entrepreneurial director of the nonprofit D.C. Central Kitchen, an agency for the disadvantaged in Washington, D.C., noted that in 1983 there were 35 soup kitchens and food pantries in New York City; in 2003, the number had grown to 967 (Egger, 2004, p. 44).

Organizational and service fragmentation has prompted a reassessment of the way in which services are provided, especially among funders and policymakers who worry about the effectiveness and efficiency of the services and programs offered by nonprofit organizations (see Egger, 2004). This reassessment has encouraged nonprofit staff and volunteers and funders to push for greater collaboration among agencies as a strategy to reduce duplication and enhance service efficiency.

The interest in collaboration has also been spurred by the broad reform effort under way among scholars of public management, policymakers, and public officials. This call for reform has been called the "New Public Management" (NPM) and in the U.S. context is part of the "reinventing government" movement sparked by the book of the same name by David Osborne and Ted Gaebler in 1992. While NPM has many aspects, a central feature is the perception that public managers need to be more collaborative and participatory (Osborne and Gaebler, 1992; Behn, 2001; Hood, 1991; Khademian, 2002; Wondolleck and Yaffee, 2000). While much of the NPM literature is focused exclusively on public organizations, it has affected nonprofit agencies in three important ways. First, nonprofits are perceived to represent citizens and local communities, so the push for more collaboration within the public sector has meant new opportunities for collaborations and partnerships between public and nonprofit agencies. Second, the emphasis on collaboration and teamwork has led public managers to require collaboration among their nonprofit grantees, often as a condition of receiving a grant or contract. Third, NPM has indirectly influenced the thinking of nonprofit managers and scholars by suggesting new ways of enhancing the effectiveness and efficiency of nonprofit organizations through collaboration.

Collaboration and teamwork are also a central part of contemporary thinking about management in the private, for-profit sector. The noted management scholar John Kotter (1996) observes that successful organizational change requires creating a culture of cooperation and collaboration within the organization. The general theme is echoed in the work of Katzenbach and Smith (1993) in their best-selling book, *The Wisdom of Teams*. Peter Senge (1990) emphasizes the importance of collaboration to the creation of a successful learning organization. And James Austin (2000) argues that businesses and nonprofit organizations can realize substantial benefits through collaboration.

The value of collaboration as an organizational strategy and its direct relevance to nonprofit organizations is strongly reinforced by the research on social capital of Robert Putnam (2000, 2003). His research indicates that formal and informal nonprofit organizations encourage greater cooperation at the local level and hence promote the creation of social capital, which can then help a community develop economically, respond effectively to unexpected threats and disasters, and encourage greater accountability and effectiveness in the delivery of public and nonprofit services. By implication, collaboration and partnerships of various types—public-nonprofit, nonprofit-nonprofit, and business-nonprofit—can be beneficial to the health and vitality of a community.

The Distinctiveness of Nonprofit Organizations

Despite the widespread enthusiasm for collaboration among funders, scholars, and practitioners, the unique characteristics of nonprofit organizations present special challenges in forging collaboration and partnership. These challenges include: the problem of ownership, scarce resources and undercapitalization, and the importance of mission.

In for-profit companies, ownership is well-defined and relatively straightforward, at least in principle. For publicly traded companies, the ultimate owners are the shareholders, and for private companies the owners are simply the individuals who control the company. But ownership in nonprofit organizations is much more complicated. First, most nonprofit 501(c)(3) organizations do not have members with voting rights to elect the board of directors. Instead, the board of directors is self-perpetuating, with board members chosen and elected by the board. Second, the board of directors is typically volunteer and meets for a relatively brief amount of time during the course of the year. Third, nonprofit 501(c)(3) organizations are tax-exempt organizations that receive tax subsidies from government in exchange for their charitable works. As a result, government and by extension the citizenry have a certain ownership stake, albeit an indirect one. Fourth, many nonprofits serve vulnerable client populations or disadvantaged communities. Many of these client groups and communities are represented on nonprofit boards; even when they are not in the majority they can be very influential in organizational affairs.

Thus, ownership is not straightforward and can be contentious. Indeed there is much debate among scholars, policymakers, and nonprofit personnel regarding who are the true owners and who can speak for the nonprofit. For instance, mergers among hospitals—the ultimate form of collaboration among two nonprofits—have been halted by state officials concerned about the merits of the merger and its impact on the public. Nonprofits may have difficulty responding quickly to collaboration opportunities because the board is divided and no other members exist to provide a mandate or a push to the board to form a particular partnership.

A second complication can be scarce resources common among many nonprofits, especially smaller, newer nonprofits. Collaboration among nonprofits and other organizations can be time-intensive and require a sustained commitment of staff and volunteers. But many nonprofits have very modest budgets and are undercapitalized. Consequently, they may find it quite difficult to devote the necessary resources to undertaking and maintaining a collaborative initiative. Volunteers can be useful depending upon the situation, but many types of partnerships require a forceful presence of key staff of the agency.

A third key factor affecting the ability of nonprofits to engage in collaboration and partnerships is the mission-based focus of nonprofits. Indeed, one of the most distinctive aspects of nonprofits is the mission, which serves as a guiding statement for the organization and serves to attract individuals for paid and volunteer positions (Wolf, 1999). The mission thus offers "purposive" incentives to individuals to join the organization, by giving individuals a compelling reason or purpose (Wilson, 1973). The additional "solidary" benefits of the fellowship and satisfaction of working with like-minded people is a factor prompting people to join (Wilson, 1973; Mason, 1996). Consequently, many individuals working in paid and volunteer positions in nonprofits are in the organization not primarily for the material benefits (which is typically the case in a business) but for the nonmaterial purposive or solidary incentives.

This passion and commitment can be a tremendous benefit for nonprofits with few resources. But this same enthusiasm and dedication means that many individuals may be reluctant to collaborate or partner with other organizations because of the concern that a partnership might compromise or undermine the mission of the organization. For example, the staff of a nonprofit "Save the Salmon" might be worried that a partnership with the fishing industry might compromise the organization's values and ideals. Or a child welfare agency serving at-risk youth might be worried that an alliance with a much larger nonprofit would dilute their distinctive services and compromise quality. The passion for the organization among board members also means that many board members may feel an obligation to maintain the separate identity of the organization and enhance the competitiveness of the organization rather than pursue collaborative initiatives.

Despite these obstacles and challenges, nonprofits have a greater incentive than ever to undertake collaborations and partnerships. The next section details the different types of partnerships as a framework for understanding the trade offs involved in various partnership arrangements and the issues for policymakers and nonprofit staff and volunteers to consider in developing and sustaining successful and effective partnerships.

Collaborations and Partnerships: Defining the Landscape

A collaborative effort can be defined as "a mutually beneficial and well-defined relationship entered into by two or more organizations to achieve common goals" (Mattesich, Murray-Close, and Monsey, 2001). Further, three different levels of collaboration can exist: 1) cooperation (project-specific relationship), 2) coordination (informal relationship), and 3) collaboration (formal relationship). Collaboration can occur through several different types of organizational mechanisms, including alliances, consortia, coalitions, federations, networks, collaboratives, and partnerships (Hill and Lynn, 2004; Austin, 2000; Kohm, 2004). All of these different mechanisms can be informal, meaning that no legally incorporated entity exists; instead, the different parties are bound together by mutual interest in a specific topic or concern such as wetlands preservation or human services. Even as an informal arrangement, these different organizational entities may receive funding from donors, although sizable grants are typically channeled through a fiscal sponsor and the money regranted. Formal organizations have boards of directors, bylaws, and funding from donors or members. Frequently, collaborative initiatives start as informal entities and then move to legal incorporation and greater formalization as they become larger and their funding becomes more substantial.

Collaboration can be a two-party relationship between a nonprofit and one other organization, such as the partnership between CARE and Starbucks (Austin, 2000). But many collaborations today are multiparty initiatives with many different nonprofit, public, and sometimes for-profit organizations. Typical examples include a community health partnership focused on reducing substance abuse in a local community, and a citywide collaboration to foster economic development in disadvantaged areas of the city.

Importantly, Austin (2000) and others have noted that collaboration between nonprofits and business can be conceptualized along a continuum from philanthropic to integrative. The former begins with a loose relationship characterized by an exchange of resources and donations from the business to the nonprofit. The collaboration can remain at this level, but over time it may evolve in a much more integrated relationship with, for example, an exchange of personnel on the respective boards of directors. These much more intense and complicated collaborations are much rarer than philanthropic collaborations, but they can nonetheless be very rewarding for both parties, if designed correctly.

Key Organizational Considerations in Developing Collaborations and Partnerships

Despite the complexities of collaboration, a tremendous surge in various types of collaborations has occurred in recent years. The sheer complexity and variation in these collaborations is quite striking and leads to several observations on the lessons learned from this outpouring of collaborative initiatives. This section focuses on these lessons with a particular focus on the commonalities among successful and effective collaborations and partnerships. The following characteristics appear to be especially important: 1) shared purpose, 2) appropriate institutional design, 3) sustained leadership support, 4) adequate resources, 5) effective technical assistance and support, and 6) proper accountability. While collaborations vary greatly, these general lessons are applicable to designing effective collaborations regardless of the level of formality or substantive focus.

SHARED PURPOSE

As noted, Robert Putnam (2000, 2003) has written extensively about the value of social capital, or shared networks of cooperation in a community, in contributing to beneficial social, economic, and political outcomes in a community. For example, communities with high levels of social capital have higher levels of participation in voluntary associations and higher levels of contributions to charitable organizations. Likewise, research indicates that collaboration among nonprofit and other types of organizations is more likely in communities with higher levels of social capital. Cooperative social networks—the essential component of social capital—allow individuals to exchange information and resources and develop bonds of trust that then encourage greater collaboration (Huxham, 2003). Trust promotes collaboration even in the absence of targeted resources for collaboration.

Some examples—both unsuccessful and successful— will illustrate this point well. In the first instance, the city of Hartford, Connecticut, in conjunction with several nonprofit service agencies, received a grant of over $7 million in 1999 from the Federal Department of Labor. The grant was a "Youth Opportunity" (YO) grant, designed to improve the delivery of services to at-risk youth in Hartford through a new collaborative approach. All of the various public and nonprofit agencies agreed to participate in the grant application process and the basic collaborative approach. But no preexisting bonds of cooperation existed among the participating agencies, so predictably, after the grant was awarded and the work of the collaborative begun, the working agreement among the parties unraveled, with open public feuding among the participating agencies. YO Hartford continues to exist and has received new grants to support its work, but it took years for the collaboration to create trust and shared purpose among the participants (Kennedy School of Government, 2002).

Elsewhere, an economically declining community in Oregon received a number of targeted grants to reverse this trend. The grants required a collaborative approach by several public, nonprofit, and for-profit organizations. But the community lacked a spirit of cooperation and consensus on the appropriate strategies to reverse their economic slide. As a result, the nonprofit and public organizations in the community could not sustain their collaborative efforts (Hibbard, as cited in Mattessich and Monsey, 1997, p. 24).

The third unsuccessful partnership example is an effort to create collaboration among hospitals. In this instance, the advent of Medicaid managed care had created intense competition among the hospitals as well as conflict over financial objectives. As a result, collaborative efforts faltered because of a lack of trust (Shortell et al., 2002, p. 77).

Successful partnerships and collaborations demonstrate the importance of cooperative social networks. Putnam (2003) chronicles the story of Tupelo, Mississippi, where decades of collaborative efforts led by the local Community Development Foundation (CDF) have facilitated and promoted extensive community involvement and participation as well as collaboration among many different organizations in the community and region.

Wondolleck and Yaffee (2000) note that, in Northern California, a group of individuals representing environmental organizations, timber interests, fishing groups, and local public organizations met for a substantial period of time in a local library to discuss issues of mutual concern. This informal group, dubbed the Quincy Library Group (QLG), forged a local consensus on important environmental issues which then led directly to new proposals on forest management and other important natural resources issues.

Importantly, shared purpose does not necessarily mean shared or common objectives. Many types of collaborations bring together nonprofits and other organizations with fundamentally different objectives and missions. But the collaboration may be successful in engaging the various parties if each party believes that it is a productive exchange and offers sufficient "gains from the trade" of information and resources. Environmental collaborations, for example, can bring together individuals with extremely divergent goals. Yet, collaborations are possible nonetheless if the various parties believe that they will each receive some benefit for participation (albeit different benefits). For instance, the National Wild Turkey Federation (NWTF) and the multinational timber company, Georgia-Pacific (GP), entered into a partnership in 1993 whereupon NWTF trains GP foresters in ways to enhance wild habitat in areas where GP is logging. To date, it has been a very successful partnership (Wondolleck and Yaffee, 2000).

Another example is the partnership between CARE and Starbucks, ongoing for several years. Starbucks has supported CARE through direct cash donations, publicity, and initially through the sale of speciality coffee with a certain percentage of the proceeds donated to CARE. For their part, CARE publicized Starbucks and its leadership and their support for CARE programs, especially in the regions where Starbucks bought coffee (Austin, 2000).

Creating a shared vision can sometimes take years. Thus, it is imperative that the leadership of the partnerships take special care to keep the partner organizations and individuals engaged long enough to build trust. For example, a partnership of several agencies involved in substance abuse prevention may be reluctant to participate in a collaboration, since achieving a significant decline in drug use may be many years away. However, these partner agencies may be very willing to participate if tangible benefits or "small wins" can be achieved in the short term. For this reason, it may also be advisable to focus initially on points of agreement and wait to tackle more controversial issues after the necessary trust has been created. A good example is the evolution of the Nanticoke Watershed Alliance, a nonprofit membership organization comprised of many nonprofit, public, and for-profit businesses interested in watershed protection of the Nanticoke River basin in southern Delaware. In the beginning, the Alliance membership was extremely polarized, with profound distrust existing among members. But gradually trust developed, as the member organizations worked together on Alliance projects. Successful projects encouraged more staff and volunteer participation and more funding support and helped convince the original partner agencies to remain committed to the Alliance (Frech, 2004).

APPROPRIATE INSTITUTIONAL DESIGN

Collaboration can be complicated and challenging, making it especially imperative that collaborative initiatives be carefully designed (Hill and Lynn, 2004). Indeed, inappropriate institutional design is a major reason for the collapse of many collaborations and partnerships. One frequent area of difficulty is the governance and management of the partnership. Many collaborations begin informally with the staff and volunteers of nonprofit organizations and their partners. Often governance and management are not the immediate priorities; instead, the initial focus is relationship building, the exchange of information, and problem-solving. Over time, though, many collaborations evolve into more formal entities, especially if the collaboration seeks public or private funding. Many multiparty collaborations, such as a community health partnership or a collaboration of agencies to help at-risk youth, will seek formal 501(c)(3) legal status in order to receive grants and increase their ability to sustain their operations. With incorporation, these partnerships are required to create a board of directors and bylaws governing the organization. Unfortunately, this step can be perilous and often the governance structure represents a variety of political compromises that may create problems in managing the collaboration (and its grants). For instance, the YO Hartford partnership created a governance structure at the outset that was so complicated that it was unworkable, leading to serious staff problems. Eventually, the entire governance structure was significantly reworked in order to save the partnership (Kennedy School of Government, 2002).

Even collaborations without extensive funding such as YO Hartford need to be very cognizant of their governance structure. Many collaborations rely upon a fiscal sponsor, especially in their early years, to act as the organization of record for the receipt of a grant supporting the activities of the collaboration. For example, a collaboration involving several agencies concerned with AIDS prevention might obtain a grant to support a collaborative effort. Instead of creating a new organization, these agencies might decide to have the grant administered by an existing organization such as a local foundation or hospital. But these fiscal sponsorship arrangements can quickly go awry if the various parties are not completely clear on their respective responsibilities. Further, some fiscal sponsors may actually be politically controversial, making the work of the collaboration more difficult.

Another key institutional design question for collaborations is membership and voice. In multiparty partnerships, it is especially critical that appropriate mechanisms are developed to allow the various parties to exercise their "voice" and feel part of the collaborative process. For instance, a health partnership comprised of community organizations, school districts, and hospitals experienced serious difficulties in making progress toward their goals because the partnership was unable to create adequate opportunities for the disparate and diverse members of the community to effectively participate (Shortell et al., 2002). A much more positive example is the Dudley Street Neighborhood Initiative (DSNI), a Boston-based collaboration of many different nonprofit agencies in the Dudley Street area. From the outset, DSNI aggressively recruited neighborhood residents to help them participate in the leadership of the initiative and actively courted their input on key decisions affecting the community (Putnam, 2003; Mattessich and Monsey, 1997).

Ensuring effective participation requires thinking creatively about organizational mechanisms to involve citizens and local organizations and groups. A rural health partnership created special advisory committees to guarantee that certain groups and organizations would be included. And the partnership's steering committee was comprised of representatives of all of the agencies potentially interested in improved health, transportation services, and better medical assistance (Shortell et al., 2002). In some natural resources partnerships, positions have been created to coordinate the various activities of multiple partners. For instance, the U.S. Forest Service created a full-time, volunteer partnerships agreement coordinator at Michigan's Huron-Manistee National Forest. The primary responsibility of this coordinator was to work with the many different citizen groups and district forest rangers to promote effective partnerships and to ensure adequate representation of all concerned parties. Many successful partnerships also combine creative structures such as advisory committees with a detailed Memorandum of Understanding (MOU) to guide the work of these committees (Wondolleck and Yaffee, 2000, p. 93).

The importance of appropriate structures and institutions reflects two key considerations in forging successful collaborations: 1) developing and sustaining effective participation is challenging, so partnership structures need to support participation as much as possible; and 2) partnerships and collaborations can be very time-consuming; thus, staff support can be very helpful in facilitating the collaborative process. Completely volunteer collaborations are very difficult to sustain.

UNDERSTANDING THE INSTITUTIONAL LIFE CYCLE

Over the years, many scholars have commented on the concept of organizational life-cycle (Daft, 1992; Quinn and Cameron, 1983; Simon, 2001). In creating effective partnerships, understanding the life cycle of the partnership can be particularly useful. As noted, many collaborative initiatives involving nonprofits begin informally and then proceed to a much more formalized stage with substantial funding and staff. Then, at the more formal stage, the leadership of the collaboration must be able to mobilize the necessary support and participation from involved groups and organizations. In effect, partnership leadership needs to overcome the collective action dilemma that can hinder adequate participation. Partnership leadership needs to be skilled at starting new initiatives and inspiring interested staff and volunteers about the potential benefits of collaboration. But once established, the collaboration must turn its attention to managing a sometimes complex operation. New board members may also be necessary. As a result, the leadership skills and governance structure needed at a more mature phase of the collaboration are likely to be much different than the talents needed at the outset.

An excellent example of this life cycle is Manna, Inc., a community development corporation (CDC) in Washington, D.C. Initially, Manna was a small, neighborhood-based organization; but over time, it has grown into a complicated, citywide development organization with a board of directors, an advisory committee called the Manna Leadership Committee, and a for-profit subsidiary overseen by a small board (Zdenek, 2004). CDCs are a good example of a new type of nonprofit that because of its diversified revenue base and type of service—housing and community development—needs to cooperate with many different nonprofit, public, and for-profit entities on an ongoing basis.

Understanding the institutional life cycle also means moving the collaboration along toward its goals. Partnerships can get "stuck" at the initial organizing stage and never really make it to the next stage. Many partnerships, especially initiatives organized in response to a specific event or grant award, can begin with widespread enthusiasm and initially significant participation by the different organizations and groups involved in the initiative. But many partnerships have difficulty moving beyond discussion of joint activities to the actual program development and implementation. These partnerships may then find that they have built greater cooperation but have not had much impact on the target problem, such as substance abuse or AIDS prevention, that provided the initial spark for collaboration. Successful partnerships are capable of moving the staff and volunteers along the life cycle and advancing to the programming stage.

This important point regarding life cycle also applies to collaborations between nonprofits and business. For instance, Starbucks and CARE entered into their partnership in the early 1990s when Starbucks was relatively small and CARE was a huge organization. But Starbucks is now a huge enterprise, dwarfing the still substantial size of CARE. The needs and priorities of CARE and Starbucks for the partnership have changed significantly as a result. In order to remain vital, the partnership needed to evolve as well to reflect the profound changes in the two organizations (Austin, 2000).

LEADERSHIP SUPPORT

Many scholars writing on the subject of partnerships and collaboration have noted the importance of leadership (Smith, 1998; Fawcett et al., 2004; Weiner and Alexander, 1998; Zdenak and Steinbach, 2000, 2004; Wondolleck and Yaffee, 2000). More specifically, Shortell et al. (2002) call attention to three components of leadership common to successful partnerships: 1) committed core leadership, 2) a consistent "organizational driver," and 3) the practice of subsidiary leadership. The first component reflects in part the complicated nature of collaborations. In the context of nonprofit organizations, collaborations often require leadership to inspire and motivate countless staff, volunteers, and citizens, even in the absence of bonds of trust and cooperation. This type of leadership requires an ongoing commitment, typically embodied in a paid executive director with adequate support resources. Not surprisingly, leadership turnover in the midst of the development of a partnership or collaboration can seriously undermine a partnership.

The second component—a consistent organizational driver—is a crucial, often overlooked factor in facilitating successful collaborations. A few examples illustrate the point. In the 1980s and 1990s, City Year, a national organization working with at-risk youth, developed a partnership with Timberland, the large outdoor clothing and equipment company. The partnership benefitted from excellent leadership but it also had the full support of the respective boards which ensured that the partnership was pushed along (Austin, 2000). Shortell et al. (2002) concluded that a key factor in the ability of a successful community health partnership in the American Southwest to achieve its goals was the ongoing political and financial support of the local hospital foundation.

More generally, many nonprofit collaborations involve the active involvement of local government, even if it is not in a direct partner capacity. For instance, a collaboration involving several nonprofit agencies engaged in reducing homelessness is likely to require a positive response by local government if it is to succeed. Local government can also be essential in helping support the initial organizing effort. Indeed, Smith (1998) conducted a study of collaborations and partnerships focused on substance abuse prevention and found that the support of local government was essential to partnership success. One noteworthy collaboration of nonprofit and public youth agencies, Hampton 4 Youth, was directed by an individual employed by the city of Hampton, Virginia, and the nonprofit benefitted greatly from the sustained support of the city for the work of the collaboration.

The third component—subsidiary leadership—is especially crucial in complicated multiparty partnerships and collaborations. This type of leadership involves the ability of the partnership leadership to delegate authority and decision-making to other members of the partnership. Subsidiary leadership, in the context of community collaborations, relies upon programmatic and administrative opportunities, such as a public awareness campaign or a fundraising initiative, to help train citizens and the representatives of participating organizations for leadership positions in the collaboration (Shortell et al., 2002). Further, Chaskin et al. (2001) observe that this leadership approach is also critical to building community capacity for action and collaboration.

RESOURCES

Many collaborations rely completely on volunteers. Other collaborations may be developed by paid employees, but the collaborative effort may be outside regular job responsibilities. Many organizations also depend upon full-time paid employees. Regardless of the situation though, successful partnerships and collaborations are more likely if sufficient resources are devoted to supporting the collaboration, both at the formulation and the implementation stages (Wondolleck and Yaffee, 2000; Smith, 1998; Shortell et al., 2002; Mattesich and Monsey, 1997). To be sure, some partnerships begin with no money, but inevitably, successful collaborations require a partner organization and/or an individual to take responsibility for raising the necessary funds. Even relatively simple tasks such as communication among agencies and members require funding and staff time. Little will be accomplished without funding (Mattessich and Monsey, 1997; Smith, 1998; Shortell et al., 2002).

To be sure, too much funding can be overwhelming and even inadvertently sabotage a partnership. Collaboration involving nonprofit agencies, such as a community health partnership or a community development project, requires agency staff and volunteers to trust each other and jointly build the project. But large grants can introduce a host of perverse incentives into the collaboration, actually making the process of creating cooperation among different parties much more difficult. As a general rule, funding needs to be on an appropriate scale for the collaboration and its particular point in the organizational life cycle. Indeed, community partnerships with extensive citizen participation may be well-advised to gradually build funding as they develop programs (Mattessich and Monsey, 1997; Smith, 1998; Shortell et al., 2002).

The level of resources is a visible measure of organizational commitment. Sustainable alliances and collaborations require that the various parties institutionalize their support and provide adequate material incentives to keep everyone engaged (see Austin, 2000). Further, many alliances grow and evolve in complexity over time, making it even more imperative that collaborating organizations develop strategies to institutionalize their commitment. Possibilities include jointly raising money from outside funding organizations and integrating their operations so that collaboration becomes routine.

Importantly though, institutionalizing the commitment of collaborating organizations is likely to require those organizations to think very clearly about evaluation and effectiveness. Many partnerships go awry through inattention to evaluation and outcomes. A sustained commitment to evaluation will help keep the collaboration on track and build the case for continued funding. For instance, drug prevention partnerships supported by private foundations and federal agencies in the 1990s often suffered from diffuse programming and mission and did not collect the appropriate data to allow them to adjust and refine their programs as the partnership developed (Smith, 1998).

TECHNICAL ASSISTANCE AND SUPPORT

Collaborations and partnerships evolve and change over time. And it is complicated, sometimes frustrating work. As a result, technical assistance can be especially useful in providing corrective and supportive feedback. (See for example, Paine-Andrews et al., 2000.) Regarding the former, it is very important that collaborations receive help on the programmatic issues since partner agencies may bring very different levels of knowledge and skill to the collaboration. In order to move forward and achieve collaboration objectives, ongoing counsel and feedback for the partner agencies can be especially valuable. For complicated, multiparty partnerships, such as a community health partnership, the technical assistance role can be filled by an outside evaluator who is hired to assess collaboration outcomes. These partnerships are often supported by grants from private foundations and government agencies that will sometimes support hiring a "coach" to provide regular advice. (One example is the Urban Health Initiative supported by the Robert Wood Johnson Foundation; see www.urbanhealth.org).

The staff and volunteers of collaborative projects can also benefit from technical assistance with organizational concerns related to sustainability and effectiveness. For instance, the staff and volunteers involved in partnerships may not necessarily have skills in fundraising and revenue diversification. Thus, enlisting the help of fundraising consultants can be very beneficial. Similarly, partnerships, especially as they become more formalized, can benefit from advice on the implementation of new management systems and structures.

Significantly, partnerships may be able to enlist expert help through outreach efforts that may build broader political support. For example, the Nanticoke Watershed Alliance has successfully reached out to many scientific experts for specific advice on a range of technical environmental issues (Wondolleck and Yaffee, 2000, p. 201). Austin (2000) profiles several nonprofit-business collaborations where business executives provide regular support and guidance to the nonprofit partner.

ADEQUATE ACCOUNTABILITY AND EVALUATION

Effective and sustainable collaboration requires focus (Shortell et al., 2002; Smith, 1998). Maintaining a focus on program goals and outcomes requires adequate accountability and regular attention to outcome evaluation. Despite the importance of accountability, many nonprofits find it to be problematic. First, many collaborations begin informally or start in response to a specific event or crisis; identifying appropriate outcome measures or institutionalizing data collection to inform program operations may not be the top priority. As a result, the partnership may not be in a position to assess its operations as it matures since it will not have the necessary data. To avoid this problem, the staff and volunteers of collaborations must be conscious from the very beginning of the need to collect the appropriate data.

Second, collaboration should be viewed as a supplement rather than an alternative to conventional decision-making processes. For instance, a group of nonprofit youth agencies might come together to develop new programs for at-risk youth. It is important that the process of reaching decisions within the collaboration be connected in some way to the decision-making processes of the individual nonprofit organizations. Making this connection can be very helpful in creating broader support for the collaboration, although all parties need to ensure that the decision-making process does not become too complicated with too many players and potential stakeholders (Wondolleck and Yaffee, 2000).

Third, accountability requires a targeted and appropriate programmatic plan. Many collaborative initiatives, especially multiparty efforts, are at great risk of being overly expansive and diffuse in their programming. For instance, a collaboration of several nonprofit and public agencies in a southern state was founded to address the serious problem of substance abuse in a large urban area. But the partnership was unable to move forward effectively because it initiated programming in many different areas. And much of this programming was often quite fleeting and short-lived and thus did not build lasting trust to help keep the partnership together (Smith, 1998). This type of programming also made it impossible for the partnership to adequately assay its impact.

Fourth, ongoing attention to evaluation is essential because nonprofit executives and board members need to carefully weigh the costs and benefits of collaboration. Multiparty collaborations involving nonprofits can have very high transaction costs with substantial staff and volunteer time required. Moreover, in terms of specific outcomes, the experience of many multiparty collaborations has often been quite disappointing (Kreuter, Lezin, and Young, 2000; Shortell et al., 2002; Smith, 1998; Annie E. Casey Foundation, 1996). Unsuccessful partnerships tend to suffer from diffuse or overly complex goals, unrealistic timetables for program implementation, and a failure to focus the partnership on achievable outcomes (see Kreuter, Lezin, and Young, 2000). Given the potentially high costs of collaboration, nonprofits should be very clear about their reasons for undertaking such efforts and the expected benefits that they hope to achieve. A continual focus on these benefits and measurable outcomes also keeps partners engaged and promotes adaptation and course correction if necessary.

This general point about carefully weighing costs and benefits is also noted by Austin (2000) in connection with nonprofit-business collaborations. He argues that a key ingredient in high-performance collaborations is the need to systematically focus on *"defining, generating, balancing, and renewing value"* (p. 178). In practice, this focus on value means constantly evaluating the work of the collaboration, assessing the impact of collaboration activities, and carefully considering the costs and benefits of the collaboration on a regular basis.

Future Directions and Trends

The substantial growth of nonprofit organizations in the last ten years combined with stagnant or declining revenues suggests that collaboration and partnership are likely to remain important topics for nonprofit managers and volunteers in the coming years (if for no other reason than that funders will demand it). As a result, nonprofit organizations need to be well-positioned to take advantage of appropriate partnerships that will benefit their organizations and their communities. Nonprofits can help themselves to be better potential partners through a number of steps. First, nonprofits should analyze their governance structures in order to enhance their connections to their communities, including other public and private organizations. Many nonprofits tend to have small boards and weak community connections, leaving them with thin cooperative social networks. Indeed, Pietroburgo and Wernet (2004) recently concluded that the availability of compatible partners was one of the key predictors of successful restructuring in nonprofit hospice organizations. To create these networks, several possible strategies exist, including changes to the membership of the board, ongoing outreach to local public officials and business leaders, creating new advisory committees and affiliated entities, and participating in community forums and events. These networks could also have a number of positive spin-off benefits, including greater charitable giving to the organization.

Second, nonprofits may want to consider merger, rather than try to collaborate to produce a joint activity or service. Mergers offer potential efficiencies and may be the only way that some programs can survive. Mergers are often difficult in the nonprofit sector due to conflicting agendas and the ambiguity on ownership; nonetheless, a combination of two organizations may lead to a healthier and more sustainable combined organization. Two nonprofits might even explore a partial merger that only affects administrative and back-office functions, rather than direct program services (Kohm, 2004).

Third, funders may need to adapt their own procedures in order to promote effective, sustainable partnerships. Public and private funders are often key organizational drivers in successful collaborations (Shortell et al., 2002), but they can inadvertently undermine the collaboration process by mandating and/or encouraging inappropriate governance structures (See Hill and Lynn, 2004). Government funders may also threaten to terminate or reduce service contracts, thus discouraging two nonprofits from collaborating (Kohm, 2004).

Finally, nonprofits would be well-served to think broadly about collaboration and its effects. Many collaborations may not be able to achieve concrete outcome goals, such as reduced smoking or improved economic development. Yet, collaborations, even relatively informal collaborations, may help build social capital and, more broadly, the community connections of nonprofit agencies. In the long run, these connections can be very beneficial in building and sustaining political and community support for the nonprofit organization and provide an excellent basis for other collaborative initiatives.

References

Austin, James E. 2000. *The Collaboration Challenge*. San Francisco: Jossey-Bass.

Behn, Robert D. 2001. *Rethinking Democratic Accountability.* Washington, DC: Brookings Institution Press.

Casey Foundation, Annie E. 1996. *The Path of Most Resistance.* Baltimore: Annie E. Casey Foundation.

Chaskin, Robert J.; Prudence Brown, Sudhir Venkatesh, and Avis Vidal. 2001. *Building Community Capacity.* New York: Aldine de Gruyter.

Daft, Robert L. 1992. *Organizational Theory and Design.* St. Paul, MN: West Publishing.

Egger, Robert. 2004. *Begging for Change: The Dollars and Sense of Making Nonprofits Responsive, Efficient, and Rewarding for All.* New York: HarperCollins.

Fawcett, Stephen B., et al., 2004. "Leadership and Group Facilitation," *Community Toolbox.* www.ctb.lsi.ukans.edu/tools.

Frech, Lisa Jo. 2004. "A Case Study in Forming a Grassroots Watershed Organization." Nanticoke Watershed Alliance. www.nanticokeriver.org.

Hill, Carolyn J., and Laurence E. Lynn, Jr. 2004. "Producing Human Services: Why Do Agencies Collaborate?" *Public Management Review,* 5, 1 (March), pp. 63–82.

Hood, Christopher. 1991. "A Public Management for All Season?" *Public Administration,* 69, pp. 3–19.

Huxham, Chris. 2003. "Theorizing Collaboration Practice," *Public Management Review,* 5, 3 (September), pp. 401–424.

Independent Sector. 2003. *The Nonprofit Almanac.* Washington, DC: Independent Sector.

Katzenbach, Jon, and Douglas K. Smith. 1993. *The Wisdom of Teams.* Boston: Harvard Business School Press.

Kennedy School of Government. 2002. *The Challenge of Multi-Agency Collaboration: Launching a Large-Scale Youth Development Project in Hartford.* Kennedy School of Government Case Program. Case #1673.

Khademian, Anne M. 2002. *Working with Culture: The Way the Job Gets Done in Public Programs.* Washington, DC: CQ Press.

Kohm, Amelia. 2004. *Cultural Clashes in Nonprofit Partnerships: What's Going On and What Can We Do?* Chicago: Chapin Hall Center for Children at the University of Chicago.

Kotter, John. 1996. *Leading Change*. Boston: Harvard Business School Press.

Kreuter, Marshall W.; Nicole A. Lezin, and Laura A. Young. 2000. "Evaluating Community-Based Collaborative Mechanisms: Implications for Practitioners," *Health Promotion Practice*, 1, 1 (January), pp. 49–63.

Mason, David. 1996. *Leading and Managing the Expressive Dimension: Harnessing the Hidden Power Source of the Nonprofit Sector*. San Francisco: Jossey-Bass.

Mattessich, Paul, and Barbara Monsey. 1997. *Community Building: What Makes It Work?* St. Paul, MN: Amherst H. Wilder Foundation.

Mattessich, Paul; Marta Murray-Close, and Barbara R. Monsey. 2001. *Collaboration—What Makes It Work*. St. Paul, MN: Amherst Wilder Foundation.

Osborne, David, and Ted Gaebler. 1992. *Reinventing Government*. New York: Plume.

Paine-Andrews, Adrienne, et al. 2000. "Some Experiential Lessons In Supporting and Evaluating Community-Based Initiatives for Preventing Adolescent Pregnancy," *Health Promotion Practice*, 1, 1 (January), pp. 66–76.

Pietroburgo, Julie, and Stephen P. Wernet. 2004. "Joining Forces, Fortunes, and Futures: Restructuring and Adaptation in Nonprofit Hospice Organizations," *Nonprofit Management and Leadership*, 15, 1 (Fall), pp. 117–137.

Putnam, Robert D. 2000. *Bowling Alone*. New York: Simon and Schuster.

———— 2003. *Better Together: Restoring American Community*. New York: Simon and Schuster.

Quinn, Robert E., and Kim Cameron. 1983. "Organizational Life Cycles and Some Shifting Criteria of Effectiveness," *Management Science*, 29, pp. 31–51.

Senge, Peter M. 1990. The Fifth Discipline: *The Art and Practice of the Learning Organization*. New York: Doubleday.

Shortell, Stephen M.; Ann P. Zukoski, Jeffrey A. Alexander, Gloria J. Bazzoli, Douglas A. Conrad, Romana Hasnain-Wynia, Shoshanna Sofaer, Benjamin Y. Chan, Elizabeth Casey, and Frances S. Margolin. 2002. "Evaluating Partnerships for Community Health Improvement: Tracking the Footprints," *Journal of Health Politics, Policy and Law*, 27, 1 (February), pp. 49–91.

Simon, Judith Sharken. 2001. *Five Life Stages of Nonprofit Organizations*. St. Paul, MN: Amherst H. Wilder Foundation.

Smith, Steven Rathgeb. 1998. *Lessons Learned from Community Coalitions to Prevent Substance Abuse*. Boston: Join Together.

———— 2002. "Social Services." In Lester M. Salamon, (ed.), *Nonprofit America*. Washington, DC: Brookings Institution Press.

Smith, Steven Rathgeb, and Michael Lipsky. 1993. *Non-Profits for Hire: The Welfare State in the Age of Contracting*. Cambridge, MA: Harvard University Press.

Sosin, Michael R. 1990. "Decentralizing the Social Service System: A Reassessment," *Social Service Review*, 64, pp. 617–636.

Weiner, Bryan J., and Jeffrey Alexander. 1998. "The Challenges of Governing Public-Private Community Health Partnerships," *Health Care Management Review*, 23, 2, pp. 39–55.

Wilson, James Q. 1973. *Political Organizations*. New York: Basic Books.

Wolf, Thomas. 1999. *Managing a Nonprofit Organization in the Twentieth-First Century*. New York: Simon and Schuster.

Wondolleck, Julia M., and Steven L. Yaffee. 2000. *Making Collaboration Work: Lessons From Innovation in Natural Resources Management*. Washington, DC: Island Press.

Zdenek, Robert O., and Carol Steinbach. 2000. "The Leadership Challenge: Creating an Enduring Organization," *Shelterforce Online* (November–December) at: www.nhi.org/online/issues/114/zdenak.html.

Zdenek, Robert O. 2004. "Remarks on Institutional Collaborations and Transformations." Biennial conference of the National Center for Nonprofit Entrepreneurship (NCNE), Washington, DC.

8

Mobilizing for Public Sector Support

Elizabeth J. Reid
Center on Nonprofits and Philanthropy
The Urban Institute
Washington, DC

Introduction

Nonprofit organizations are the backbone of civic and political expression in contemporary American politics. They bring a wide array of issues to public attention and compete and collaborate with other players in national, state, and local policymaking. Their vigilant advocacy has shaped the social contract between government and citizens and contributed to improvements in the quality of life for a broad cross section of Americans, including traditionally underrepresented constituencies, such as minorities, the poor and working poor, women, children, and immigrants. Both here and abroad they have helped to open institutional decision-making to new voices and issues. Cross-national networks of activists on issues such as the environment, health, poverty, and transparency have spawned nonprofits in other countries, enlarged the voices of women and the poor, and transformed policymaking in governments and international institutions (Boris and Krehely, 2003).

The diverse array of organizations shaping public understanding of issues and influencing public outcomes is daunting. A handful of large charitable organizations are highly visible in Congress and state legislatures and instrumental in shaping budget and policy priorities in their policy areas. Policy coalitions and networks provide a means for many smaller, less politically active community organizations to be involved in the policy process. Increasingly, nonprofit organizations emphasize their work in policy networks and coalitions as a way to coordinate scarce resources and reduce political competition. Some nonprofits are membership organizations with inclusive governance; others have few ties with the constituencies they represent. Some have professional staff with political skills, while others rely primarily on board members and community leaders to generate interest and support for policy initiatives.

Groups go about their work as advocates in many different ways. In aggregate, few charitable nonprofit organizations engage in activities that directly attempt to influence policymaking and elections, such as lobbying or get-out-the-vote activities. Emphasis on providing services in the large and growing nonprofit service economy and strict limitations on the political activity of charitable organizations constrain their willingness and available resources to advocate. Many do, however, see public outreach and education as part of their work. They contribute substantially to raising public awareness on issues and shaping public understanding of viable solutions to those issues.

In a national election year, nonprofit organizations that are not 501(c)(3) organizations, and therefore operating under more liberal political regulations, surface as influential actors in elections. Large, regular political players often have one foot in the policy process and the other in elections. These organizations, such as the Sierra Club or National Rifle Association, are structured, financed, professionally staffed, and technologically ready to conduct policy advocacy. They join coalitions to contribute to the building of electoral majorities in a political system characterized by weak political parties.

This chapter discusses challenges facing nonprofits as policy advocates and their organizational response to these challenges. The diversity in size, scope, and purpose of nonprofit sector organizations complicates an assessment of the impact of and response to these challenges. Practical insights and workable strategies are often specific to groups and their policy goals. The impact of environmental factors, such as a laggard economy and conservative political environment, suggests "business as usual" will not suffice. In a time of tax cuts and diminishing support for public goods, particular challenges arise for nonprofits that seek to gain support for public expenditures.

Challenges for Nonprofit Advocates

Like other problems of nonprofit management, there are short-term and long-term dimensions to building organizational capacity for advocacy. Nonprofit organizations need the flexibility to adapt to the short-term volatility of the politics of economic uncertainty, political support and opposition, national elections, and significant events. Changing actors and priorities on budget and policy decisions require an organizational commitment to weather change, the creativity to quickly devise new strategies, and the flexibility to adjust demands to emerging political opportunities.

Over the long term, organizations need the resources, skills, knowledge, and networks to sustain campaigns for policy reform. Policy networks and coalitions that can cross social and economic boundaries are central to altering levels of participation, influencing policy, and shaping electoral outcomes. As policy cycles play out over time, organizations need to be able to pursue their advocacy in different venues: framing issues, partnering in strategic alliances, muscling through budget and legislative decisions, and addressing new social realities that arise as policies and programs are established and mature.

Contradictions and uncertainties in the economic and political environment challenge nonprofit advocates. An enlarged national deficit, a slow economy, and an ideological preference for limited government all constrain public expenditures in favor of market incentives. Additionally, the emerging reality of a prolonged war on terrorism, with the potential of restructuring the relationship between individuals, groups, and government, shifts the public's attention to issues of public safety, civil rights, and civil liberties. Further, recent Congressional hearings on issues of nonprofit organizational accountability have generated debate within the nonprofit sector about whether additional oversight of the sector will result in government overreaching and an increased politicization of the sector.

Charitable social service organizations that have become financially interdependent with government are particularly affected by economic uncertainty. Watchdog organizations, like OMB Watch, contend that nonprofits face a growing and long-term financial and organizational crisis resulting from federal and state budget deficits. Nonprofits are being called upon to fill the gaps resulting from government cutbacks at the same time that they have less funding from government to provide services. Many are calling for a more responsible and equitable tax policy as a fundamental step to restoring health to the nonprofit sector. These shifts in government priorities, taxation, and provision of public goods raise questions for charitable organizations. What issues will legislators address? What strategy will build public and political support for reforms that require an expenditure of public dollars? How will reforms be administered in an understaffed government? How can new programs be funded? At the same time, the policy legacy of devolved national government or new federalism has meant that states and localities are salient arenas for advocacy, policy innovation, and change.

The regulatory system for exempt organizations presents additional challenges. Tax and political regulations for exempt organizations are complex, confusing, and in flux. Most nonprofit advocates proceed cautiously, if at all, in the present regulatory environment. Definitions of permissible political activity and limitations are unclear, annual reporting is complex, and enforcement of standards is erratic. The level of lobbying by nonprofit organizations has been relatively steady over the past ten years, with only two percent to two-and-a-half percent of groups reporting lobbying expenditures (National Center for Charitable Statistics, 2004). Political scientist Jeffrey M. Berry and other nonprofit sector watchdog organizations make the case for full implementation of simplified reporting of lobbying expenditures as a way to remove a regulatory barrier to lobbying by charitable organizations (Berry with Arons, 2003).

Additional changes in regulation may be necessary. Poor coordination between the Internal Revenue Service and the Federal Election Commission undermines public transparency about the role of organizational expenditures for political activity. Some improvements have been instituted, but increased regulation of the nonprofit sector also creates controversy over its potential impact on civic engagement. However, new requirements for better disclosure and reporting of political expenditures by Section 527 organizations shed light on the funding of election-related activity; yet these new regulations did not slow the growth, fundraising, or expenditures of these groups during the 2004 elections. Campaign finance reforms to clean up soft money in politics, while a step in the right direction, have nevertheless put some tax-exempt groups in the spotlight as vehicles for raising and spending soft money in elections. Their practices likely will be addressed by campaign finance reform advocates and elected officials.

Increased media, Congressional, and regulatory scrutiny of nonprofits has created an aura of uncertainty about the risks associated with advocacy and demands for nonprofits to justify their privileges and exemptions. In some cases, the oversight is justified. The Nature Conservancy came under scrutiny by the press and public for cronyism in their financial and accounting practices, resulting in an overhaul of organizational practices. But far too often, groups face a less visible scrutiny based on the ideological preferences of those in power. A report by OMB Watch documents the widespread impact of restrictive rule-making and revenue cuts, that when observed in aggregate, amounts to a wholesale attack on organizations that provide essential programs, such as family planning or health assistance for AIDS (Bass, Guinane, and Turner, 2003).

Generating the resources for policy advocacy remains a challenge. While record amounts of hard money are raised by political action committees (PACs) and political parties in national elections, resources for policy advocacy remain difficult to attract. This challenge has several dimensions. Individuals, members, governments, corporations, and foundations have benefits and drawbacks as sources of support for advocates. A recent study by Mark Chaves and his colleagues suggests that financial support by government does not necessarily constrain political activity, but groups report anecdotally a dampening affect on types of advocacy activities and strategies pursued as reliance on government increases (Chaves, Stephens, and Galaskewicz, 2004). Corporate donors may agree on the need for social change but be reluctant allies when tax reform and public expenditures are required to carry out necessary reforms. The National Committee for Responsive Philanthropy (NCRP), an outspoken critic of underspending by foundations for groups engaged in advocacy, has documented differences in patterns of giving in conservative foundations that benefit conservative organizations and the advancement of conservative policy agendas (NCRP, 2004). The study begs the question as to whether patterns of giving by mainstream and liberal foundations undermine the ability of liberal groups to achieve their policy goals. Regardless of the source of revenue, organizations that engage in policy advocacy need to manage the ideological and strategic preferences of donors.

Organizations and leaders do not stand apart from their environment, but are shaped and challenged by its character and vicissitudes. The contemporary legacy of the charitable arm of the nonprofit sector with its emphasis on addressing need and emulating sound business practices is improved management but not necessarily improved public engagement. Most nonprofit organizations are not structured for advocacy and lack leaders with the political skills to operate in the competitive and partisan environments characterized by contested and divisive national and state politics. Instead, leaders are trained to be efficient administrators of service programs. Many lead with compassion but have never been active politically, rarely appreciate the art of politics, or dismiss the potential of political reform as costly, outside of their organizational missions, and mostly unattainable. In a nonprofit sector filled with small and medium-sized organizations, other organizational priorities compete with advocacy. The prospect of building political support to move forward political goals, either through bipartisan consensus or partisan muscle, or finding ways to lead and engage boards and constituents, requires retooling leadership skills and organizational capacity.

These challenges need to be examined in light of democratic governance. On one hand, a call rings out for expanding citizen participation and amplifying the voices of nonprofit organizations on issues as a way to secure public programs that incorporate sound solutions to address the needs and reflect the sentiments of the body politic. On the other, the political system is stifled by many competing interests and approaches in the policymaking process, and there are few power brokers or other mechanisms to mediate competition, aggregate interests, and find consensus. No one organization or leader is dominant or persuasive enough to carry the day in an era of organizational competition, diffused power, and constrained resources. However, policy entrepreneurs or organizational leaders with the skills and connections to form and nurture strategic partnerships, coalitions, state associations, policy networks, and other forms of collaboration give people ways to expand exchange on policy topics, unite in common cause, reduce interorganizational competition, coordinate strategies, and generate public and private resources for change.

Organizational Responses to Restore Public Sector Support

Challenges not withstanding, nonprofit advocates may affect how policy is made by influencing the speed at which the political system addresses problems and aggregates public preferences. They can also influence the way in which policies attract support, by the way they frame issues and align support or opposition for change. Sometimes nonprofits, like other institutions with set routines and preferences, do more to explain the dampening rather than the amplifying of political processes. Even for change-oriented organizations, collective action strategies may fail in certain contexts. Strategies for surmounting these difficulties include well-honed organizations, selective incentives for joining and participating, the strategic cooperation among potential allies, and politically active organizational entrepreneurs. This section draws on examples and insights from nonprofit practice and research to illustrate ways nonprofits are becoming more prepared, flexible, engaged, strategic, and change-oriented in shaping budget and policy decisions.

BUILDING INSTITUTIONAL CAPACITY FOR ADVOCACY

Nonprofits that engage in advocacy need organizational structures, financial resources, skilled leadership, and active constituencies to conduct policy work. As a first step, advocacy organizations need to answer the question "capacity for what?" By answering this question, organizations can be more strategic about building clout to achieve their budget and policy goals. But where do groups begin?

Toward that end, the National Council of Nonprofit Associations (NCNA) launched a campaign calling for one-third of the expected three percent increase in government revenues to be applied to domestic services and other services that impact people's lives. Audrey Alvarado, executive director of NCNA, notes:

> We need a new vocabulary, a common language, that speaks to what we in the non-profit sector do for our communities, society, and the promotion of democratic ideals. And we need organizational capacity and knowledge to initiate public policy that supports a domestic agenda to build and strengthen our communities. (Alvarado, 2004)

Building on an earlier public policy initiative designed to strengthen NCNA's affiliate state associations of nonprofit organizations, Building Capacity for Advocacy and Public Policy (BCAPP), the campaign will utilize the policy expertise of the state associations. The BCAPP initiative, in partnership with Independent Sector, helped state associations establish decision-making structures for policy work, commit additional resources to policy work, employ technology to enhance their communications, and develop sectorwide policy agendas. They also engaged in more activities on issues of concern, expanded relationships with policymakers and increased the participation of other nonprofits in state association-sponsored policy activities. Some aspects of policy work were more stubborn to tackle. After an infusion of training, grants, and technical assistance, organizational communication with association members and with legislators remained low. Finding the resources for policy work and meeting the changing demands of policy engagement are also challenges groups will need to address to sustain their efforts.

"Organizational Factors Influencing Advocacy For Children," a recent state-level study conducted by researchers at the Center on Nonprofits and Philanthropy at the Urban Institute, supports the BCAPP findings and adds several additional insights on advocacy capacity (DeVita et al., 2004). Being strategic about determining issue priorities was found to be important for two reasons. Groups focus limited resources for maximum impact. In multi-issue human service coalitions, prioritizing also prevented groups from being pulled in different directions by competing interests. It allowed them to play lead and support roles in the coalition, depending on their issue preferences and organizational resources. The study also found that while the tools for measuring effectiveness are imprecise, a multilayered process of assessing policy and organizational change at the end of the year allowed groups to determine the costs and benefits of policy engagement and identify future strategies of action

BUILDING PARTNERSHIPS FOR CHANGE

Strategic partnerships are designed to take advantage of the growing interface between nonprofits, government, and business. By identifying shared interests and goals across sectors, institutions leverage networks of influence to build the public, financial, and political support for new priorities for public expenditures and policy reforms. Generally, these multisector collaborations are nonpartisan, and the campaigns are financed with corporate, as well as, individual contributions.

Experiences from a campaign to improve early childhood education by the Foundation for Early Learning, a public foundation in Washington State, demonstrate the benefits and the challenges of strategic partnerships. In 2001, the foundation started a collaborative of funders, the Early Care and Education Coalition (EC2), to increase public awareness of the importance of the first five years in a child's success in school and life. The EC2 coalition steering committee is comprised of six foundations and a corporate sponsor (Boeing Corporation) and a twenty-five-member advisory committee comprised of providers, professionals, and parents. EC2 decided to focus its efforts on a statewide public engagement campaign and a public policy initiative to provide preschool for all four-year-old children in Washington State.

Collaboration among high-profile foundations and corporations eased fundraising for a statewide campaign. EC2 committee members initially contributed to a support fund for the public awareness campaign and for a project director to staff it. Two years into the campaign, a parallel policy track emerged when the Gates Foundation gave a $500,000 grant to the League of Education Voters (LEV) to conduct a fundraising campaign for an initiative to reform the educational system to support preschool through Grade 16. The EC2 coalition became a strategic partner in the development of policies addressing the needs of preschool education. Widespread and influential support for reform accelerated the pace of the campaign. The initiative was voted down in the November 2004 elections, though a portion of its intent has been reconstructed as legislation to create an Early Learning Council. Success on the P–16 initiative came with some organizational costs for the EC2 partnership. The EC2 public awareness campaign was put on hold when the P-16 initiative was jump started by the Gates grant to LEV. Additionally, the project director for EC2 spent a great deal of staff time on the LEV campaign, and EC2 members became concerned about the lack of focus for the public awareness campaign. Competition for funding increased, with two organizations needing support for early care and education campaigns.

Different organizational structures, policy approaches, leadership styles, membership, and strategies of action can create tensions within coalitions and the policy process that, when well-managed, should not prevent cooperation on policy reform. The Foundation for Early Learning worked hard at assembling and mediating the variety of interests in their strategic partnership. Jeanne Andersen, executive director of the Foundation for Early Learning, sees the trade offs for her foundation this way: "It's important to be strategic, but it is also important to be mission driven" (Andersen, 2004). Balancing policy goals and organizational goals can be tricky. For example, as the P–16 campaign heated up, EC2 members were concerned about the lack of policy attention to one of their primary organizational goals, the first three years of a child's life, yet supported progress on early learning that could be made by P–16.

VOLUNTEER ACTION WHEN GOVERNMENT FAILS

Many nonprofit organizations are faced with a harsh reality. Years of government cuts in basic services and public programs leave nonprofits with the dual job of addressing need and advocating for renewed vision and commitment from government. For environmentalists, recent years have been particularly frustrating as policy progress has been stifled on clean air and water, toxic waste cleanup, sustainable energy policy, land conservation, and wildlife protection, and some hard-fought gains have been undermined by administrative action.

The Institute for Conservation Leadership trains leaders to build volunteer organizations to protect and conserve the earth's environment. Volunteer activists provide a defense against government failures, such as poor government enforcement, poor public data on air and water quality, and lack of funding for maintenance of public parks and protected areas. Citizen watchdogs have documented and publicized environmental problems in ways that pressure government to be more responsive. Volunteers have filled the gap when government cuts eliminated vital data collection on air and water quality. They collect data previously gathered by government agents or correct inaccuracies in government data to ensure that the public is not misled by official studies. Nonprofits muster the volunteer support for national parks when waning public support results in declines in staffing, law enforcement, and facilities maintenance.

The Institute for Conservation Leadership has seen organizations strained when they must split their mission between performing service functions that they believe should be the purpose and scope of government, and advocating for public sector support to protect public health, document need and progress on environmental concerns, and safeguard precious resources. Diane Russell, executive director of the Institute, sees the contributions volunteers make to environmental progress, yet knows its limits in the long run.

> Empowerment comes from playing the watchdog or collecting and publicizing independent data and these influential citizen contributions can lead to more effective advocacy. But volunteerism is not a substitute for public sector support for the environment. Sustaining a sufficient level of volunteerism to do the work of

government is not possible unless private resources flow into the public arena. (Russell, 2004)

BROADENING AND DEEPENING VOTER TURNOUT

Elections present a window of opportunity for nonprofit organizations to highlight their issues and educate and motivate voters to elect sympathetic representation. Attention is at its highest among the electorate, and there is an implicit division of labor between candidates and groups during elections as they attempt to maximize voter turnout in a low voter turnout nation. Candidates generally appeal to the ten percent of the voters who are less partisan—swing voters—while groups make a targeted appeal on issues of concern to identify and motivate broad groups of voters and ensure their presence at the polls.

It is easy to overlook the contributions nonprofit organizations make to voter participation in elections. While partisan activity for charitable organizations is prohibited, voter information and registration are permissible when conducted in a nonpartisan manner. Many charitable organizations, unclear about regulatory restrictions or fearful of generating internal organizational divisions, refrain from nonpartisan election-related advocacy or voter education. Some organizations, however, have found ways to work within the current legal and regulatory framework.

Independent Sector and the National Council of Nonprofit Associations have renewed efforts to encourage organizations to register voters, enact voter-friendly personnel policies, shape party platforms, sponsor candidate forums, get voters to the polls, and a host of other permissible nonpartisan election-related activities. Post-election results show the impact of strategic planning at the community level on voter turnout. The Community Voting Project, launched by the Center for Community Change in partnership with community groups, demonstrated the ability of grassroots groups to do high-impact voter mobilization. Together they built voter lists, registered 147,029 new voters, and mobilized another 128,655 "occasional" low-income and minority voters in targeted precincts.

Large organizations that are regular policy advocates often create organizational structures to finance partisan activity through related, but legally separate, tax-exempt organizations (Reid and Kerlin, 2003). For example, the Sierra Club and the National Rifle Association have organizational structures that include multiple tax-exempt entities. Charitable organizations are sometimes deliberative membership organizations or alternatively may primarily fundraise and conduct educational programs and engage in limited lobbying. Related 501(c)(4) social welfare arms engage in lobbying and sometimes in permissible but limited partisan political activity. Related to the social welfare arm may be political action committees for raising and donating hard money campaign contributions to candidates and parties. Separate Section 527 organizations may be used for partisan get-out-the-vote activity, because they are not covered under recent campaign finance reform and are thus able to raise and spend soft money.

New prohibitions on soft money expenditures by national parties in federal elections resulted in a windfall of soft money to liberal and conservative 501(c)(4) and Section 527 organizations. Taking a lesson from the successes of conservative groups and politicians, liberal groups retooled for the 2004 elections and illustrated the potential for resources, technology, and better coordination between constituency-based organizations on increased voter turnout. America Votes, a coalition of the large membership organizations that together claim to represent twenty million Americans, coordinated voter registration and public education on liberal issues to turn out their members. Americans Coming Together used door-to-door voter contact to persuade occasional voters to go to the polls. Labor unions formed an adjunct membership organization, Working America, to sign up community members who were not covered by labor contracts at work but wanted to support a pro-labor agenda. While they did not tip the balance of voters in favor of the Democrats, the innovative practices used by these organizations and the challenges their activity pose to the regulatory framework for nonprofit political engagement will surely be discussed and studied by regulators, academics, and political strategists in years to come.

USING TECHNOLOGY TO BOLSTER REFORM

Nonprofit organizations are employing the power of technology for advocacy: creating global networks to pressure international institutions and national governments on international issues; raising money for reform campaigns and election participation; and challenging traditional media outlets with information alternatives. The Internet and other forms of cheap global communication are also being used to reinforce communication among groups in policy networks and strengthen intra-organizational communication between staff, leaders, and members in organizations.

Virtual organizations and virtual volunteering and giving may not seem tangible, but the impacts can be real. Regulators are wrestling with how to treat organizational expenditures for Internet campaigns to lobby for legislation or promote candidates. Politically active membership organizations supplement on-the-ground membership drives and calls for action with virtual opportunities to join, donate, and act. E-mails, listservs, chat rooms, and blogs bring constant updates and opinions on issues and link activists in ongoing dialogues about policy and strategy.

Still, some observers of the nonprofit sector have warned of a downside to technology. Virtual organizations with few roots in communities or among people can use marketing techniques to identify people receptive to calls for action and susceptible to persuasion on certain issues. "Astroturf" organizations are tax-exempt shells for narrow interests, formed by political consultants or law firms on behalf of clients. They are able to generate a negative public response to proposed legislation and have succeeded in slowing the pace of legislation they oppose.

Future Directions for Nonprofit Advocacy

Several dilemmas for the nonprofit sector stand out. The well-heeled partnership of nonprofits and government has had both positive and negative ramifications for political expression. Additionally, the regulatory system for tax-exempt organizations is overly complex for advocates, and yet lacks the basic transparency necessary for ensuring public trust in the political role of nonprofits. Further, some foundations contribute to building the infrastructure and activism for policy reform. More often though, foundations have ignored the centrality of politics to the construction of sound policy on issues in which they invest millions of program dollars. Finally, technology has transformed the ability of groups to raise money for causes and mobilize across national boundaries, but has created a virtual universe of organizations with few roots in the electorate.

Several lessons from practice also stand out. To start, nonprofit organizations across the board need to strengthen their capacity as advocates. They need leaders with political and organizing skills and ways to translate and project their everyday experiences into the public eye and the policy arena. Political skill training for leaders and volunteers is critical. Nonprofit management programs emphasizing advocacy as part of organizational management would help to bridge the divide between advocacy and service functions in organizations. In some ways, volunteer experience is the best teacher. Getting out of the office and into the public and political eye has the potential to transform and empower leaders and volunteers. Technical assistance in building better communication between leaders and members or constituents can lead to more inclusive, responsive, and participatory organizations and enhance legitimacy in the policy process.

Additionally, nonprofit organizations also need to build strategic partnerships and coalitions as mechanisms for coordinating visions, resources, volunteers, leadership, and participation. However, the costs and benefits of partnerships need to be understood, planned on in advance, and managed as the partnership unfolds. There is no one strategy or one kind of organization that is the key to improving public sector support for programs that address the needs of those who are served and represented by nonprofit organizations. Partisan and nonpartisan alliances have proven effective, depending on the goal and the environment. Partnering with government and business or pressuring government and business are both strategies that can work, but that require leaders with the skills and judgments to design and implement a winning approach. Drawing on the expertise of community volunteers can also lend weight to change.

Further, finding the resources for policy advocacy can be challenging. Having a diverse portfolio of resources reduces dependency and financial vulnerability to ideological or policy differences. Donor organizations can also make adjustments in how they structure their grantmaking to provide flexible core operating and long-term support to their grantees. Balancing the organizational tasks of fulfilling organizational missions, framing issues with political salience, and leveraging financial support for policy change can be tricky and requires skilled leaders and organizers to generate the ideas and momentum to attract support.

Processes and tools for assessing advocacy effectiveness need to be developed to weigh the costs and benefits of time and resources spent in pursuit of policy goals. Assessments of advocacy campaigns or policy work by organizations can be part of an internal or external review and evaluation. In some cases, large membership organizations, like the NAACP or AFL-CIO, poll to determine the impact of their advocacy activities on member and public opinions and behavior. A lower cost alternative is an annual review of policy activity by board and staff as part of the planning for next year's policy work. In any case, the assessment should be multidimensional and outside sources of information should be sought, such as the opinions of elected officials and others in government and business, as well as community leaders. Organizational impacts of policy work may include changes in membership numbers and composition, fundraising gains and losses related to policy campaigns, board cohesion and tensions on prioritizing and framing policy issues and generating the resources for them, and trade offs of staff time dedicated to policy work compared to other organizational needs. New, lost, or burnt-out leadership are potential organizational gains and losses in the wake of budget and policy campaigns. Gains or losses in the policy process are usually the most common measure of success, but may unduly narrow an assessment of the payoffs and drawbacks of advocacy engagement to legislative gains. Successes and failure in the policy process need to be measured at many pressure points along the way to change. New levels of civic participation or new allies for the cause need to be accounted for as part of organizational progress toward policy goals.

Importantly, political activism among nonprofit organizations does not appear to be enough to overcome the deficit in resources and power that nonprofits face in a political system dominated by large, special interests. Unless the capacity for political action is more widespread and cooperative and resources are available to take risks, nonprofit organizations will be less likely to engage their volunteers, clients, and natural allies to expand networks and sustain action necessary to renew public sector support for education, the environment, health care, and other public goods. They risk being ignored as a source of political vitality in an era of political cynicism. And unless nonprofits have ties to an engaged citizenry to legitimize their demands for public goods, they risk being perceived as narrowly interested.

Building the clout for budget and policy reforms backed by public support and public investment is possible, but organizations require the commitment, flexibility, and patience to make adjustments and change "business as usual." With attention to strengthening nonprofit advocacy capacity, building strategic collaborations for reform, deepening links between organizations and people, and assessing and reassessing organizational advocacy campaigns, nonprofits can be a strong, inclusive, and legitimate voice for people and contribute to sound policy and better governance in government and society.

References

Alvarado, Audrey. 2004. Remarks from panel presentation at the biennial conference of the National Center on Nonprofit Enterprise, Washington, DC., January 16 and 17.

Anderson, Jeanne. 2004. Remarks from panel presentation at the biennial conference of the National Center on Nonprofit Enterprise, Washington, DC, January 16 and 17.

Bass, Gary; Kay Guinane, and Ryan Turner. 2003. "Attack on Nonprofit Speech: Death by 1000 Cuts." Washington, DC: OMB Watch.

Berry, Jeffrey M., with David Arons. 2003. *A Voice for Nonprofits*. Washington, DC: Brookings Institution Press.

Boris, Elizabeth T., and Jeff Krehely. 2003. "Civic Participation and Advocacy." In Lester M. Salamon (ed.), *The State of Nonprofit America*. Washington, DC: Brookings Institution Press.

Chaves, Mark; Laura Stephens, and Joe Galaskewicz. 2004. "Does Government Funding Suppress Nonprofits' Political Activity?" *American Sociological Review*, Volume 69, No. 2, April.

De Vita, Carol; Maria Montilla, Elizabeth J. Reid, and Omolara Fatiregun. 2004. *Organizational Factors Influencing Advocacy for Children.* Final project report for the Foundation for Child Development.

National Committee for Responsive Philanthropy. 2004. *The Axis of Ideology: Conservative Foundations and Public Policy.* Washington, DC: National Committee for Responsive Philanthropy.

National Center for Charitable Statistics. 2003. Core and Digitized Data.

Reid, Elizabeth J., and Janelle Kerlin. 2003. "More Than Meets the Eye: Structuring and Financing Nonprofit Advocacy." American Political Science Association, Annual Conference, Philadelphia, PA.

Russell, Diane, 2004. Remarks from panel presentation at the biennial conference of the National Center on Nonprofit Enterprise. Washington, DC, January 16 and 17.

Philanthropy and the Economy: Maintaining vs. Investing in the Nonprofit Sector

James M. Ferris
Emery Olson Chair in Nonprofit Entrepreneurship and Public Policy
University of Southern California
Los Angeles, CA

Introduction

Philanthropic capacity has been growing in recent years as a result of the accumulation of wealth that has accompanied economic growth and the transmission of wealth among generations. Not only has the capacity of philanthropy been growing, but it has also received a great deal of attention from the press and the public. This has led to increased expectations about the promise of philanthropy—in particular its scale, reach, and impact. To fully understand what is possible requires an appreciation for the role of philanthropy in society: what it is and what it can be. As philanthropy grows, there are new players and new institutions that enable individuals to realize their philanthropic purposes.

The pursuit of philanthropic purpose underscores the fact that philanthropy is not merely a funding stream for needy nonprofits to tap. Moreover, despite the growth in philanthropy, it cannot keep pace with the growing number of nonprofits, the growing gaps in funding due to diminished public funding—either in absolute terms or a reduced rate of growth—or the limited opportunities for generating fees for services. This is evident in philanthropy's declining share of the operating expenditures of nonprofit organizations from nearly 50 percent in 1964, to 24 percent in 1998 (Urban Institute, 2003). Thus, the potential for philanthropy lies in its ability to provide the "venture capital" for the nonprofit sector.

This requires that philanthropy develop grantmaking strategies that strengthen the nonprofit sector and its impact in terms of making a difference in public problem-solving—through service delivery, advocacy, and/or community building. These strategies include investing in nonprofit capacity-building, sector infrastructure, or public policy engagement. In addition to grantmaking strategies, the ultimate success of philanthropy to achieve its potential in expanding its reach depends on its ability to move toward the creation of a more efficient capital market for the nonprofit sector. In effect, there is a need to develop mechanisms and change practices to facilitate the match between philanthropic dollars and nonprofit organizations. This will require a grantmaking process that rewards risk-taking and encourages performance.

The plan of this chapter is as follows. First, we examine the forces at play that shape the growth of philanthropic capacity over the long term and some of the uncertainties on the horizon in terms of public policy towards philanthropy. Second, we explore the philanthropic strategies that are emerging as philanthropy accentuates notions of venture capital in its work. Third, we review the role of philanthropy in nonprofit finance and reveal the limits of philanthropy as a mere substitute for nonprofit revenues from either government or commercial endeavors. Cognizant of this reality, we then identify several issues in grantmaking that suggest the need to view at least a portion of philanthropic dollars as investments in nonprofit organizations, the nonprofit sector, and social change. Then, we conclude with a discussion of the need to develop a more efficient capital market between philanthropy and nonprofits.

The Growing Capacity of Philanthropy

Economic trends have an important impact on the capacity of individuals to give. While the evidence suggests that the aggregate relationship between individual giving and income is relatively stable, running between 1.6 and 2 percent a year for the past few decades (AAFRC, 2004), it is clear that as individuals accumulate significant wealth they have a greater propensity to become involved in philanthropy in significant ways. Individuals with high net wealth have the opportunity to make philanthropic gifts at a greater scale with the possibility of greater, more lasting impact. This is true in instances in which they create new philanthropic foundations or make new gifts to the endowments of their existing foundations, or when they choose to make "mega" gifts to nonprofit organizations.

Indeed, the number of foundations in the U.S. increased from 32,401 in 1990 to 64,843 in 2002, an increase of 100 percent. And, the assets of these foundations grew through gifts as well as rising stock market values from $142.8 billion in 1990 to $435.19 billion in 2002, nearly a three-fold increase (Foundation Center, 2004). Moreover, in recent years we have seen a significant increase in the creation of new "big" foundations, such as the Bill and Melinda Gates Foundation, the Gordon and Betty Moore Foundation, the Open Society Institute, and the Suzanne Buffet Foundation. In addition, the assets of existing foundations burgeon as a result of new gifts to already established endowments, such as the William and Flora Hewlett Foundation and the Annenberg Foundation.

At the same time, we have also seen the increasing frequency of multimillion dollar gifts and grants to universities, hospitals, museums, and other nonprofit organizations, such as Joan Kroc's $1.5 billion gift to the Salvation Army or the Annenberg Foundation's generous grants of $100 million to both the University of Southern California and the University of Pennsylvania. For example, in 2003 there were 164 gifts in excess of $5 million made by living donors or through bequests (AAFRC, 2004).

The potential capacity for philanthropy will continue to grow over the long term as a result of emerging industries that will lead to wealth creation, the continuation of the intergenerational transfer of wealth, and a growing economy and the fortunes of the stock market. In addition, the emergence of new vehicles for philanthropic giving such as donor-advised funds, increasing sources of donor education, and efforts to develop a culture of giving are likely to help the potential for philanthropy to be realized. The only question is at what rate these economic forces and institutional developments will fuel the expansion of philanthropy over the long run.

While the long-term prospects for wealth creation and accumulation are, in general, bright, we are still faced with the challenges of short-term fluctuations in the economy. Hence, the growth in capacity is not likely to be continuous. And, the growth is unlikely to be sustained at the unprecedented rates that occurred in the 1990s, particularly in the latter part of the decade.

But beyond the economic fluctuations that will affect the pace of giving over time, the current public policy environment is creating uncertainty that can, at the margin, have an important impact on philanthropic decisions. This is especially true for those individuals and foundations with a substantial capacity to give.

Tax policy has an important impact on giving. It is a well-established fact that marginal income tax rates, together with rules on charitable deductions, have an important impact on the magnitude of giving. But even more important in the coming years, in terms of the giving of the wealthy, will be the future of the estate tax. Under current law, the estate tax rate and base is being phased to zero by 2010, followed by a reinstatement in 2011 at levels set by 1997 law (Congressional Budget Office, 2004). But will the elimination of the estate tax be made permanent? Obviously, such a provision is likely to have two impacts. Increasing the threshold at which the tax applies increases after-tax wealth that is likely to increase charitable gifts. On the other hand, as the tax rate is reduced, the marginal price of giving increases. Thus, the ultimate impact is an empirical question. Most estimates, however, suggest that current law will depress giving as well as influence the timing of those gifts. Of course, in the event that the estate tax is eliminated permanently, the impact on philanthropic giving over the long term is likely to be more substantial.

In addition to tax policy, the increased public scrutiny of philanthropic foundations by the IRS, Congress, and state attorneys general has a possibly chilling effect on the creation of philanthropic foundations. If such attention leads to increased regulation in terms of payout rates or administrative controls, board governance, and other rules, there are potential impacts on both the magnitude and form of giving (U.S. Senate, 2004). Philanthropists have a variety of options for conducting their philanthropic activities. It is quite possible that as oversight of private foundations increases, individuals will be more willing to conduct their giving through donor-advised funds—which are currently subject to fewer regulations, though additional regulations are currently being discussed—or through major gifts to nonprofit institutions.

In addition to changes in public policy that impact the long-term dynamics of giving, there is also the possibility that changes in public spending will have an impact on the giving preferences of donors. We recognize that increases in public funding tend to "crowd out" private giving. In today's environment, the opposite forces might come into play. It is quite possible that rising public budget deficits and changing budget priorities for national security will increase the funding needs of nonprofit organizations, at least in the short run, and perhaps over the longer-term, resulting in the potential for a "crowd in" effect. In essence, giving to nonprofit organizations increases as government support recedes. This impact is likely to be more pronounced in areas where donors direct their giving rather than in increases to the overall level of giving or in the areas of most acute need.

In summary, the prospects for greater philanthropic capacity are bright. The economic underpinnings for wealth accumulation and growth over the long term are sound. With an increasing range of philanthropic mechanisms to choose from and a greater consciousness about philanthropy and its impact, there is reason to believe that this greater capacity will eventually translate into greater philanthropy. But, it is clear that there are no assurances that the trajectory of philanthropy will be smooth and there is little to guide us in predicting how high it might be. Actions to ensure a higher path are likely to have a payoff. However, it is also important to understand that with this growth in philanthropy there are likely to be changes in the nature of philanthropy itself. Philanthropy at a greater scale—gifts and grants of greater magnitude—will present greater opportunities for philanthropy to make a difference. But that will require a set of philanthropic strategies and concerted action.

Emerging Philanthropic Strategies

Beyond the increased capacity for philanthropy that accompanies economic growth and economic fortunes, significant forces are at work that impact philanthropic strategies. Over the past decade and a half, we have seen new players enter the world of philanthropy and bring with them entrepreneurial models that seek to leverage assets for outcomes (Center on Philanthropy and Public Policy, 2002). This is best personified by the venture philanthropy movement, which has stressed the importance of leveraging philanthropic assets for demonstrable results, including high engagement on the part of donors.

In effect, philanthropy is seen as an investment in desirable social outcomes rather than simply as charity or doing good deeds. Philanthropic assets are leveraged to create outcomes that advance the objectives of philanthropists and the institutions that they have created. These assets include more than just dollars; they also include knowledge and networks. Philanthropists are willing to invest these assets to produce the outcomes that advance their missions.

A key element in putting all of their assets into play is to tap their own knowledge and skills to help build the capacity of the organization. And while not all of the new players in philanthropy have the time to be as hands-on as they might wish, there is a sense that they are actively engaging in the selection of grantees and working with them to realize the desired impacts.

Another important facet of viewing philanthropy as an investment is the focus on outcomes. There is a desire to be able to demonstrate not only the outputs that result from giving, but also the outcomes in terms of social objectives. Obviously, the process of measuring outputs and outcomes is easier in some areas than in others. Nevertheless, the focus on outcomes provides a discipline to choosing strategies and tactics that can best lead to the desired objectives.

This is not to say that issues of leverage, engagement, and outcomes were not of concern prior to the beginning of the venture philanthropy movement. After all, some argue that many in "traditional" philanthropy were working on these issues prior to the emergence of this movement. But with the introduction of new players in philanthropy at a time of heightened scale and pace, there was a confluence of events that underscored the shifting focus to view philanthropy as an investment with many of the attributes of the venture philanthropy model.

The emerging sense that philanthropy is an investment has a dramatic impact on grantmaking. In an effort to make a difference, the inclination is to direct giving to those organizations that have the opportunity to make a difference in terms of the general objectives of philanthropy. As this happens, there is a tendency for philanthropy to try to produce outcomes by leveraging resources. This often entails focusing on new programs that can be demonstrated to be the direct result of grantmaking and, in many instances, on efforts by grantmakers to induce recipients to generate additional resources for giving. This suggests that those who view their philanthropy as an investment are not going to be interested in simply providing resources to nonprofits that are experiencing funding gaps as a result of changing public spending levels and priorities.

Philanthropy in the Context of Nonprofit Finances

Philanthropy is an important source of nonprofit finances. Yet, it comprises only a small portion of nonprofit revenues, and one that has declined over time. An examination of nonprofit revenues reveals that fees for services are the major source, accounting for 37.5 percent of nonprofit revenues in 1997. Government funding represents 31.3 percent of nonprofit revenues; philanthropy—private giving from individuals, foundations, and corporations—contributes 19.9 percent of nonprofit revenues; and revenues from other sources account for 11.4 percent (Urban Institute, 2003). In contrast, in 1977 the relative shares of nonprofit revenues were: fees for service—37.5 percent; government funding—26.6 percent; philanthropy—26.3 percent; and other sources—9.6 percent.

The role of philanthropy varies across industries within the nonprofit sector. For example, philanthropy plays a larger role in the finances of nonprofit arts organizations than it does in the case of health care organizations. In 1996, philanthropy accounted for 41 percent of the revenues of nonprofit arts organizations, while fees accounted for 45 percent and public funding provided 14 percent (Salamon, 1999). In contrast, health care organizations received

54 percent of their revenues from fees for service, 41 percent from government, and 5 percent from philanthropy.

Moreover, philanthropy encompasses all gifts from individuals, foundations, and corporations. Individuals account for the great majority of private giving in the United States. Of the $240.72 billion in private giving in 2003, $179.36 billion (74.5 percent) came from individuals; and another $21.6 billion (9 percent) came from bequests of individuals. Foundation giving totaled $26.30 billion (10.9 percent) and corporation giving through foundations and grant programs totaled $13.46 billion (5.6 percent) (AAFRC, 2004).

In the case of individual giving, most of the gifts are small and made by many individuals. However, what captures the imagination of the public—especially with the media attention that they generate—are the large multimillion dollar gifts of individuals that establish endowments at foundations or nonprofits, underwrite the construction of buildings, or finance major programs and initiatives. The growth of the number of "mega" gifts, whether from individuals or foundations, is creating a sense of greater philanthropic scale. But these gifts cannot substitute in any measurable way for other funding sources on a sectorwide basis. Even these largest gifts often pale in comparison to the magnitude of government funding or fees generated from the delivery of services. It is public funding and fees for service that have underwritten the expansion of nonprofit organizations in recent decades in both numbers and size. Indeed, as philanthropy has grown, the number of nonprofits has also grown. But the increase in philanthropy has not been commensurate. As a consequence, nonprofits have become more reliant on public funding, and increasingly, commercial activities (Young and Salamon, 2002).

Thus, in an era when philanthropy is growing, its relative importance in the balance sheets of nonprofits is not. This creates a challenge for philanthropy to be relevant and raises the question: What is the appropriate role of philanthropy? It is clear that to merely think of philanthropy as a substitute for other funding sources is to limit its role and create unrealistic expectations.

First, given the small slice of nonprofit finances that philanthropy represents, it is not reasonable to expect it to fill in gaps, whether they result from changes in economic conditions, public funding, or commercial opportunities. After all, philanthropy is not countercyclical. Philanthropy tends to decline when the economy does. Individuals are less likely to give during periods of declining income and wealth. And although foundations may seek to provide some cushion to their grantees in the short term to weather economic downturns, they are not anxious to increase their payout as their endowments decline. To view philanthropy as a funding stream interchangeable with public funding and commercial activities would shortchange the potential of philanthropy—both in terms of the important role philanthropy can play in social change, and in terms of making it less attractive for those with the capacity to give.

The promise of philanthropy lies in its ability to provide "venture capital" for the nonprofit sector—the resources to create change in society—whether in the context of organizational or sectoral capacity, public policy engagement, or innovative programs. But even accepting this "venture capital" role, it is important to recognize that not all segments of the nonprofit sector have equal access to the various funding sources. Some nonprofits have missions and activities that more closely match public spending programs. Some nonprofits generate goods and services for which there are consumers with a capacity to pay for services. And other nonprofits are closely aligned with the interests of philanthropists and foundations.

To summarize, philanthropy is not a general source of capital for the nonprofit sector. While it is a source of venture capital, it is linked to particular missions of philanthropists and philanthropic institutions. Thus, nonprofits working in areas of interest to philanthropy are better positioned to tap these resources. But the focus on leverage and making a difference tends to favor new efforts and programs rather than the maintenance of ongoing activities.

Grantmaking as Investment

As philanthropy grows and is accentuated by efforts to make a greater impact, there is an array of strategies to consider. While some strategies focus on the possibility of more philanthropic dollars being granted to nonprofits, others are more concerned about the use of grants to strengthen the capacity of nonprofits and the sector as a whole. In effect, what are the strategies for leveraging philanthropic assets to have an impact that exceeds the dollars invested? Here we consider a range of philanthropic strategies related to the magnitude of grantmaking such as the payout decision, as well as strategies for nonprofit capacity-building, public policy engagement, and sector infrastructure.

THE PAYOUT RATE

One of the most fundamental strategic choices for a foundation's grantmaking is the payout rate—the rate at which they spend from their endowment for grantmaking and associated administrative expenses. This decision frames what is possible in terms of the grantmaking budget for the foundation and creates a time frame for the work of the foundation (e.g., a fixed time horizon such as twenty-five years, or in perpetuity). In the case of private foundations, a foundation's payout decision is constrained by the minimum payout required by law (5 percent). Foundations have generally set their payout rate close to the mandated minimum (Deep and Frumkin, 2003).

During the recent period in which the endowments of foundations have expanded with the fortunes of the stock market, there has been renewed focus on what the appropriate payout rate should be, both in terms of what individual foundations might choose to do on their own and what federal law should be. Some argue that as the economy prospers, foundations should increase their grantmaking beyond the automatic increase that occurs with a given payout rate as endowments grow in value. In effect, foundations should increase their payout rate. Some have gone a step further to argue that the minimum payout rate mandated by law should be increased either directly or indirectly, as in the case of recent proposals to disallow certain administrative expenses in calculating "qualifying distributions." In this instance, the "effective" payout rate increases at the same time incentives are provided for controlling administrative costs. Such an approach was apparent in HR 7 from the 108th Congress, and continues to be discussed in terms of proposals to adopt policies pertaining to the nonprofit sector (U.S. Senate, 2004).

Running throughout the arguments in favor of an increase in the payout rate, in particular the federal mandate, is the notion that foundations should increase the amount of their grantmaking rather than continue to accumulate wealth in terms of growing endowments as a result of the prosperous 1990s. While this argument was advanced during good times, the continued push during a period of declining foundation assets and diminished public budgets seems to suggest that foundations are viewed as an alternative funding source rather than as a source of "venture capital." Of course, the opponents of an increased payout rate focus on the value of differentiating foundations from other institutions by ensuring that they exist into perpetuity. Of course, some founding donors have an explicit desire to have the foundations they create sunset after a number of years.

More recently, the issue of the payout rate has been framed in terms of the particular mission of a foundation. In effect, the payout rate is a strategic choice for a foundation. Foundations may choose to exist into perpetuity, but there is nothing sacrosanct about the perpetuity of a foundation. This approach suggests that the choice of payout rate should be determined by the foundation's mission. For example, a foundation committed to eradicating particular diseases such as AIDS should direct its resources to that mission in the near term, rather than preserving its assets for grantmaking over the long term. On the other hand, foundations with more general missions, such as improving quality of life, may choose payout rates that ensure the ability to fulfill their mission in perpetuity (Deep and Frumkin, 2003; Meehan, Kilmer, and O'Flanagan, 2004). This new approach is helpful to a foundation making strategic decisions, in particular at the creation stage of a foundation. However, it does little to resolve the public policy issue of what is the appropriate payout rate that should be required by law.

NONPROFIT CAPACITY-BUILDING

Increasingly, there is a concern that in the current environment nonprofit organizations do not have sufficient capacity to carry out their missions. Recently, some grantmakers have made an effort to help nonprofit organizations improve their performance. This strategy focuses on investing in nonprofit organizations that the foundation then works with to enable them to be more effective. The interest in this area is underscored by the creation of an affinity group of funders focused on effective nonprofit organizations as well as foundations themselves— Grantmakers for Effective Organizations (GEO).

Capacity-building encompasses many activities that are designed to enhance the organization's capacity to fulfill its mission. These activities might include instituting basic accounting and financial management systems, building more effective governing boards, developing strategic plans, or enabling strategic restructuring. Grantmakers have also taken an interest in helping nonprofits to achieve organizational efficiencies through mergers or sharing certain administrative functions (La Piana, 1998). Foundation initiatives to build nonprofit capacity take several forms. These include efforts to fund infrastructure organizations that work with nonprofits to improve capacity; the direct provision of technical assistance to nonprofit grantees; or grants to enable nonprofits to acquire services on their own to improve capacity. Examples of infrastructure groups are BoardSource, which focuses on the best practices for nonprofit board governance; local management support organizations that provide a range of courses to improve the skills of local nonprofit organizations and their professionals; or state associations of nonprofits that provide programs and professional development activities. Other foundations tend to focus their efforts on their own grantees, either by providing programs or services to them directly, or by making grants available to nonprofits to undertake their own capacity-building efforts.

The net returns on investment in capacity-building will be contingent on the current state of organizational development. And in many instances, these investments will not entail significant dollars, but will yield substantial returns. While there is increasing recognition of the importance of nonprofit capacity-building, it has come as the result of a concerted effort to raise the issue (Light, 2004). This effort has been critical to counter a common view that such investments divert resources from the program activities of nonprofit organizations. The strength of nonprofit organizations will be critical as nonprofits compete for philanthropic dollars. Foundations are reluctant to make grants to organizations that they view as organizationally risky. A stronger nonprofit is also likely to be well positioned to compete for public funds and service-related fees where such opportunities exist.

PUBLIC POLICY ENGAGEMENT

Another strategy for foundations to increase their impact is to engage in public policy. Foundations seem to be increasingly interested in pursuing their missions not simply through the delivery of services, but through policy change. Given that many areas of foundation interest are also areas of governmental interest, there is an opportunity for foundations to leverage their dollars, as well as their knowledge and networks, to impact their programmatic interests by engaging public policy (Center on Philanthropy and Public Policy, 2003).

Foundation engagement in public policy is not new. There has been a long-standing interplay between philanthropy and government, given the common objectives each sector shares in addressing public problems. Foundations have long realized that their dollars pale in comparison to public budgets. One model suggests that foundations fund successful demonstration projects that governments then adopt and take to scale. Yet, foundation engagement in public policy is more expansive and complicated than this model suggests.

Foundations that choose to engage the policy process have a variety of points at which they may enter and participate. The differing stages in the process, the venues where public policy decisions are made, and the level of government (local, state, and national) where issues are considered, all offer options for pursuing policy goals. Foundations must also choose how to engage the process. Many foundations fund work of policy relevance, including policy analyses and program evaluations, pilot programs, and technical support. However, such activities alone are not likely to have much impact on policy issues. A foundation that seeks to drive public policy will want to consider playing a more active role in influencing the policy environment, including investing in nonprofit advocacy groups and policy networks.

In addition, given the dim political prospects for major government initiatives with big price tags and a polarized public, foundations are beginning to work directly in partnership with government to aid their capacity to govern (Ferris and Melnick, 2004). This is counter to earlier foundation efforts, which have typically focused on working from the outside to influence public policy through funding grassroots organizations that are policy advocates, or funding policy networks and elites that help to frame issues and shape public policy debates.

Public policymaking is a complex process. It is messy, unpredictable, and uncertain; beyond the control of any individual or organization; and an open-ended proposition in that public policies are always subject to change. Foundations that choose to engage public policy understand that it involves risk, both in terms of being able to yield desirable outcomes and its ability to invite public scrutiny and controversy. Some foundations simply invest in the work of others including researchers and think tanks, policy networks, and advocacy groups. But others are willing to play an entrepreneurial role, incurring risks by taking a proactive role. They seek out partners that will create policy ideas and build networks. In some instances, they will help to create these ideas and networks. In addition, they are willing to build and leverage their own connections or political capital with policymakers to realize policy change.

SECTOR INFRASTRUCTURE

Finally, foundations have an interest in building the capacity of the sector as a whole. It is clear that there is a need not only to build the capacity of nonprofit organizations, but also of foundations. But, in addition to building the capacity of individual organizations, there is a need to strengthen the capacity of the sector as a whole—locally, regionally, nationally, and internationally— including professional associations and academic research centers (*Nonprofit Quarterly,* 2004).

As nonprofits and foundations have grown in number, there is an increasing recognition that it is advantageous for them to share information, join membership groups, and even work together. There have been a number of infrastructure groups in existence for decades, such as the Council of Foundations, the Foundation Center, and Independent Sector. But we have seen a growing number of entities in recent years catering to varied dimensions and interests of the sector. For example, there has been growth in the number of regional associations of grantmakers and statewide associations of nonprofits that seek to build the sector at a subnational level. In addition, an increasing number of grantmaker affinity groups have emerged based on issues and interests such as education, health, Hispanics, and women. Common organizational issues are addressed by, for example, the Association of Small Foundations and Community Foundations of America. There is also an increasing number of organizations focused on organizational governance and management, such as BoardSource and local management support organizations.

Beyond these membership organizations, in recent years we have seen networks, alliances, and collaboratives emerge to drive action. Two examples are Funders for Smart Growth, an affinity group, and Los Angeles Urban Funders, a local collaborative (Hopkins, 2005). These efforts have been funded, and even spearheaded, by foundations. Again, they are examples of trying to leverage assets—dollars and otherwise—to make a bigger difference than through the actions of any single organization.

SUMMARY

The magnitude of philanthropic grants is driven in large part by economic fortunes. Given the tendency of foundations to hover around the minimum payout rate of five percent, grantmaking by existing foundations increases with the value of foundation endowments. In addition, as wealth is accrued, particularly beyond the amount that is needed for personal gain, there is an increased likelihood that existing foundations will receive new gifts to their endowments and new foundations will be formed. In effect, grantmaking reinforces rather than counteracts economic prospects.

The instance in which grantmaking may provide a countercyclical impact is where foundations view their primary function as funding the service delivery needs of nonprofits. During periods when community needs are most acute and nonprofit partners are in distress, foundations may be willing to increase their payout. There is an indication that some foundations pursue such a strategy.

In recent years, however, there seems to have been a growing tendency among funders to strengthen the capacity of the nonprofit sector through a set of grantmaking strategies such as building the capacity of their grantees, engaging in public policy, and building the sector's infrastructure. These grantmaking strategies are viewed as investments in the field, rather than merely funding the work of nonprofits that deliver services, advocate for policy, and build communities. Given the undercapitalization of the sector, the enduring question is: What is the appropriate allocation between investment in the sector and funding the important work of nonprofits, today and in the future.

Implications for Philanthropy and the Nonprofit Sector

Beyond the macro question of the appropriate level and mix of investments, there is the question of how the available resources should be directed to nonprofit organizations. This is the challenge of developing a more efficient "capital market" for the nonprofit sector. How are philanthropic resources matched to the opportunities and needs of the varied nonprofit organizations?

Unlike traditional capital markets where those who supply the funds are concerned with rates of return and indifferent to other outcomes, philanthropic markets work on multiple dimensions. There is an interest in outcomes that range from service delivery to social change, from nonprofit capacity to healthy communities, and from local impacts to national implications. And foundations, in recent years, have increased their demands for demonstrable results since the impacts are not self-evident, as is the case with financial returns.

Thus, transaction and information costs associated with philanthropic grantmaking are considerable. Both grantmakers and nonprofits incur costs in the process. Grantmakers incur costs in identifying those nonprofits that are able to produce results that further the funder's mission, as well as in assessing the probability that the nonprofit will likely be successful. In the case of nonprofits, there are considerable costs in acquiring information about funding opportunities. The expanded capacity of philanthropy has generated more sources of funds and more types of grantmaking vehicles, as well as more strategic grantmaking. Together, these trends result in a more complex philanthropic landscape that increases the costs of acquiring information about funding opportunities.

On the other hand, there are an increasing number of resources that, at least related to particular types of philanthropic funds, enable nonprofits to acquire information about the process. Resources such as Guidestar and the Foundation Center's *Foundation Directory Online* are increasingly accessible to nonprofits as a result of the Internet. But they do not provide as much helpful information about increasingly important forms of giving such as donor-advised funds or corporate support via marketing budgets.

But it is not simply a matter of lowering the transaction costs. In order for the capital market of the nonprofit sector to work better, it will require a more concerted effort on the part of philanthropy to fund innovation, reward risk, and hold grantees accountable for performance and outcomes (Silverman, 2004). Moreover, it will be important to move such strategic action beyond the larger foundations to the vast array of players in philanthropy—both individuals and institutions—if the full potential of the nonprofit capital market is to be realized (Bernholz, 2004; Meehan III, Kilmer, and O'Flanagan, 2004).

What do these philanthropic trends and emerging strategies mean for nonprofit organizations? Nonprofit organizations that rely on philanthropic grants for substantial revenues must understand not only the general trends in grantmaking, but also the strategies of funders that are most interested in their organizations and the work they do.

In those instances where nonprofit organizations are seeking support from new funders, there is a considerable amount of information gathering and relationship building that is required. The same is true for nonprofit organizations that are seeking funds for new programs.

Conclusion

We are in the midst of an era of tremendous growth in philanthropy and the emergence of new institutions and forms of giving. In this environment, there is an opportunity to consider strategies that will realize the promise of philanthropy well into the future. The promise is not simply a matter of the scale of philanthropy—the dollars—but also the reach and impact of philanthropy.

Given the motivations, strategies, and passions of philanthropies and their relative numerical "insignificance" in the balance sheets of nonprofit organizations, it is critical that philanthropy undertake strategies that accentuate its role as a critical social institution and its relevance to the nonprofit sector. Philanthropists and the foundations they create must recognize the unique role they can play in strengthening the capacity of the sector and building the capacity of the organizations that comprise it.

To play this role requires that they view their role not merely as another funding stream, but as investors in nonprofit organizations and the nonprofit sector— through capacity-building, infrastructure development, and public policy engagement. It also requires an understanding of their role, collectively, to work to build a more efficient "capital market" that will enable the nonprofit sector to continue its unique functions as a service innovator, policy advocate, and community builder, rather than become a pale imitation of a government agency or a commercial enterprise.

References

AAFRC Trust for Philanthropy. 2004. *Giving USA.* AAFRC Trust for Philanthropy: Glenview, IL.

Bernholz, Lucy. 2004. *Creating Capital Markets: The Deliberate Evolution.* New York: John Wiley and Sons.

The Center on Philanthropy and Public Policy. 2002. *What is "New" About New Philanthropy?* Los Angeles: University of Southern California.

The Center on Philanthropy and Public Policy. 2003. *Foundations and Public Policy: Leveraging Assets for Public Problem Solving.* Los Angeles: University of Southern California.

Congressional Budget Office. 2004. *The Estate Tax and Charitable Giving.* Washington, DC: U. S. Government Printing Office.

Deep, Akash, and Peter Frumkin. 2003. "The Foundation Payout Puzzle," Kennedy School of Government, unpublished paper.

Ferris, James M., and Glenn A. Melnick. 2004. "Improving the Health of Californians: Effective Intersectoral Strategies for Challenging Times: A Summary of a Roundtable on Philanthropy and Health Policymaking," *Health Affairs,* May–June 2004, pp. 257–261.

The Foundation Center. 2004. *Foundation Yearbook,* Foundations Today Series, 2004 Edition. New York: The Foundation Center.

Hopkins, Elwood. 2005. *Collaborative Philanthropies: What Groups of Foundations Can Do That Individual Funders Cannot.* Lanham, MD: Lexington Books.

Klauser, Michael. 2003. "When Time Isn't Money: Foundation Payouts and the Time Value of Money," *Stanford Social Innovation Review,* Spring 2003, pp. 51–59.

La Piana, David. 1998. *Beyond Collaboration: Strategic Restructuring for Nonprofit Organizations.* San Francisco: The James Irvine Foundation.

Light, Paul. 2004. *Sustaining Nonprofit Performance: The Case for Capacity Building and the Evidence to Support It.* Washington, DC: Brookings Institution Press.

Meehan III, William; Derek Kilmer, and Maisie O'Flanagan. 2004. "Investing in Society," *Stanford Social Innovation Review,* Spring 2004, pp. 34–43.

Nonprofit Quarterly. 2004. *Funding Infrastructure: An Investment in the Nonprofit Sector's Future.* Volume 12, Special Issue. Boston: Nonprofit Quarterly.

Salamon, Lester M. 1999. *America's Nonprofit Sector: A Primer,* 2nd ed. New York: The Foundation Center.

Silverman, Les. 2004 "Building Better Foundations: Q and A with Ralph Smith," *The McKinsey Report,* January 2004.

The Urban Institute. 2003. *The New Nonprofit Almanac.* Washington, DC: Urban Institute.

U.S. Senate, Finance Committee Discussion Draft. June 2004. Available at: http://www.senate.gov/~finance/hearings/testimony/2004test/062204stfdis.pdf.

Young, Dennis R., and Lester M. Salamon. 2002. "Commercialization, Social Ventures, and For-Profit Competition." In Lester M. Salamon (ed.), *The State of Nonprofit America.* Washington, DC: Brookings Institution Press, pp. 423–426.

10

Holistic Grantmaking

Greg Cantori
Executive Director
The Marion I. and Henry J. Knott Foundation
Baltimore, MD

Introduction

Holistic grantmaking involves not only traditional grants, but also other financial, technical, and collaborative assistance tools that, strategically combined, assist a recipient organization in advancing its mission in ways and to a scale not otherwise possible. This array of grantmaking tools creates new paradigms in financial assistance for the lending/granting organizations themselves, and also assists their evolution by identifying new needs and opportunities.

Although most nonprofits and foundations are somewhat familiar with one or two specific funding tools, few are aware of the total universe of tools currently available to them. Even fewer have the required skills or internal capacity to use these tools in comprehensive, coordinated ways that fill the gaps left by traditional grantmaking.

Major sections of the recently completed Council of Foundation's "Stewardship Principles for Family Foundations" formally recognizes the advantages holistic grantmaking holds for both foundations and grantees. It looks specifically at how foundations can use combinations of support systems—for example, combining a challenge grant with an outright grant and a loan to tide a recipient over until more funds are received. The principles also include the concept of grantmakers using "tools" in assisting grantees:

The author thanks Rick Schoff for putting into context the panel presentation on "Holistic Grantmaking" that included Rodney Christopher, associate director for program and product development at the Nonprofit Finance Fund, and Syrinda Paige of Wachovia Bank, during the biennial conference of the National Center for Nonprofit Enterprise, January 16–17, 2004 in Washington, DC. The author also thanks Rodney Christopher for his comments and suggestions. The author is solely responsible for the contents.

Principle: "We consider multiple strategies to further our mission."
Options to strengthen performance:

- learn best practice models and compare practices against others in the field

- consider a range of financial support options that could include: general operating, project, capital, research, scholarship, endowment, multiyear and challenge grants, and funds to respond to emergency or other unanticipated needs

- collaborate with others who fund similar work

Other tools:

- provide technical assistance to grantees and other nonprofits

- invest in ways that further the mission (e.g., program-related investments, microcredit loans, socially responsible investing, proxy voting/shareholder resolutions)

- convene community leaders, nonprofits and/or other funders doing similar work

(Council on Foundations, 2004, p. 2)

Nationally, foundation assets invested in program-related investments (PRIs) increased 90 percent between 1990 and 2000 from $222 million to $421 million. Although increasing quite dramatically, PRIs still accounted for less than 1 percent of the $30.5 billion in grants paid in 2001 by private foundations (Foundation Center, 2003). Not only do PRIs still represent only a fraction of grantmaking, most PRI activity is still the domain of the largest foundations, with many loans exceeding $1 million per organization. As we will see, however, there are vast opportunities for much smaller PRIs, made by smaller foundations, that can strategically advance both the foundation's and grantees' missions.

We will briefly discuss these many tools and how they can be used sequentially, simultaneously, or in unique combinations to structure powerful support systems.

Current Practices

To create a base for our discussion, we provide a summary review of the many funding tools currently used by funders. This list is always in flux as new tools are discovered. The majority of funders use some of these exclusively while other tools are rarely used and then only by funders willing and able to apply the financial and human resources needed to make those tools effective.

We begin with traditional *project grants.* These are by far the most frequently used tool. They are typically *outright grants,* as there is no strict expectation of deliverable products in order for an organization to receive its funds. However, sometimes specific conditions are attached, such as reaching some threshold in volunteer participation, completing a project phase, or receiving additional funds (see *challenge grants* below). Project grants typically allow a minimal percentage of funding to be used for operational overhead.

Operating grants help to offset the difficulty many nonprofits have in successfully implementing their project grants. Operating grants typically pay for consultant and staff costs which may include strategic planning, board development, upgraded technology, staff/board training, executive coaching, and even basic operating costs such as rent and utilities. More specialized operating grants may address capacity-building, such as management assistance to help with a potential merger and/or acquisition of another nonprofit, and executive transitions. Mergers and executive transitions have become so important to both the funder and grantee communities that several organizations, such as CompassPoint in San Francisco and the Maryland Association of Nonprofits, have set aside permanent funding pools for these purposes. They have also carefully selected a pool of experienced consultants to help nonprofits navigate these highly stressful and disruptive events.

Funders may also issue *matching grants* to encourage grantees to generate additional funding. *Challenge grants* are more demanding than matching grants because they are "all or nothing," that is, the nonprofit receives nothing unless it raises a specified amount from other sources. This tool is used to aggressively spur the grantee to identify new sources of funding or increase its current funding.

Although matching and challenge grants are usually initiated by the funder, some astute nonprofits request them up front to improve their odds in meeting fundraising goals. Either way, funders need to be aware of the potential pitfalls in overusing these funding tools. As Kramer (1999) notes:

> The leverage, or added value, of a matching grant is often only illusory. Matching grants do not change the allocation budgets of other foundations. Consequently, they do not increase the total amount of money that foundations give or that charities receive—they just redirect some of the dollars from one project to another. Matching grants are a zero-sum game.

Multiyear grants are a powerful tool because they strengthen the mutual engagement of funders and grantees. With such grants, each year's progress is evaluated and compared to that of the previous year, and the next year's goals are appropriately modified before further funding is released. Multiyear grants frequently allow for mid-course corrections based on the learning that occurs, as mistakes and successes are recognized and acted upon. Funders and grantees have more opportunities to learn about each other, potentially increasing the level of trust and therefore grant effectiveness. With closer collaboration comes a greater likelihood that a nonprofit might receive additional funds, if needed, to increase its operational effectiveness. Often, multiyear grants include a declining allocation each year as a way to "wean" grantees from relying too much on a foundation's long-term support. Multiyear grants usually include waypoints, or required outcomes, for their continuation. Examples include specific deadlines, reports, and/or objectives that must be met before the next round of funding becomes available.

Funders can also use *microgrants* for highly specific needs such as a new computer, staff training, or emergencies. These grants frequently range from one hundred to several thousand dollars each and are normally less burdensome in both the application process and reporting.

To help keep geographically dispersed board members connected, to explore new grant opportunities, or to respond to emergencies outside of a foundation's normal grant cycle, *discretionary grants* are often the tool of choice. These grants give program officers, executive directors, and/or individual board members the authority to designate funding up to a specified annual limit. Such grants are retroactively approved by the full board. Unfortunately, discretionary grants have a high potential for abuse precisely because of this lack of prior approval by the board and the fact that they are not granted through a full participatory board process. These grants sometimes create grantee confusion when discretionary funding appears to contravene overall foundation grantmaking (Born, 2001).

Because of events such as 9/11, the December 2004 tsunami in Indonesia, and the 2005 hurricanes in the U.S., *emergency grants* have become a widely recognized funding tool. These grants are usually made within predetermined parameters to respond to natural or man-made disasters, theft, or even unplanned management transitions. To avoid poor administration or even public criticism, as the Red Cross suffered after 9/11, it is crucial that guidelines, polices, and procedures be carefully conceived and established for emergency grantmaking.

Now that we've completed a brief summary of these tools, let's look at an example in how they were used in combination in Baltimore. No formal process existed for funders in the Baltimore area to coordinate on emergency grant situations. However, the Association of Baltimore Area Grantmakers (ABAG) was in a unique position to coordinate the work of these funders.

There were several nonprofit emergency funding needs during the winter of 2003—roof collapses, flooding, heating loss, etc. One example involved the homeless shelter I Can Inc. Without heat for three weeks, the shelter needed to immediately raise $45,000 to replace a boiler. Temperatures hovered just above freezing throughout the building. Residents huddled together while eating their meals so they could share body heat. (The shelter is also a convalescent release site for several area hospitals.)

It took lots of foundation and I Can Inc. staff time to identify, call, and coordinate the emergency funding request with other funders. In the end, I Can Inc. was able to raise the needed funds within a week using a combination of matching, discretionary, and emergency grants.

Another nonprofit was burglarized twice within a week, requiring immediate emergency funding for new computers, a security system, window bars, and new locks. In working with these cases, the Knott Foundation learned of both the emergency funding abilities and restrictions many foundations have.

An Emergency Grant Coordination Program was created so that each emergency grant request would have a self-designated "lead" foundation to do the necessary grant research. That lead foundation would validate the request with an organizational, financial, and circumstance review and perhaps a site visit. Foundations wishing to participate would then "opt-in."

The participating foundations agreed on a clear definition of "emergency," as follows: the organization had no reasonable way to know the emergency would occur; the nature of the emergency requires funding before normal grant cycles; other funding is not obtainable that will meet the emergency need; if the emergency is caused by a loss of anticipated funding, the lost funding had been fully committed to the organization and it was not foreseeable that it would be lost.

Problems that arise due to poor planning and management are not considered emergencies, under this definition. Foundations will be able to check the ABAG members-only site for updates on the status and funding for any given crisis.

Periodic e-mails to opted-in foundations can direct them to the site and be used to provide instant updates.

Just as a *common grant application form* is used to help nonprofit organizations save time in applying to multiple foundations, this new Emergency Grant Coordination Program will serve a similar purpose as a more efficient way to serve area nonprofits with an emergency need.

The ABAG example shows how foundations can leverage their funding tools through intermediaries. Other examples of intermediaries include *community development finance institutions* (CDFIs), which have grown tremendously over the past decade. CDFIs take both social and for-profit investor monies and lend them at advantageous rates to community development corporations and projects. Community credit unions behave in much the same way except that they are focused on individual banking services as well.

Foundations also have found it mutually beneficial to participate in *funding collaboratives* where they can pool their financial and human resources to serve specific funding needs. These pools often become subsidiary grantmaking organizations in and of themselves.

In addition to various grantmaking tools, foundations have a unique ability to make PRIs, charitable loans that are favorably treated for tax purposes. Examples of PRIs include:

- *Equity Sharing:* Where the funder acquires a percentage of the equity appreciation (or loss) as a second loan or as a "cloud on the title."

- *Loan Guarantees:* A partnership with a lending institution, usually with the lending institution taking the lead role, to reduce the overall cost of borrowed funds. Note, although guaranteed funds are set aside as restricted assets they are not considered PRIs unless and until the loan defaults and the funds are called.

- *Direct loans*
  - *Cash flow loans:* Assist with temporary cash shortages due to slow paying receivables or other cash emergencies.
  - *Bridge loans:* Provide interim funding while a grantee awaits a public funding take-out or is selling property and needs cash before settlement.

- *Pooled loans:* Include community development finance institution (CDFI) loans, community loan funds, or formally structured funder collaborative loans.

- *Linked deposits:* Security-based credit lines maintain investment returns while also allowing the use of the credit line for PRIs. This tool allows grantmakers to leverage their assets in making PRIs.

A New Way of Thinking

As we can see, there is already a tremendous variety of funding tools available to foundations. However, only a small number of foundations actually use many of these tools, aside from traditional project-based grants.

Properly used, microgrants or discretionary grants are great ways for a foundation to dip a toe into a grantee's "pool" and quickly learn key details about the grantee's operations. Frequently, these small grants create less formal working relationships between the parties because the amounts of money at risk are relatively small and results are often seen much sooner. For both parties, proposal and reporting requirements are simpler and less burdensome. A well-focused and applied microgrant can make a surprisingly big impact, although it's not always clear why. Perhaps it is because funds are clearly earmarked for immediate needs, or because small "wish list" projects often receive funding this way. In the latter case, particular staff may be very committed to seeing their "pet" programs succeed.

Some newer strategies provide grants and loans based on an increasingly popular social investment model which assumes that grantees can generate earned income (Smith, 1996). Several how-to manuals and books have been published, and foundations are increasingly likely to assist nonprofits looking to these new revenue sources. Because income-generating businesses within a nonprofit can create tremendous stresses—such as mission drift, new distractions, difficulty in determining fair compensation for staff, and likely negative cash flows for the first few years—Community Wealth Ventures, a business plan and technical assistance developer, is assisting local foundations and their grantees with this approach. Applicant nonprofits are looking for capital for their new or expanded ventures, and PRIs, perhaps in combination with project or operational grants, fill that need exceedingly well. As these ventures develop and thrive, debt repayment becomes possible, freeing foundation assets for additional loans while allowing nonprofits to create new income sources.

Over the past ten years, "venture philanthropy" has become a more familiar practice, especially among younger foundations whose wealth was created through successful entrepreneurship in the technology field. This form of philanthropy consists of high-engagement grantee-grantor relationships in the form of strategic assistance, board and executive recruitment, coaching and development, assistance in raising capital, accessing networks, and facilitating partnerships.

Nature of the Challenge

A primary challenge to holistic grantmaking is foundations' awareness of the many funding tools available to them and the latent demand that exists for those tools and funding strategies. Less than 30 percent of 1,192 foundations surveyed by the Urban Institute had solicited any type (anonymous or not) of feedback from grantees over the past two years (Ostrower, 2004). Without knowing what types of grants or loans their grantees would find useful, foundations tend to remain complacent about their current grantmaking models.

The vast majority of foundations are unstaffed or understaffed, limiting the time they have to learn about these tools, much less put them into practice. Unless a foundation is willing to temporarily step off the proposal treadmill, and unless smaller foundations are determined to adopt alternative tools, traditional reactive grants will continue to dominate the grantmaking landscape.

Local or regional associations of grantmakers increasingly serve as important forums for discussing these tools, sometimes deliberately, but often indirectly as facilitators of discussion among their member funders who share new initiatives with their peers. In addition, many national organizations such as the Council on Foundations, Grantmakers for Effective Organizations, the Foundation Center, and the Center for Effective Philanthropy provide cutting-edge research and information on experiences with alternative grantmaking.

Nonprofits are often unaware that foundations can provide these additional resources for them. Hence, they simply don't ask for such help. Because nonprofits aren't asking, foundations presume there isn't a need (Ostrower, 2004). Both entities are missing substantial opportunities in relating to one another in more powerful and mutually beneficial ways.

One way to combat this problem is to inform and educate grantees on how foundations could provide alternative funding and technical support. Once a more informed grantee knows what to ask for, foundations will experience emerging demand for these products and services. Perhaps slowly at first, foundations will try these new approaches. If they have access to careful research and freely shared boilerplate templates and programs, and with the lessons learned from their peers, foundations should find these tools a good way to enhance their own effectiveness.

Grantees are sometimes astonished to discover that a loan or alternative grant from a foundation is possible. At the Knott Foundation we have heard statements such as, "I never realized foundations had so many ways of helping." The past experience of grantees has always been to identify foundations with a compatible mission, submit a letter of inquiry and/or proposal, and hope for the best. The dynamic resulting from a holistic grantmaking experience is altogether new and exciting and yet brings new challenges. This is a real paradigm shift.

A primary obstacle lies in the traditional barriers between a foundation's investment committee and its grant committee. The former sees their domain solely as the preservation and growth of assets, very frequently with only passing recognition that 95 percent of a typical foundation's corpus is invested in nothing even closely related to its mission. An exception to this apparent lack of mission-related investing is the use of social and/or proxy screens where an investment committee may set boundaries preventing investments in companies involved in weaponry, or nuclear or tobacco production. Proxies can also be voted on in such a way as to send a message to companies that a foundation will not approve of actions that might prove contradictory to its mission. However, these social and/or proxy screens just scratch the surface. Most foundation assets are invested in various domestic and international companies and markets unrelated to projects the grant committee is funding. On the other hand, grant committees rarely, if ever, ask the investment committee to consider investing in their giving areas. The barrier between these committees is therefore both psychological and structural and remains very real and difficult to overcome as these committees see their foundation's work from opposite perspectives.

A second obstacle, even within traditional grantmaking, lies with the fact that funders are increasingly searching for financial or outcome-based results while grantees often remain uncomfortable with financial models of accountability and rely instead on program descriptions to make their case. This disconnect becomes clear when grantees extol the virtues of their work using only *outputs* (such as number of seminars held or clients served) rather than the measurable *outcomes* foundations increasingly are looking for. In addition, grantees often put together project budgets that are not well thought out, or too simplistic or rudimentary, often because they lack the accounting processes or capacities suitable for accurately tracking project income and expenses.

A third challenge to alternative grantmaking is inadequate foundation staff capacity. Many foundations have refrained from hiring additional staff while others have reduced staffing levels in response to asset losses over the past five years. This has created a major barrier to alternative grantmaking practices. Brody and Miller (1996) make the case that any type of more proactive work with grantees entails additional human and financial resources. Foundations need to reconcile these additional costs before moving forward. However, with the continuing debate on whether foundation administrative expenses should continue to count toward the mandated IRS 5 percent payout requirement, many foundations favor the more fiscally conservative approach of limiting staff. This means that only the most determined foundations will allocate the necessary administrative resources to launch and maintain a holistic loan and grant program. The future staffing outlook could become even more challenging if the current regulatory reviews and discussions result in the separation of administrative costs from the 5 percent required payout.

A fourth challenge lies in how to frame and reconcile grantmaking and investment decisions within the foundation. In particular, foundations will need to make some basic decisions on whether to treat these tools as investments, grants, or some combination of the two. They will also need to decide which committee or committees will have the oversight in making the ultimate investment versus charitable-use decisions. One possible way to approach this challenge is to create a third committee focused solely upon alternative grants and investments, perhaps made up of members from both the grant and investment committees. Just as PRIs straddle the investment/grant chasm, this new committee could speak to both the grant and investment committees in their respective languages about alternative grants and loans.

THE CASE FOR OPERATING AND TECHNICAL ASSISTANCE AS A KEY COMPONENT OF HOLISTIC GRANTMAKING

Organizations such as Grantmakers for Effective Organizations are playing an increasingly significant role in promoting and educating funders on the need for increasing operating and technical assistance support as a key component in making effective use of holistic grants.

Many nonprofits may need some technical and in-kind assistance to increase their credit worthiness and to better understand how to manage short-term assets/liabilities that include items such as their cash flows, interest payments, and administrative costs. They also may need help in understanding the implications of decisions affecting their long-term assets/liabilities, such as hard assets (e.g., buildings, vehicles) and soft assets such as endowments and operating reserves.

Alternative grant and loan funding dramatically changes funder/grantee relationships. Typically nonprofits may write proposals for specific projects that include many details on their ability to make a difference with that specific project, while leaving out critical information about their own total capacity, organizational health, and internal struggles. Funders who are burdened with many competing proposals frequently do not have the time or resources to investigate in any depth the underlying managerial and financial strengths and weaknesses of their potential grantees. Rather, it is expedient to examine a proposal only within its own context, i.e., budget, staffing, outputs, and outcomes, with only a cursory review of the nonprofit's overall organizational capacity. Frequently this approach works relatively well: the nonprofit receives its funding and then attempts to fulfill its many obligations to multiple funders. Funders within this typical funding scenario see the grantee with polarized lenses that are preset in such a way that only the best projects, the best news, the best-looking financials, and the best outcomes are readily submitted and accepted. In the vast majority of cases, the grantees carry out their contractual expectations reasonably well (although they rarely exceed expectations) and the funder has no need or time for further recourse and will count the grant as a success.

However, behind the scenes there is frequently another, much more challenging dynamic. To remain accountable, multiple commitments often require multiple reports. Nonprofits frequently endure funding streams that are both unpredictable and delayed. They often must juggle funding to meet inexorable monthly expenses such as rent and payroll, no matter when their funding is actually available. Too many nonprofits play a shell game with a reluctant nod from their boards in maintaining their operations with an attitude of, "As long as we do what we promised our funders, what difference does it ultimately make to use one pool of funds to temporarily fund another?"

A case in point is a ten-year-old nonprofit that helps women involved in prostitution through street outreach, shelter, and counseling. Their mission was highly compelling. Their executive director was a passionate advocate and recognized leader in the field. Many foundations provided funding because the nonprofit addressed a multitude of closely related issues—HIV/AIDS, drug abuse and drug dealing, violence against women, human trafficking, neighborhood improvement, and more. The nonprofit, in turn, made a number of highly effective presentations to both organized philanthropists as well as individual donors and religious institutions. Few, if any, questioned the organization's financial or managerial accountability. The mission was so immediately gripping and the director so impressive and impassioned that those matters appeared almost trivial. In fact, many may have felt they were imposing themselves upon a hard-working nonprofit. As one funder put it, "I guess we could be looking more carefully, but they are saving lives every day and they're just experiencing typical growing pains." In actuality, they were not growing any more. The charismatic director had given the funding community a sense of misplaced comfort in her own overall abilities. Her board and funders had overlooked just how much she was actually doing on her own. Funders didn't fully consider the board's size, their qualifications, or how they were overseeing operations. The nonprofit's own board reluctantly accepted plausible answers as to why the IRS form 990 was late and an audit hadn't been performed. Funders either hadn't asked for or internally scrutinized balance or revenue statements (they existed only as haphazardly constructed guesstimates for public funding). Perhaps because there was a staff of seven, they assumed the director must have had all the administrative aspects of her nonprofit in place. In reality, she had been doing street outreach, managing staff, doing what little bookkeeping she could, making funding and advocacy presentations, and writing and reporting on grants. Even for the most dedicated do-it-all directors, this workload was clearly unsustainable.

From a request for a discretionary microgrant for $1,000, the Knott Foundation learned of the delayed financials. This nonprofit was waiting on several vital but delayed grants from the city and state. Once the organization learned that PRI loans were available, it requested a $25,000 cash flow loan to tide them over for several months. The loan process included a review of balance sheets, income/expense streams, and a monthly one-year projected cash flow statement. All these items raised red flags. When the Knott Foundation called the contract officers responsible for providing the take-out funding, it learned of several additional concerns about delayed reports and financial statements. Things were already looking bad when we also learned that the board president had just resigned because she recently had become aware that payroll taxes were in arrears. That left a board of just three active members—far too small for the all the work needed for good governance, especially in a time of crisis.

The nonprofit was at a critical turning point. Quick and decisive decisions were needed by both funders and the nonprofit if the latter was to continue as a going concern. All options were discussed, including fully informing all other funders, laying off staff, merging, and even bankruptcy. Through this technical assistance, a plan emerged that would include a capacity-building grant.

A request for an alternative type of grant or cash flow loan opens an entire new way of working with a nonprofit organization. Suddenly, instead of suggesting all the wonderful things that will be accomplished with a traditional grant by a wonderful organization that has its act together, *an alternative grant or loan request can, in and of itself, be an admission that something may not be quite right.* That takes courage, and it behooves the potential funder to be ready and willing to offer appropriate technical assistance if, and only if, the nonprofit is also willing to accept it.

All kinds of probing questions issue forth from a request that may involve a funding intervention. In particular, the nonprofit must ask itself:

- Are we truly ready and willing to bare all to our funders?

- Are we prepared to carefully listen to and heed any advice?

- What are we doing to show we are already working diligently on the issue?

And the foundation must ask:

- What's happening to create this need?

- Does their board and staff know the situation in full?

- Is this a regular occurrence or a one-time crisis?

- Is the need the result of a funder being habitually late in issuing a contract or check?

  - If so, might we call upon them asking its status and perhaps why they are habitually late? Foundations have to remain sensitive as to why many nonprofits are loath to aggressively collect their grant receivables. With fierce competition for funding, these squeaky wheels could become blacklisted in direct or subtle ways.

  - Might the foundation take an aggressive stance in helping the nonprofit collect its receivable(s)? Foundations often have much clout within their local communities. They can use that reputation to their grantees' advantage with a simple phone call or letter of inquiry to the appropriate contract officer or public official.

Further questions for the foundation to consider are:

- Do we want to be known as a proactive and/or capacity-building funder?

- As a matter of policy, are we generally willing to take a stand on behalf of nonprofits and of a particular nonprofit? For example, would we call and demand that a delayed payment from a grant or government contract be made immediately to a nonprofit that is owed the funds?

- Are we in a favorably strategic position with our peers to advocate for this nonprofit?

- Are we ready for the increased risks of unrecoverable loans or grants to organizations that don't meet their contractual objectives?

- Are we willing to provide additional resources with no ironclad guarantee that our grant goals will be met or that loans will be repaid?

- Do we have the interest and capacity to coordinate with other funders?

- If so, are we mutually willing to share key grantee successes, concerns, and failures?

Our particular example suggests a good outline for how a single funder can holistically assist a nonprofit, as shown in Table 1.

TABLE 1. A 'SWISS ARMY KNIFE' APPROACH TO HOLISTIC GRANTMAKING

Tools	Discretionary grant	Cash-flow loan	Management assistance	Capacity grant	Project grant
Amount requested	$1,000	$25,000	None	$2,000 + $5,000 later	$17,000
Goals	To teach self-defense to women involved in prostitution (to help fight off a known serial murderer).	To tide the NPO over until a major state grant is issued.	To evaluate the need for layoffs, merger, acquisition or bankruptcy.	To pay for board development and executive coaching.	To increase street outreach efforts in two neighborhoods.
Results	Learned of the NPO, its mission, and the perils of prostitution.	Became aware of deeper organizational issues, and denied loan.	Convened other funders. Hired consultants to review and correct financials.	Helped the NPO positively address operational fundamentals.	Delayed until organization is stronger and able to realistically add to current workload.
Outputs and Outcomes	30 women and staff were trained. No one was killed or injured.	Recognition of capacity-building needs.	Action plan created.	Staffing cut, director establishes priorities.	Next step if capacity grant is proven successful.

What is also remarkable about this approach is that it is just a starting place for ongoing nonmonetary assistance. Draper (2004) outlines how a foundation's talented staff can give not only guidance and advice, but might also be "loaned" for a specified period. Foundations can also leverage their extraordinary networks with hosted lunches, gatherings, and seminars. As mentioned earlier, they can also serve as advocates on behalf of a specific nonprofit, or on behalf of nonprofits in a given field of service, to local, state, and national governmental agencies and policymakers. The Knott Foundation has also provided office space free of charge for small, start-up nonprofits as well as free use of a conference room for nonprofit retreats and board meetings. The foundation also provides free storage. For example, a children's theater's props and sets needed a home while the organization located new theater space after their relocation plans fell through.

A foundation's nonmonetary impact is limited only by creativity and the willingness to help nonprofits work through sometimes very stressful changes. The bottom line is that as funders help nonprofits in these holistic ways, those funders also learn much more about the grantee's strengths and weaknesses and how they can be more effective in advancing the mutual social missions of foundations and their nonprofit clients.

Future Directions

The future holds some exciting new ways for funders to make a difference. We've seen here how a single foundation can make a substantial impact by offering a number of funding and technical tools to their grantees. Perhaps an even more attractive model than a single foundation providing holistic grants is the involvement of multiple funders as partners or within collaboratives. Each partner provides its individual expertise and strengths, leading to an increase in the overall quality and quantity of technical resources, dollars, and tools available to grantees.

Working through a Regional Association of Grantmakers (RAG) and/or an affinity group greatly facilitates any collaborative project. The RAG serves as the information disseminator and coordinator, with a particular foundation playing a lead role to do the necessary due diligence, especially when a funding emergency occurs. The lead foundation can then disseminate through the RAG a summary report of findings that address key operational issues, needs, and lessons learned from the grantee. A common Holistic Funding Form, filled in jointly by the lead foundation and grantee, would serve as the natural outgrowth to the common grant application forms that many RAGs already have in place. This form would indicate assistance already given and the current gaps requiring additional assistance. These gaps could include nonmonetary and technical assistance as well as loans and grants. Foundations could indicate their interest in "opting in" to such a process well before a holistic funding need is identified.

In an analysis of the readiness of foundations for emergency grantmaking post 9/11 Steuerle (2003) noted:

> Some doubt was raised as to whether a "committee approach" could ever resolve the confidentiality and organizational limitations on this scale. One participant noted that the charitable sector often was not collaborative and warned of ignoring this fact of life. Another noted that disaster relief and social welfare groups have different ways of operating and do not easily hand off to each other. Yet another noted that even the question of who could convene had to be addressed. Perhaps legislation would be required, but the precise nature of any language was not discussed. No one suggested that all tensions could be removed, only that some could be relaxed.... Documentation of what happens was agreed to be valuable. While some documentation of September 11 activities has taken place, it still was not clear how much might be falling through the cracks. Nor was it clear that a formalized system had been established so the charitable sector would be ready and able to document its reactions to emergencies on a continual, improving basis.

Clearly, we need a way to document and learn from our experiences in holistic grantmaking.

After Action Reports are a long-standing response to creating a learning organization methodology in the military. Such reports would serve holistic grantmakers very well. As illustrated in Table 2, these reports entail six very simple but powerful questions.

TABLE 2. AFTER ACTION REPORT: HOLISTIC FUNDING AND TECHNICAL ASSISTANCE INTERVENTION

1. What was our aim?	*4. What should be changed?*
To assist NPO clients and staff with self defense training.	NPO board and funders need to review financials in more detail, evaluate executive director regularly, and ensure board has good depth and skills and experience. Bring other funders to table.
2. What actually happened?	*5. What did we learn?*
Discovered that management and board were overextended, financials in disarray.	Always look closely at financials—they can tell a tale otherwise uncovered. Ask if director has been evaluated at least annually.
3. Why did it happen?	*6. What do we want to sustain?*
Charismatic leadership, inexperienced board, distracted funders.	Create or keep a holistic grant program in place that includes technical assistance.

Such reports can be entered into a relational, searchable database so anyone about to enter into a similar situation has immediate access to the funding streams and technical assistance lessons previously learned. Using a tool such as an After Action Report will improve upon the trial and error approach most foundations and grantees are currently using.

This systemic way to ask for, and get, appropriate and ongoing technical assistance, including creating new collaborations, raises the further question: How do we cover the additional costs of handling gifts, grants, and other expenses for grantees that require additional back-office services? Foundations might charge a sliding fee based both on the nonprofits assets or income and/or on the number of transactions it handles (Cohen, 2004). This model might especially help community foundations that are dealing with the increasingly popular use of large institutional donor-advised fund programs that are now competing for a community foundation's donor market share (Steuerle, 1999).

It would be useful to investigate exactly which foundations use which funding tools, including how often and for what type of projects or programs. That data could then be correlated with factors such as a foundation's geographic and funding priorities, a foundation's corpus, and its staffing philosophy. From this information, we might better understand why so many apparently useful tools remain underutilized.

Another much needed development would be to standardize holistic funding terminology, pro formas, applications, and reporting forms. Along the lines of the widely used common grant application forms, standardized formats would allow all parties (funders, RAGs, grantees, other lending/granting institutions) to spend more of their very limited time on the particular holistic funding issue rather than on the mechanics of locating appropriate funders, completing applications, or approving funding requests.

Ultimately, as funders and grantees develop their mutual ability to identify and use holistic funding tools, they can begin to use program and operational performance management approaches, such as Balanced Scorecards, Net Impacts, and integrated, ongoing evaluation methods that make complex grant/loan structures understandable, manageable, and accountable.

Finally, it's essential that funders take a lead in making the nonprofits aware of the tools available through clear and collaborative local and national marketing efforts. Intuitively, and anecdotally, we know the market for holistic funding exists. This is a real "create the opportunity and they will come" situation. What we also need is more empirical evidence to demonstrate to reluctant funders and unaware grantees that it makes sense to dedicate or reallocate resources within a holistic funding process.

Conclusion

Although most nonprofits and foundations are somewhat familiar with one or two specific funding tools, few are aware of the total universe of tools currently available to them. Even fewer are able to use these tools in comprehensive, coordinated ways that fill in the gaps left by traditional grantmaking. Through good business planning and monitoring, these organizations can signal their ability and willingness to take on these more complex funding and technical assistance structures. As we have seen, a single funder can offer a myriad of financial, technical, and other nonmonetary assistance options to its grantees. Perhaps even more promising is the use of funder collaboratives and partnerships to address the needs of single and multiple grantees within specific fields. By fully embracing these new tools, funders and grantees are likely to see a dramatic increase in their overall effectiveness in advancing their mutual missions.

References

Born, Jason C. 2001. "Discretionary Grants: Encouraging Participation . . . or Dividing Families?" National Center for Family Philanthropy, September, p. 4.

Brody, Frances, and Scott Miller. 1996. "How Much Does It Cost to Make a PRI?" Paper prepared for the MIT Project on Social Investing, January, 1996, and reprinted with permission in Christie I. Baxter, *Program Related Investments—A Technical Manual for Foundations.* New York: Wiley, 1997.

Cohen, Todd. 2004. "Foundation for the Carolinas Creates Service Centers." *Philanthropy Journal,* September 2004.

Council on Foundations, "Stewardship Principles for Family Foundations." Adopted by the committee on family foundations, September 2004.

Draper, Lee. 2004. "Achieving Impact Without Giving Cash." *Foundation News and Commentary,* September/October, 2004, pp. 28–32.

The Foundation Center, September 2003

Kramer, Mark. 1999. "Foundations Shouldn't Play with Matches." *Chronicle of Philanthropy,* November 18.

The Foundation Center. 2003. *The PRI Directory: Charitable Loans and Other Program-Related Investments by Foundations,* 2nd ed. New York: The Foundation Center.

Hamilton, Deborah Brody. 2004 "Becoming More Than We Are—Ten Trends in Family Philanthropy." *Passages,* Volume 6:3, National Center for Family Philanthropy.

Ostrower, Francie. 2004. "Attitudes and Practices Concerning Effective Philanthropy." Center on Nonprofits and Philanthropy at The Urban Institute, April 2004.

Smith, Steven Rathgeb. 1996. "New Directions in Nonprofit Funding: Alternative Revenue Sources, Prospects, Requirements and Concerns for Nonprofits." *New Directions for Philanthropic Fundraising,* Number 12, Summer 1996.

Steuerle, C. Eugene. 1999. "Will Donor-Advised Funds Revolutionize Philanthropy?" *Policy Briefs/Charting Civil Society.* Washington, DC: The Urban Institute, September 1, 1999.

————— 2003. "Preparing for the Next Emergency—Some Lessons for Charities from September 11, 2001." *Policy Briefs/Charting Civil Society.* Washington, DC: The Urban Institute, September 30, 2003.

11

Engaging Business with Nonprofits

Alison Louie and Arthur C. Brooks
The Maxwell School of Citizenship and Public Affairs
Syracuse University
Syracuse, NY

Introduction

Most nonprofits face a fairly uncertain landscape of financial support. While the sector as a whole receives a third of its funding from government, 20 percent from private donations, and the rest from earned income, these percentages are highly variable with respect to the type of nonprofit and to each organization's unique ability to raise each type of funds (Brooks, 2004). Perhaps most volatile of all is private charitable support. In 2002, nonprofits received about $241 billion in contributions, including $12 billion in corporate giving (AAFRC, 2003). However, charitable support ranges from 6 percent (to health organizations, on average), all the way up to 84 percent (to religious organizations).

Complicating matters, the data on private donations do not include information on nonmonetary support, which is particularly relevant with for-profit corporations. For example, no data exist on the value of the benefits from in-kind exchanges derived from for-profit ventures, strategic partnerships, and market transactions. Nonprofit managers are cognizant of these benefits and increasingly seek relationships with the for-profit sector as a result (Young, 2004). However, as we argue in this chapter, these benefits are often poorly understood, as are the best means to cultivate them.

This chapter seeks to organize and synthesize the most salient thinking on relationships between nonprofits and for-profits. After summarizing types of engagement, we discuss the potential costs and benefits of each and what nonprofit managers should consider when making a decision about collaboration. This leads us to several conclusions and suggestions for nonprofit managers who seek to build corporate partnerships.

Forms of Engagement

A number of authors have created taxonomies of the interactions between for-profits and nonprofits. In general, the major contributors to the literature have identified three types of relationships. First, for-profits can donate goods, services, money, time, or expertise to nonprofits. Second, they can interact with them commercially. Finally, they can act as partners toward a common goal.

Andreasen (1996) labels the three types of collaboration as transactions, licensing, and joint-issue relationships. *Transactions* occur between the two sectors when the for-profit purchases or sells services, supplies, or equipment to or from a nonprofit (perhaps at subsidized rates), or when a for-profit includes a nonprofit in the net proceeds from its regular market transactions. (In this way, Andreasen's "transactions" overlaps significantly with what other writers think of as philanthropy.) An example of this last type of transaction relationship is the 1983 campaign in which American Express donated one dollar for every new account (and one cent for every transaction) to the foundation that was renovating Ellis Island and the Statue of Liberty.

Licensing can be similar to a transaction, except that the nonprofit explicitly sells the use of its name and logo for a fee or a percentage of the sales. Colleges and universities have been licensing their names and logos for decades. More recently, other organizations have entered into this type of relationship. For example, SmithKline—maker of Nicoderm (a smoking cessation product)—and the American Cancer Society have been featured in advertisements as partners to help people quit smoking. The American Cancer Society said that they do not endorse any products, but was paid $2.5 million for use of the logo.

In contrast to transactions and licensing, *joint-issue* promotion does not necessarily entail a transfer of funds from one to the other. Instead, the nonprofit and the for-profit join forces to combat a single issue, working jointly to distribute products or promotional material.

Sinclair and Galaskiewicz (1997) describe the three types of possible relationships in a slightly different way, labeling them commercial, strategic/civic, and philanthropic. In a *commercial* partnership, a corporation purchases either the use of a nonprofit's name, its services, or technology. There is little altruism in this type of relationship because the corporation fully expects a tangible benefit from engaging with the nonprofit. Tuckman (2003) addresses why and how nonprofits are increasingly compelled to enter into commercial ventures of this nature. Increasingly, funding challenges have caused nonprofits to consider this type of venture as a means for financial security. Andreasen's licensing is an example of Sinclair's and Galaskiewicz's commercial engagement. A corporation sees that the use of a nonprofit's name and logo can positively affect the sale of its product by increasing the consumer base or the legitimacy of the company. A similar type of commercial partnership relies on a tangible asset, rather than the nonprofit's name. For example, universities can patent scientific breakthroughs and then license them to private companies. In these cases, universities do not treat the income as a charitable gift. Rather, they treat it as an earned revenue source and the corporation enters the collaboration with the expectation of increasing its profits.

Sinclair's and Galaskiewicz's category of *strategic* partnerships is comparable to Andreasen's joint-issue relationship. *Civic* partnerships, on the other hand, differ from strategic partnerships in that the measurable benefits do not accrue to the corporation, but rather to the community, and the corporation benefits from the improved community relations.

Philanthropic partnerships refer to what most people think of as corporate philanthropy: unrestricted gifts from corporations to nonprofits. These types of relationships may be publicized for community relations, but organizations benefit directly from the favorable tax treatment they induce.

Austin (2000b) develops the basic taxonomy further, asserting that there is a collaboration continuum. By so doing, he argues that one can understand the type of relationship that exists between the nonprofit and the for-profit as well as how the relationship is developing, giving a better sense of where the relationship can go. Austin notes that for-profits and nonprofits may or may not progress linearly through the stages, but suggests that progression is desirable.

In the *philanthropic stage* (Stage I), a business donates money or supplies to a nonprofit. This stage is characterized by a low level of engagement between the two collaborators, a narrow scope of activities, infrequent interaction, and a peripheral importance to the mission of the collaborators. Sinclair and Galaskiewicz's philanthropic partnership is typical of a Stage I relationship. In the *transactional stage* (Stage II), benefits flow to and from each partner. This stage can also be identified as "commercial" because both partners are focused on a specific transaction. In this stage, the missions and values of the partners begin to overlap and there is a reciprocal exchange of resources. In the *integration stage* (Stage III), each organization considers not only what is in the best interest for the individual organization but also for the partnership (or collaboration). Through the increased interaction and resource sharing, the organizational cultures are interwoven. The chief difference between the second and third stage is that in the third stage the organizations are combining efforts instead of exchanging resources. Table 1 summarizes the three basic types of interactions, with examples from the literature.

TABLE 1. ENGAGEMENT TYPES BETWEEN NONPROFITS AND FOR-PROFITS

Engagement type	Examples
Philanthropic (Stage I)	Grants
	Sponsorships
	Profit-sharing
Commercial/transactional (Stage II)	For-profits supply nonprofits
	Nonprofits supply for-profits
Integrative/partnerships (Stage III)	Co-branding and licensing relationships
	Joint-issue marketing
	Civic partnerships

Benefits and Costs of Engagement

We now turn to the costs and benefits of relationships between nonprofits and for-profits. Our principal conclusion in this section is that, while benefits appear simple and costs complex (particularly from integrative partnerships) for nonprofits, the reverse tends to be the case for for-profits.

The chief reason for any organization to engage in cross-sector collaboration is the belief that the partnership will provide the organization with added net value. Therefore, we first identify potential benefits and costs of collaborative relationships. Next, we provide a framework to help with decisions regarding collaboration, by defining added value, considering the effect collaboration will have on both the mission and profitability of organizations, and understanding risk.

Nonprofits benefit from partnerships with businesses in terms of resources, volunteers, and expertise. Clearly, the monetary benefits that accrue from, say, corporate philanthropy are easy to understand. Slightly less transparent are the nonmonetary benefits—usually in human resources—that come from integrative relationships. Co-branding, licensing, and joint-issue marketing can provide manpower to a nonprofit, but also business expertise—from financial and legal advice, to improved design and marketing of services. The relationship between Timberland (an outdoor clothing retailer) and City Year (a nonprofit that promotes community service) provides an example of the benefits a nonprofit can receive from partnering with a corporation. City Year solicited Timberland in 1989 for a donation of boots for their youth service corps, and Timberland's initial donation provided supplies. However, in subsequent years, an integrative partnership progressed: Timberland provided not only uniforms, but also volunteers for City Year projects. As the two organizations continued to work together in a co-branding relationship, Timberland's human resources vice president provided expertise to City Year. Other Timberland executives also engaged in City Year's planning, including City Year naming Timberland's COO to their board of directors (Austin, 2000b).

For-profits also receive benefits from collaboration, although these benefits tend to be more indirect than what nonprofits see. In the preceding case, for example, Timberland's involvement helped to solidify its brand identity and corporate culture. The benefits to corporations can include improved corporate image, human capital development for managers, sites for business experimentation and innovation, tax deductibility, policy influence, and increased product demand (Austin, 2003). Marx (1999) found that a majority of for-profits claim to manage their philanthropic programs strategically, presumably to maximize these benefits. The benefits of a good corporate image include improved employee morale, recruiting, retention, and skill development; greater consumer and investor loyalty; and technology refinement and development (Austin, 1998b; Kanter, 1999). And indeed, research has found a positive relationship between corporate social performance and profit (Bloom, Hussein, and Szykman, 1995; Conference Board, 1993; Dechant and Altman 1994; Lewin and Sabater, 1996). When a nonprofit represents a community of actual or potential consumers, corporations that collaborate with that nonprofit can increase their demand through goodwill and exposure to the market base (Abzug and Webb, 1999).

Other corporate goals for strategic giving include high quality of community life, improved community services, and racial harmony. Businesses can also benefit from collaboration if they think of these organizations as ground for innovation, learning valuable lessons from their engagement with nonprofits which they can bring to their own operations (Kanter, 1999).

While there are substantial benefits to both nonprofit and for-profit organizations from collaboration between sectors, there are also costs involved. The potential hazards for nonprofits include loss of control over mission, loss of credibility, a clash between corporate cultures, opportunity costs, competition for funding and clients, and resource dependence.

Nonprofits can lose flexibility and control over their mission when they partner with a for-profit, because the joint governance can take decisions away from the nonprofit (Andreasen, 1996). Additionally, corporations may have certain requirements with which nonprofits must comply in order to receive funding or maintain a partnership. Similarly, nonprofits risk losing credibility when they pair with corporations. While for-profits gain an associational identity with nonprofits and hope to increase their audience, the stakeholders of the nonprofit may feel that the organization is "selling out," threatening its legitimacy (Phillips, 2002). For example, in 1997, the American Medical Association (AMA) agreed to put its logo only on products of the Sunbeam Corporation in exchange for a percentage of sales revenues. When the public and members of AMA found out about the deal, there was such an outcry that the AMA felt compelled to back out of the contract, costing the organization almost $10 million (Associated Press, 1998; Bartling, 1998).

There is also the complication that nonprofits and for-profits can be liable for each other's actions since they have entered into a contract. For example, pairings between nonprofits and for-profit health product manufacturers (such as the venture described earlier between SmithKline and the American Cancer Society) have come under scrutiny because the general public presumably sees the collaboration as the endorsement of a treatment by a credible body. However, not all licensing relationships draw the same scrutiny (Abelson, 1999).

The risk of culture clash is also possible. When two or more organizations work together they must establish joint governance. If in doing so, they do not allow for some flexibility and resiliency, the partnership is difficult to alter and may lead to its demise if each partner cannot sustain the collaborative effort (Takahashi and Smutny, 2002).

Creating a strategic alliance requires time and the consideration of the senior leadership. Consequently, if the alliance fails to form or does not function successfully, there is an opportunity cost (Austin, 2003).

Competition is another risk. In one scenario, corporate funding may crowd out private donations. In the case of government grants, Brooks (2000) found that crowding out occurs most often in social service and health nonprofits. The displacement of private dollars suggests that donors react to potential recipients' receipt of other funding sources. Similarly, corporate support may threaten individual donations, which could lead to the nonprofit becoming increasingly dependent on the corporate partner for funding. This may be dangerous, because it lowers funding diversification and increases the nonprofit's exposure to market instability. Competition is also a concern—e.g., when the for-profit and nonprofit compete for clients they are often hesitant to share information or work together to improve services (Austin, 2003).

While the costs to nonprofits are real, they are complex and somewhat opaque. Costs to for-profits from partnerships, on the other hand, are much easier to comprehend. In general, for-profits may see collaboration with nonprofits as a business investment with low return. Part of this perception may be simply due to the difficulty in measuring the intangible benefits that flow from these relationships. However, it may also be the case that the returns—even if properly measured—are actually quite low. In a weak economy, examples of the hard decisions firms face as they calculate their expected returns on nonprofit partnerships are not difficult to find. For example, ExxonMobil recently withdrew from its corporate sponsorship of PBS's Masterpiece Theatre after spending over $300 million on the show over a thirty-five-year period. This is not an isolated case; PBS has seen one third of its corporate sponsorships disappear in the past decade. Underwriting a PBS show is an expensive undertaking without the same audience base and commercial time as buying advertising time on commercial television. The return on investment was simply judged to be too low for ExxonMobile (Saunders, 2004).

Evaluation of Engagement

In the last section we suggested that to decide whether collaboration is the right decision, managers should understand the impacts on their organizations. More specifically, managers must consider the effects of an alliance on their mission and net revenue and then compare the risk with the result and, ultimately, what the added value of the alliance would be (Young, 2004; Austin, 2000b). Once managers decide that collaboration is appropriate, the key to sustaining a successful alliance is understanding the value added and how to sustain productive collaborations.

While organizations should be able to list the benefits (for example, technical assistance for nonprofits, and employee motivation for for-profits) that flow from collaboration, it can be much more difficult to specify the monetary value of these benefits. Young (2004) suggests that for-profit and nonprofit managers should consider the following questions: 1) How much will an alliance enhance or hinder my mission? 2) How much does an alliance increase or decrease my net revenues? Answers to the first question can be grouped into three categories: mission-enhancing, mission neutral, and mission-interfering. Alliances that are mission-enhancing are attractive while mission interference should be avoided if possible. Answers to the second question are: profitable, break-even, and loss-making. One notes that the effect on mission usually has a qualitative answer, while profitability can be estimated quantitatively. Managers should consider the answers to both questions when considering whether to engage in collaboration.

In considering both questions, it is helpful to think of the mission consequences in win/lose scenarios. It is obvious that if partnering would enhance the mission and increase profitability (win-win), it is the obvious course of action. Even if an alliance is mission-neutral but profitable (neutral-win), it would be wise to further consider the option. However, if the venture would be mission-enhancing but would create a loss (win-lose), the organizations would have to think about both the short- and long-term profits and losses, and whether the enhanced mission would warrant the expected loss in revenues. Framing a decision to form an alliance in this way helps prevent the formation of alliances for the sole intent of increasing profitability while detrimentally affecting the mission.

Another set of questions concerns potential rewards versus the risks from seeking these rewards. Every decision a manager makes regarding his or her organization has risks. Collaboration requires substantial investments of time and/or money; therefore, a small increase in returns should only be pursued if it is a low-risk activity. However, depending on the relative size of the returns, a manager may deem it worth taking more risk when the potential payoff is large.

In sum, consideration of whether to engage in an alliance requires the following steps:

1. Identify the costs and benefits.

2. Determine how collaboration would affect the mission and profitability. (If collaboration would create a scenario where it would be detrimental to either, managers must seriously consider whether the loss incurred would be less than the value added.)

3. Ascertain the level of risk associated with the collaboration and whether the expected return is worthwhile.

Methods of Engagement

Given the fact that net benefits from engagement tend to be easier to identify for nonprofits than for-profits, it is not especially surprising that we typically see the former pursuing these relationships with greater zeal than the latter. This brings us to the managerial implications of this chapter. How can nonprofits engage for-profits most effectively? Understanding the drivers of alliances, and how to create and balance the added value among the alliance participants, establishes the foundation for engagement strategies that organizations can use to connect with other sectors. Here we identify strategies that capitalize on this understanding. First, nonprofits can actively market the benefits of these relationships to for-profits—benefits that for-profits might not have identified themselves, including enhancing mission, marketing, and acting for sites for innovation and skill development. Second, nonprofits can leverage market power to increase the perceived cost to for-profits from *not* partnering. Nonprofits can do this by illustrating how collaboration can positively affect a for-profit's business, and therefore, show the *opportunity cost* of not forming an alliance.

To begin with, nonprofits must think bilaterally: they must focus not just on the benefits they receive, but also on those they create for their for-profit partners. Focusing only on what they receive will not sustain the interest and involvement of for-profits in the long run (Cropper, 1996). But when both sides are devoted to advancing the whole partnership, higher levels of engagement and value can be achieved (Rackham, Friedman, and Ruff, 1996).

Nonprofits can begin by illustrating the improved community relations that follow from a partnership. An example of this is the Hand in Hand promotion in the early 1990s, in which the National Cancer Institute, the American College of Obstetricians and Gynecologists, and the American Heart Foundation effectively showed *Glamour* magazine and Hanes hosiery how a breast cancer awareness campaign could portray the corporate partners as concerned with women's health—not just their money. The campaign consisted of in-store promotions, including free informational materials on breast health that were included in Hanes hosiery purchases. A follow-up study found that the material increased the target audience's understanding of breast health and helped position *Glamour* and Hanes with the target demographic population (Andreasen, 1996).

Nonprofits can also stress the benefits of collaboration to for-profit executives in the form of board involvement. Austin (1998a) found that 81 percent of business leaders at Fortune 500 companies are involved with nonprofits and that 57 percent were board members. The executives said they learned new skills and perspectives from the philanthropic work and widened their networks. This involvement—in addition to the skills the executives bring directly to nonprofit governance—can stimulate other types of partnerships down the line because trust builds as the relationship progresses. Indeed, considerable research has found that trust, built over time, is an indispensable component for collaboration (Waddock, 1988; Wasserman and Galakiewicz, 1994; Ring and Van de Ven, 1994; Kanter, 1994; Rackhan, Friedman, and Ruff, 1996; Dickson and Weaver, 1997; Burke, 1999).

In an effort to facilitate engagement by for-profit executives, some organizations match corporate executives with nonprofits in their field of interest (Austin, 1998a). For example, boardnetUSA is a New York-based group that connects nonprofit boards with emerging leaders. Boardnet believes that young businesspeople can develop managerial competencies on a board while assisting the nonprofit. This win-win approach can make service appealing to corporate executives (Boardnet, 2004).

Corporate volunteer programs can be marketed by nonprofits as a means to develop human resources below the level of corporate management. Employee volunteer programs can be formal or informal, regular or ad hoc. Descriptive research praises these programs as reducing employee absenteeism and bolstering company loyalty. Whether or not these claims can be substantiated, getting large numbers of employees to participate certainly opens a gateway for greater collaboration across sectors (Tschirhart, 2004).

The preceding strategies have focused on carrots, but nonprofits might also choose to use "sticks." For example, if a nonprofit (or a group of nonprofits) is the main customer of a business, it can use its market power to gain corporate engagement. Savvy businesses are attuned to the needs and desires of their stakeholders, and nonprofits can use this fact to their advantage. For example, the Nonprofit Coordinating Committee of New York, a consortium of over 1,300 nonprofits, uses its market power to get member organizations discounts on airfare, legal advice, insurance, office supplies, and payroll processing. A nonprofit does not necessarily have to be the main customer of a for-profit to have usable market power, however. Indeed, an organization can leverage its credibility with the community. For example, a nonprofit can push communities that trust them toward—or away from—corporations that cooperate (or do not) with the nonprofit.

Once the cross-sector collaboration process begins, there are several factors that are key to sustaining the relationship, including communication, attention, mutual expectations, and accountability (Kanter, 1994; Austin, 2000a, 2000b). These management practices act as a foundation for a productive collaboration. Each organization must continue to focus attention on the collaborative effort. This means that the project should involve decision-makers and have a high level of visibility in the organization. Additionally, organizations must strive for open communication. The collaboration must become a part of the organizational system so that leaders and employees come to view participating in the collaboration project as part of their jobs. Also, the leaders of organizations all must have the same expectations (for which communication plays an important role). Mutual expectations mean that each partner will work towards the same goal, and consequently, each organization is accountable to the other for its efforts.

Conclusions and Future Research

In this chapter, we have synthesized a body of research on the spectrum of relationships between nonprofit and for-profit organizations. Given the desire of many nonprofits to engage corporate partners for support or collaboration, we have outlined the types and benefits and costs of collaboration. We have also provided a framework with which to think about whether a potential collaboration is advantageous, and we have outlined the strategies nonprofits can adopt to explain the net benefits of these relationships to potential for-profit partners.

Our discussion here has taken place at a fairly general level, not limited to any particular type of nonprofit or for-profit organization. We expect that certain engagement approaches would be more or less effective, depending on the activities, size, and location of each potential partner. For example:

- *Activities.* Partnership between, say, for-profit and nonprofit health care providers such as a for-profit hospital and a nonprofit nursing home (which offer related services) would require different considerations than a partnership between a manufacturing company and an environmental group.

- *Size.* The size of organizations affects potential partnerships, because the larger the organization, the more people, organizational units and levels must move through the different stages of engagement. (Small organizations with relatively few employees could attain buy-in and integration with greater ease.)

- *Location.* Certain locations encourage engagement between the sectors, such as the North Carolina Research Triangle, which has a high concentration of for-profits, nonprofits, and government entities.

To take this discussion to a more precise level, case studies are needed that investigate both successful and unsuccessful cross-sector collaborations. The proximate goal of more specific information on for-profit/nonprofit collaborations would be to establish a set of best industry practices—born of real-world examples—and a "dashboard" of indicators that is germane to each industry.

References

AAFRC. 2003. *Giving USA.* Indianapolis, IN: Center on Philanthropy. www.aafrc.org.

Abelson, Reed. 1999. "Marketing Tied to Charities Draws Scrutiny from States." *The New York Times,* May 3, A1.

Abzug, Rikki, and Natalie J. Webb. 1999. "Relationships between Nonprofit and For-Profit Organizations: A Stakeholder Perspective." *Nonprofit and Voluntary Sector Quarterly,* 28, pp. 416–431.

Andreasen, Alan R. 1996. "Profits for Nonprofits: Find a Corporate Partner." *Harvard Business Review,* 74, pp. 47–59.

Associated Press. 1998. "Broken Deal Costs AMA $9.9 Million." *The New York Times,* August 2, A12.

Austin, James E. 1998a. "Business Leaders and Nonprofits." *Nonprofit Leadership and Management,* 9, pp. 39–51.

———— 1998b. "The Invisible Side of Leadership." *Leader to Leader,* 8, pp. 38–46.

———— 2000a. "Principles for Partnership." *Leader to Leader,* 18, pp. 44–50.

———— 2000b. "Strategic Collaboration between Nonprofits and Businesses." *Nonprofit and Voluntary Sector Quarter,* 29, pp. 69–97.

———— 2003. "Institutional Collaboration." In Dennis R. Young (ed.), *Effective Economic Decision-Making by Nonprofit Organizations.* New York: The Foundation Center and National Center on Nonprofit Enterprise.

Bartling, Charles. E. 1998. *Strategic Alliances for Nonprofit Organizations.* Washington, DC: American Society of Association Executives.

Bloom, Paul N.; Pattie Yu Hussein, and Lisa R. Szykman. 1995. "Benefiting Society and the Bottom Line." *Marketing Management,* 4, pp. 8–18.

Boardnet. 2004. boardnetUSA. www.boardnetusa.org.

Brooks, Arthur C. 2000. "Is There a Dark Side to Government Support for Nonprofits?" *Public Administration Review,* 60, pp. 211–8.

Brooks, Arthur C. 2004. "The Effects of Public Policy on Private Charity." *Administration and Society,* 36, pp. 166–85.

Burke, Edmund M. 1999. *Corporate Community Relations: The Principle of the Neighbor of Choice.* Westport: Praeger.

The Conference Board. 1993. *Corporate Volunteer Programs: Benefits to Business* (Report No. 1029). New York: The Conference Board.

Cropper, Steve. 1996. "Collaborative Working and the Issue of Sustainability." In Chris Huxbaum (ed.), *Creating Competitive Advantage.* London: Sage.

Dechant, Kathleen, and Barbara Altman. 1994. "Environmental Leadership: From Compliance to Competitive Advantage." *Academy of Management Executive,* 8, pp. 7–19.

Dickson, Pat H., and K. Mark Weaver. 1997. "Environmental Determinants and Individual-Level Moderators of Alliance Use." *Academy of Management Journal,* 8, pp. 404–425.

Lewin, David, and J. M. Sabater. 1996. "Corporate Philanthropy and Business Performance. In Dwight F. Burlingame and Dennis R. Young (eds.), *Corporate Philanthropy at the Crossroads.* Bloomington, IN: Indiana University Press.

Holston, Noel. 2004. "End of an Era? Clock Ticks for 'Masterpiece'," *Newsday,* July 9, 2004, A12.

Kanter, Rosabeth Moss. 1994. "Collaborative Advantage: The Art of Alliances." *Harvard Business Review,* 72, pp. 96–108.

Kanter, Rosabeth Moss. 1999. "From Spare Change to Real Change: The Social Sector as Beta Site for Business Innovation." *Harvard Business Review,* 77, pp.122–32.

Marx, Jerry D. 1999. "Corporate Philanthropy: What Is the Strategy?" *Nonprofit and Voluntary Sector Quarterly,* 28, pp.185–198.

Phillips, Ruth. 2002. "Is Corporate Engagement an Advocacy Strategy for NGOs? The Community Aid Experience." *Nonprofit Management and Leadership,* 13, pp.123–137.

Rackham, Neil; Lawrence Friedman, and Richard Ruff. 1996. *Getting Partnering Right: How Market Leaders Are Creating Long-Term Competitive Advantage.* New York: McGraw-Hill.

Ring, Peter Smith, and Andrew Van de Ven. 1994. "Developmental Processes of Cooperative Interorganizational Relationships." *Academy of Management Review,* 19, pp. 90–118.

Saunders, Dusty. 2004. "'Masterpiece' Looks Priceless; No One's Stepped Forward to Pick up Tab for PBS Series," *Rocky Mountain News,* February 7, 4d.

Sen, Sankar, and C. B. Bhattacharya. 2001. "Does Doing Good Always Lead to Doing Better? Consumer Reactions to Corporate Social Responsibility." *Journal of Marketing,* 38, pp. 225–243.

Sinclair, Michelle, and Joseph Galaskiewicz. 1997. "Symposium: Corporate Philanthropy: Law, Culture, Education, and Politics; Article: Corporate-Nonprofit Partnerships: Varieties and Covariate." *New York School Law Review.*

Takahashi, Louis M., and Gayla Smutny. 2002. "Collaborative Windows and Organization Governance: Exploring the Formation and Demise of Social Service Partnerships." *Nonprofit and Voluntary Sector Quarterly,* 31, pp. 165–185.

Tschirhart, Mary. 2004. "Employee Volunteer Programs." In Jeffrey L. Brudney (ed.), *Emerging Areas of Volunteering:* Association for Research on Nonprofit Organizations and Voluntary Action (ARNOVA) Occasional Paper.

Tuckman, Howard P. 2003. "New Ventures and Strategic Philanthropy." In Dennis R. Young (ed.), *Effective Economic Decision-Making by Nonprofit Organizations.* New York: The Foundation Center and National Center on Nonprofit Enterprise.

Turban, Daniel B., and Daniel W. Greening. 1997. "Corporate Social Performance and Organizational Attractiveness to Prospective Employees." *Academy of Management Journal,* 40, pp. 658–672.

Waddock, Sandra A., and Samuel B. Graves. 1997. "The Corporate Social Performance-Financial Performance Link." *Strategic Management Journal,* 18, pp. 303–319.

Waddock, Sandra A. 1988. "Building Successful Social Partnerships." *Sloan Management Review,* 64, pp. 20–24.

Wasserman, Stanley, and Joseph Galaskiewicz. 1994. *Advocates in Social Network Analysis.* Thousand Oaks: Sage.

Young, Dennis R. 2004. "Corporate Partnerships: A Guide for the Nonprofit Manager." National Center on Nonprofit Enterprise Working Paper. Available at www.nationalcne.org/papers/ corp_partner.htm.

12

The Distinctiveness and Efficiency of Pro Bono Volunteering

Jeffrey L. Brudney
University of Georgia
School of Public and International Affairs
Department of Public Administration and Policy
Athens, GA

Introduction

"Pro bono volunteering" consists of donations of services to nonprofit organizations at no cost or minimal cost by individuals or firms with high levels of specialized expertise. A common misconception is that the term means "for free," when in fact it derives from *pro bono publico,* meaning "for the public good." Although a variety of professionals and organizations engage in pro bono work, including those in the fields of finance and accounting, marketing and public relations, research and fundraising, and web design and information technology (Cravens, 2004; Zeisel and Estes, 1979), the term is most closely associated with the legal field.

Time contributed by attorneys is normally identified as pro bono volunteering. Rule 6.1 of the ABA Model Rules of Professional Conduct, entitled "Voluntary Pro Bono Public Service," states that, "A lawyer should aspire to render at least (50) hours of *pro bono publico* legal services per year." The Rule encourages attorneys to donate their time to persons of limited means or to organizations designed primarily to address the needs of persons of limited means, and to

The author thanks Allen R. Bromberger, Gerald B. Chattman, and Andrew Smiles for insightful remarks and observations presented at a panel on "Volunteerism and Pro Bono Work" at the National Center for Nonprofit Enterprise biennial conference, January 16–17, 2004, Washington, DC. I am very grateful to Pam Robinson for her assistance, and also thank Beth Gazley, Mark Pocock, and Dennis Young for excellent comments and suggestions. The author is solely responsible for the contents.

activities for improving the law, legal system, or legal profession. Rule 6.1 also endorses the "delivery of legal services at no fee or substantially reduced fee to . . . charitable, religious, civic, community, governmental, and educational organizations in matters in furtherance of their organizational purposes, where the payment of standard legal fees would significantly deplete the organization's economic resources or would be otherwise inappropriate." It is to this type of pro bono activity that this chapter is directed.

Despite the importance of this donated expertise and its large scale—indeed, in addition to the ABA, state bar associations, most law schools, and state associations of attorneys, as well as many law firms, expect or require their members to perform pro bono work on an annual basis—the topic has received comparatively little research attention. This chapter aims to address gaps in our knowledge of pro bono volunteering, especially as it relates to work performed and donated by business attorneys to nonprofit organizations. It examines common methods by which attorneys can be matched efficiently and effectively with nonprofit organizations so that the attorneys, the recipient organizations, as well as the law firms themselves realize benefits from the exchange.

The chapter is organized into three major sections. The first describes the characteristics that differentiate pro bono activity from more traditional forms of volunteering. For purposes of this chapter, the latter consist of donations of time by individuals to host organizations to assist with routine clerical, service delivery, and maintenance functions, activities that generally call for significantly less specialized expertise than pro bono volunteering. The next section presents and evaluates four of the most common arrangements for matching attorneys with nonprofit organizations, with an eye toward efficiency and effectiveness. These mechanisms consist of individual law firms, pro bono organizations, volunteer centers, and Internet technology. The literature and practice of pro bono volunteering and of traditional volunteering have developed separately with little, if any, cross-fertilization. Based on this observation, the chapter concludes by showing that administrators of the two types of volunteer programs have much to learn from one another.

The Distinctiveness of Pro Bono Volunteering

Pro bono work for nonprofit organizations differs from more traditional forms of volunteering, such as the donation of routine clerical, service delivery, and organizational maintenance activities, in several important ways. We can classify these distinctions according to the three major actors involved: 1) the volunteer;

2) the nonprofit organization to which she or he donates time; and 3) the employer of the volunteer, who also has an abiding interest in the pro bono assignment. Table 1 summarizes these distinctions.

TABLE 1. PRO BONO VOLUNTEERING VERSUS TRADITIONAL VOLUNTEERING

Party to the Volunteer Relationship Characteristic	Pro Bono Volunteer	Traditional Volunteer
Volunteer		
Expertise required	High	Average but variable
Job desired	Specific	Variable
Primary motivation	Work or task, organizational mission	Advance organizational mission through activities
Nonprofit Organization Receiving Volunteer Assistance		
Type of activity	Project	Ongoing but increasingly short-term
Number of volunteers needed	Few	Many
Importance of the work	High	Average but variable
Hours required	High and concentrated	Low
Employer of the Volunteer		
Need for recognition and benefits	High	*
Need to accommodate volunteer	High	*
Direct interest in volunteering	High	*

*The employer of the volunteer is typically not involved in the traditional volunteer-nonprofit organization relationship.

THE VOLUNTEER

Perhaps the characteristic that most clearly distinguishes the activities of pro bono volunteers from more mainline forms of volunteering is the significant technical expertise and professional training required. In pro bono volunteering to nonprofit organizations, the recipient agency seeks specialized voluntary assistance to aid or spearhead the performance of specialized tasks, such as legal, financial, marketing, information technology, and the like. By contrast, the tasks carried out by volunteers in general are both remarkably vast and varied. In a series of biennial national surveys conducted during the 1990s, about half of all adult Americans claim to have done some kind of volunteer work in the past year (Weitzman et al., 2002, p. 73). However, these duties generally do not require a large investment in formal education or training, such as an advanced degree.

Related to the technical knowledge or expertise dimension, the two groups of volunteers seem to differ on their outlook toward volunteer service. Whereas prospective "traditional" volunteers might well approach a recipient organization without a definite job or even a particular area of agency operations in mind, pro bono volunteering is much more specific, dictated by the professional training or skills of the volunteer. In the former, the volunteer typically has a "try before you buy" attitude that leaves her or him open, or at the least, indifferent to a variety of agency work assignments. By contrast, in the latter, the volunteer seeks to benefit the host organization by fulfilling a specific pro bono assignment that requires professional training and technical skills and that also has the potential to enhance or expand these skills. In this respect, pro bono work is one of the clearest examples of the "volunteers as unpaid staff" model that is dominant in the U.S., but by no means accepted as the only model of volunteering universally, particularly in Europe (Meijs and Hoogstad, 2001).

Finally, no volunteer will work long or hard for an organization whose mission she or he does not share, or at least tolerate. "An otherwise willing volunteer might have some difficulty doing pro bono work for a nonprofit whose mission runs contrary to the lawyer's beliefs" (Marron, 2002, p. 2). ABA Rule 6.2 on "Accepting Appointments" reiterates that all lawyers have a responsibility to assist in providing *pro bono publico* services (ABA Rule 6.1), but acknowledges that, "A lawyer ordinarily is not obliged to accept a client whose character or cause the lawyer regards as repugnant." In her discussion of pro bono volunteering, Jayne Cravens (2004) counsels donating individuals and firms to consider carefully in advance their reasons and strategy for engaging in pro bono activity, including the number, type, mission, and even the culture of nonprofit organizations deemed worthy or eligible for contributed services. Yet, pro bono work seems equally a rational response, to build skills of the attorneys involved—and build loyalty to the employing firm—as well as to enhance the business prospects of the firm.

According to Sean Delany, executive director of Lawyers Alliance for New York, an organization that matches pro bono lawyers with nonprofit clients, "Firms are asking for more sophisticated pro bono transactions" (in Chen, 2003, p. 94). Vivia Chen (2003, p. 94) writes, "What's motivating the deal-makers at the nation's top firms to do good deeds? One quick answer: It's the economy, stupid. With the dearth of deals in the current markets, some firms are parking associates in volunteer work." Esther F. Lardent (2002, p. 6), president and chief executive officer of the Pro Bono Institute at Georgetown University Law Center, similarly observes that some law firms use pro bono work to deal with the problem of "excess capacity" of legal talent that results from a volatile economy. In response to an economic downturn, she reports,

> Rather than letting their young lawyers leave, several Boston firms helped them to find transactional pro bono work that used and honed their skills and improved their contact with the city's business and banking community. The results: lawyers with a strong sense of loyalty and gratitude to their firms who, once the economy improved, had the skills and contacts to handle the influx of complex real estate matters.

Understanding the complicated web of motivations that guides volunteers to certain host organizations and particular jobs within them is a daunting task. Nevertheless, with respect to the pro bono attorney, so long as the mission of the recipient nonprofit organization is not inimical to her or his own values or beliefs, and does not pose a conflict of interest for the firm the attorney represents, a coequal, if not primary motivator to the mission may well be the functions or the work to be performed and the experience to be gained. For the pro bono volunteer, the job assignment and the benefits that she or he may derive from it (such as the chance to acquire new skills, enlarge expertise, expand contacts, build a resume, etc.) may be at least as satisfying and motivating as the policy area or goals of the organization itself. Sometimes the motives are mixed, even in official publications of the ABA. For example, the ABA's *The Path to Pro Bono: An Interviewing Tool for Law Students* offers,

> Pro bono is an important part of your future career. It will provide you excellent training and an opportunity for frontline experience that may be more difficult to realize in other cases. You will also achieve the professional satisfaction of actually making a difference in the life of an individual, a family, or even a community, by being the last hope of the least fortunate among us.

By contrast, traditional volunteers are typically more drawn to the mission or policy area of the organization (environment, human rights, youth, etc.) and the aspiration "to make a difference" in that area. The job or task itself is of lesser consequence (especially in the early stages of the assignment), so long as the volunteer perceives that it furthers the mission. Of course, attorneys also volunteer their time as a way to promote the political and social causes or missions they favor; lawyers and law firms turned out in droves to donate their assistance in the wake of September 11 and its aftermath (Lardent, 2001). Yet, the literature reviewed on pro bono volunteering leaves the unmistakable impression that the opportunity to perform challenging, career-enhancing work commands equal, if not greater, priority.

THE RECIPIENT NONPROFIT ORGANIZATION

The next set of characteristics in Table 1 addresses the needs of the nonprofit organization for pro bono assistance. Pro bono volunteering to nonprofit agencies is usually organized around specific projects that have a certain urgency and importance for the recipient (for example, an advertising campaign, a strategic planning exercise, preparing and filing for 501(c)(3) status with the Internal Revenue Service, a merger or acquisition, etc.). Project assignments can be highly labor intensive, especially in the short run, with a critical result or outcome to be attained. Although traditional volunteering is increasingly episodic and short term, it is much more likely to be an ongoing, open-ended arrangement consisting of the donation of modest hours per week. According to survey research over the past fifteen years, the average volunteer in the United States gives about three to four hours per week (Weitzman et al., 2002, p. 73). The typical volunteer job also has no clear project goal or other outcome to signal the end of contributed service.

Second, in the normal course of organizational events, many more service volunteers will be needed than pro bono volunteers, yet the work of the latter is probably more crucial to the agency. The nonprofit organization is likely to have relatively few projects to enlist specialized pro bono volunteers, especially in comparison to its needs for more traditional volunteer assistance with organizational support and service delivery. Even so, a weighty legal issue may well touch on the long-run health, if not the very survival, of the nonprofit organization. Writes Allen R. Bromberger (2003, p. 1), president of Power of Attorney, an organization that promotes and supports intermediary organizations that match business lawyers with nonprofit organizations that need their services, "Just as business people in the for-profit sector rely on a cadre of trained professionals to keep them moving toward their goals, managers of nonprofits also need help navigating the rocky fiscal and legal shoals of an increasingly complex environment." It is no denigration of service volunteering to recognize that the provision of routine clerical, service delivery, and organizational maintenance activities is necessary to organizational operations, but less crucial to organizational viability. It should be acknowledged, however, that a nonprofit organization may also see in this activity the chance to gain services through donation rather than payment. That is, the contributed time and expertise may not be that vital to goal achievement, but simply helps the nonprofit agency to meet the bottom line more easily.

THE EMPLOYER OF THE VOLUNTEER

Given the repeated exhortations in the literature that law firms need to work harder to create and sustain a culture that supports pro bono volunteering, the practice has not won universal acceptance. In those firms that have endorsed or institutionalized pro bono work, though, the involvement of the employing organization as a third party in the volunteer-nonprofit organization relationship can be crucial, and sets pro bono activity apart from most traditional volunteering. However, corporate and employee-based volunteer programs appear to be on the rise. As volunteerism expert Steve McCurley (2003) observes, "The emergence of employee volunteer programs has been one of the most significant developments in volunteerism in the past twenty years." Nevertheless, formal volunteering is normally conceived as a two-party exchange between the individual volunteer and, the host organization, with agency clients the ultimate beneficiaries. In fact, studies often lament the absence of employer support and interest in their employees' volunteering (see, for example, Urban Institute, 2004).

By contrast, the employing organization is endemic to considerations and analysis of pro bono volunteering, with no question raised regarding the direct interest and involvement of the employer in the arrangement, and the balance of costs and benefits that it may sustain. Writes Lardent (2002, p. 7), "Pro bono must be marketed within the firm as a resource that helps the firm to attain its financial goals and promote institutional integrity and resilience." Law firms and other organizations that donate services can realize a variety of benefits from pro bono work, including the opportunity to: polish their reputations as responsible corporate citizens, if not leaders, in the community; increase their visibility and attract new business; and improve client relationships and explore new market segments. Prestigious law firms also use pro bono opportunities with nonprofit organizations as an incentive to recruit and retain top graduates from law schools, supplement their training and professional development, and enhance their morale and loyalty (Cravens, 2004; Lardent, 2002, 2000). For example, in September 2003 *The American Lawyer* published "The A-List" of twenty first-tier law firms, derived according to a formula that not only took into account pro bono activity but also gave it double weight—the same weight accorded to the most important traditional factor, revenue per lawyer (Press, 2003). Just as law firms use pro bono work as a development tool to increase the skills and capacity of attorneys through consequential assignments in nonprofit organizations, consultants and businesses in other industries capitalize on pro bono projects to develop their experience, portfolio, and contacts. In sum, "pro bono is not only right, it is, indeed, good for business" (Lardent, 2000, p. 12).

With respect to costs, law firms can support pro bono activity in a variety of ways; for example, by crediting these assignments as billable (but not paid) hours, allowing paid time off, providing workday support and coverage for the pro bono assignment (including clerical and material costs), and so forth. Although detractors argue that large pro bono commitments can amount to a considerable expense, others suggest that pro bono activities may in fact be revenue neutral or even revenue-enhancing. Adherents point out that the time allocated to pro bono activity may not always constitute an opportunity cost (lost billable hours), for paying clients may not be available, and that the extended impact of pro bono work on client generation and retention must be taken into account, and may well yield positive net benefits (Lardent, 2002).

Another way in which nonprofit organizations involve attorneys as volunteers is through service on boards of directors. Nonprofit organizations frequently tap the legal community for board members, just as they seek other professionals to occupy a seat on the board—for example, those working in accounting, human resources, banking, insurance, public relations, and the media. Boards undoubtedly desire and expect these professionals to apply their job training and skills in matters where they are pertinent; for example, the board will look to a member who is an attorney for a legal opinion.

However, board volunteering is distinct from pro bono volunteering. As elaborated above, pro bono volunteering consists of donations of time and specialized expertise to nonprofit organizations. Board service is much broader. In addition to providing legal skills, the attorney, just like any other nonprofit board member, is expected to fulfill all requirements of trusteeship, such as the duties of due diligence, loyalty, and care, and to make reasoned judgments on all matters affecting the organization. The attorney's employer is also not likely to play so active a role in supporting board volunteering as pro bono volunteering, or see the need for the involvement of the firm. Finally, although attorneys may realize career benefits from association with the boards of prestigious nonprofit organizations, the career benefits of pro bono volunteering are far different; they stem from learning or enhancing job skills in applied projects or work. And in contrast to the well-heeled nonprofits that can offer prestige value to a board member, the nonprofit organizations receiving pro bono assistance are generally needy and cannot afford standard legal fees (ABA Rule 6.1).

SUMMARY

In several important ways, pro bono work differs from more mainline forms of volunteering. First, for the pro bono volunteer the work entails high levels of professional expertise and must, in itself, be motivating or stimulating. Given the specialization required, it may be difficult for the nonprofit organization to monitor performance; indeed, through the pro bono relationship the organization seeks expertise that it does not have and may lack the background to evaluate. Second, for the nonprofit agency the time contributed by the pro bono volunteer may be intended to meet a critical, perhaps, survival need. Fortunately, most organizations encounter few such contingencies, so that their demands for a pro bono volunteer may be acute, but not many volunteers are needed. Typically, the volunteer work is organized into a project with a clear result or outcome to be achieved that will signal the end of the relationship (for example, the incorporation of a subsidiary organization to engage in fundraising). In the meantime, the project is likely to require significant, concentrated time and expertise on the part of the pro bono volunteer.

Finally, a third party to the volunteer-host organization relationship in pro bono volunteering is the employing organization or firm. The employer allows or facilitates the donation of time and expertise to nonprofit organizations, and accommodates and supports the pro bono contribution internally. Not unreasonably, then, the firm anticipates benefits in return, such as favorable publicity and reputation for itself, and professional growth and development for its associates. By contrast, in conventional treatments of volunteering, the employer is not considered in what is essentially characterized as a dyadic relationship between volunteer and host organization. So peripheral to the relationship is the employer that if and when the organization does become actively involved in supporting volunteerism, the form of volunteerism is usually treated separately and explicitly as an employee-based volunteer program or "EVP." The role and necessity of third-party involvement are certainly greater in pro bono volunteering than in more traditional forms. For example, one reason (among many) that larger law firms establish pro bono committees or internal counsels responsible for oversight of pro bono activity is to ensure that pro bono work is aligned with the firm's mission and goals. These committees or counsels would make certain that pro bono activity does not present a conflict of interest with representation of other clients.

Selected Intermediaries in Pro Bono Volunteering

This discussion has shown that, on the one hand, some nonprofit firms need and seek pro bono legal assistance and, on the other, that some law firms and attorneys are interested in providing it. Thus, a market would seem to exist for these services, albeit one in which the "buyers" and the "sellers" often seem to know little about each other, even in such basic areas as their identity, wants, skills, reliability, etc. One way to bring the two parties together is through intermediary mechanisms, which already exist for this purpose. In this analysis we consider four such intermediaries: individual law firms, pro bono organizations, volunteer centers, and Internet technology.

Many law firms support pro bono work, for example, by dedicating people and resources to this function. A second mechanism is business law intermediary organizations, a growing set of nonprofit agencies that were set up expressly to negotiate the marketplace between nonprofits that find themselves in need of legal assistance at no or reduced cost and business firms and attorneys interested in providing it (Bromberger, 2002, 2003). The third intermediaries are volunteer centers, such as those sponsored by the United Way and the Points of Light Foundation. These organizations are dedicated to promoting volunteerism in local communities through volunteer placement, training, and related services (Brudney and Kim, 2003). The final intermediary is Internet technology, which is quickly emerging internationally as an electronic or online matching service linking potential volunteers and host agencies. VolunteerMatch (www.volunteermatch.com) in the United States provides matching services across a tremendous array of organizations, opportunities, and skill sets. The online service VolunteerMatch Australia (www.volunteermatch.com.au) is dedicated exclusively to pro bono volunteering in the legal domain.

Several cautions apply in analyzing and comparing the different intermediaries in pro bono volunteering. First, these forms do not comprise all possible intermediaries for business law pro bono volunteering (for example, state bar associations and law school pro bono programs also participate), although they are considered most often in the available literature. Second, the categories of intermediary vary within themselves. For example, the investment of individual law firms in pro bono activities can differ greatly from complete indifference, to exhortation (only) but no support for this work, to an active pro bono officer and/or department. *The Path to Pro Bono,* a tool distributed by the ABA to law students interviewing for jobs, admonishes, "As a prospective employee, it is important to understand the firm's culture and what will be expected of you as an employee. It is important to distinguish between those firms that claim to support pro bono and those that actually do so." Internet search and matching capabilities for pro bono volunteering likewise differ greatly (see Walsh, 2003). Pro bono business law organizations also vary widely among themselves in size, promotion, activities, types of services provided, and so on (Visser and Shmavonian, 2004). Third, although the options are presented individually in the analysis below, they can also be used in combination; for example, some attorneys might search and locate suitable pro bono assignments through the assistance of the Internet *and* a volunteer center *and* their law firm.

TABLE 2. A COMPARISON OF SELECTED INTERMEDIARIES IN PRO BONO VOLUNTEERING

Dimension	Intermediary			
	Individual Firm	Pro Bono Organization	Volunteer Center	Internet Technology
Cost to Law Firm	High	Moderate	Low	Very low
Range of Choices	Moderate	High	Low-moderate	Low
Quality of Matching Process	High	High	Low-moderate	Low
Evaluation Mechanism	High	Moderate-High	Low	Very low

Table 2 compares selected intermediaries with respect to four characteristics that would contribute to bringing together nonprofit "buyers" and legal "sellers" of pro bono services: 1) cost to the law firm, 2) range of choices for pro bono volunteering, 3) the quality of the resulting match between attorney and nonprofit, and 4) the existence of an evaluation mechanism to appraise the pro bono placement, its progress, and results. Given the caveats stated above and the fact that an analysis of this kind has not before been attempted, the conclusions must remain broad and tentative, awaiting empirical verification.

COST TO THE LAW FIRM

The first criterion for comparison of the pro bono intermediaries in Table 2 is cost to the law firm. In this analysis, cost to the firm means the costs incurred in finding a suitable pro bono assignment and placing an associate in it. The anticipated costs range from very low, if Internet technology is the (only) media chosen for this task, to high for an individual law firm. If the firm has a solid commitment to pro bono work as reflected, for example, in a pro bono department and/or officer, then the costs can be very high; if the investment of the firm is less, then costs may be lower, although other dimensions of the pro bono relationship will likely suffer as a result (see below). Volunteer centers do not normally exact a fee for linking volunteers with opportunities, but they may do so.

The literature does not yield solid information on the cost to a law firm of working through an intermediary organization rather than internally for pro bono placements. Although the costs are uncertain, they appear to be less than the firm taking on this responsibility for itself but greater than working through the Internet. The Pro Bono Institute (1998, p. 3) advises that in exchange for the significant benefits to the volunteer attorney and the firm that employs her or him on pro bono matters (for example, excellent opportunities for training, skills development, and professional growth), and in lieu of the "substantial cost for providers who develop training materials and mentor and supervise pro bono counsel" (for example, diverting staff and financial resources from other activities), "it is entirely appropriate . . . that law firms that have access to strong and well-constructed pro bono programs be asked to provide financial support as well as volunteer resources." And because funding is the most pressing and difficult issue for most pro bono intermediary organizations (Visser and Shmavonian, 2004), they are very likely to expect and exact a fee from participating law firms for their services.

RANGE OF CHOICES FOR DONATING TIME

This dimension reflects the range of target nonprofit organizations interested in receiving free or reduced cost legal assistance from pro bono attorneys—demand—and the law firms and attorneys interested in providing these services—supply. The caveat is that the demanders must be known to the suppliers for the market to function efficiently. Bromberger (2003, p. 4) describes the current situation as a market failure: "Many nonprofits, however, are stumped when it comes to the nuts and bolts of finding quality legal services. Likewise, most law firms don't know how to find good projects or can't spend the time vetting nonprofits that need their special expertise." It is this situation, he asserts, that has given rise to nonprofit pro bono matching organizations to bring interested business attorneys and needy nonprofits closer together.

The intermediaries differ along the "choice" dimension. With regard to Internet matching arrangements, it is not clear that needy nonprofit organizations know that they have the opportunity via the Internet to register those needs online to attract potential suppliers (pro bono attorneys), or that they have the capacity or interest to do so. The same reservations apply to potential suppliers in the legal community, who may also be unaware, uninterested, or incapable of seeking pro bono opportunities online. Volunteer centers may fare better on this dimension because they have a local presence and often a reputation with both nonprofit organizations and professionals for placing volunteers, so that both sides may pursue their interests in these community-based organizations.

Individual law firms with an investment in pro bono work (for example, a pro bono officer or department) are more likely to seek business law opportunities with needy nonprofits that will contribute to the development of their legal associates and the firm. But although the importance of pro bono work to firms seems to be increasing (Press, 2003; Chen, 2003), this aspect is an ancillary part of their business, and as Bromberg (2003) suggests, most law firms may not know how to find and verify these opportunities. For their part, potential recipient nonprofit organizations are likely unaware of which law firms to approach for assistance with their legal matters. The option best suited to remedy this market failure is the pro bono intermediary organization set up precisely to serve as the "go-between" to match willing legal expertise with the nonprofit agencies that require it at reduced cost (Bromberger, 2003, 2002; Visser and Shmavonian, 2004). These agencies have names that signal their interest in pro bono work, such as Lawyers Alliance of New York, Community Legal Resources (Detroit), Public Counsel (Los Angeles), Community Economic Development Law Project (Chicago), and the Community Organization Representation Project or CORP (San Francisco).

QUALITY OF THE MATCHING PROCESS

Assessments of the quality of the match achieved between the pro bono business attorney and the nonprofit agency largely mirror the conclusions reached regarding the range of choices dimension. Because the options posted for both pro bono attorneys and nonprofit agencies are likely to be limited online and the matching criteria unknown, Internet technology as yet cannot duplicate the quality of the match that can be obtained through personal knowledge, attention, and involvement. Volunteer centers do better on this dimension for just this reason, but their proficiency is limited by the fact that they are general purpose agencies concerned with many different kinds of volunteering, a variety of other activities, and participation by numerous professions (Brudney and Kim, 2003).

By contrast, individual law firms and especially pro bono intermediary agencies have the incentive and legal expertise to achieve a good quality match. To assist in this process, Power of Attorney, a national network of legal matchmakers and go-betweens, makes grants to intermediaries, sponsors semiannual meetings, provides an Internet connection for continuing contact and idea exchanges, and provides substantive training for intermediaries in fundraising, case referral, tracking systems, managing databases, and so forth. The first known survey of pro bono business law intermediaries in the U.S., based on a sample of thirty-seven organizations, found that virtually all of them engage in the critical function of case screening, though the number involved in follow-up was about two-thirds, and about half provided training (either for nonprofits or attorneys) (Visser and Shmavonian, 2004). The intermediaries facilitate the donation of attorneys' time and skills by screening each nonprofit client to determine its mission and economic eligibility (inability to pay for legal services), analyzing the legal issues, collecting relevant data and documents, and working up the case before placing it with a lawyer that has the appropriate expertise and interest (Bromberger, 2002). Says Haydee Alfonso, supervising lawyer of the Community Organization Representation Project in San Francisco, "We get it to the point where it's easy to pass over to an attorney. . . . One of the things lawyers tell us over and over again is that without the screening and matching that we do, they wouldn't be doing pro bono work. They tell us they don't have the time to go out on their own and find nonprofits and scrutinize them the way we do" (quoted in Bromberger, 2002).

EVALUATION MECHANISM

Evaluation is essential for feedback and learning in matching pro bono legal talent with the nonprofit organizations that qualify for it. The four intermediaries can be compared along this dimension.

At this writing, Internet matching systems do not provide feedback on the quality of the placement of pro bono attorneys with nonprofit agencies. This information could potentially be obtained through online survey (or other means), but a survey alone seems insufficient to tap the range and depth of the process and results of the matching for either attorney (experience gained, firm prestige, future business, etc.) or nonprofit (value of services received, organizational learning, future legal problems avoided, etc.). Similarly, volunteer centers rarely evaluate the quality of their volunteer placements (Brudney and Kim, 2003). In this instance, moreover, they normally would not have on staff the legal expertise that would allow them to conduct a valid assessment.

By contrast, a law firm with a commitment to pro bono work would have the motivation to evaluate these services to determine the costs and benefits to participating attorneys as well as to the firm itself. Assessment by the firm would likely encompass the type, amount, and quality of the work performed for the nonprofit, the final disposition of legal matters, consideration of advantages and disadvantages, lessons learned, and so forth. The results of the survey of pro bono business law intermediaries shed some surprising light on the evaluation activities of these entities. The authors of the survey study write, "In one of the most significant findings ... only two of the organizations surveyed report that they have a formal evaluation process in place to assess their work. Although many had some form of follow-up with the client (15 total), there is a clear and strong need for more formal and consistent efforts in self-evaluation and tracking of information about each program" (Visser and Shmavonian, 2004, p. 3). While the intermediaries may well recognize the importance of feedback for attracting both attorneys and nonprofits, as a group they do not seem to be routinely taking the steps necessary to yield the type of information that would help them to improve the broker function that they were created to perform.

Conclusion

This chapter has examined pro bono volunteering, defined as the donation of services by individuals or firms with high levels of specialized expertise to nonprofit organizations at no cost or reduced cost. For purposes of comparison, we refer to volunteer work that calls for much less specialized proficiency or investment in formal education or advanced training as traditional volunteering. Although a variety of professionals and organizations engage in so-called pro bono activity, the term is most closely associated with the legal field. Accordingly, this chapter focuses primarily on pro bono work performed by attorneys in the area of business law for nonprofit organizations.

The analysis shows that pro bono volunteering differs from more traditional volunteering in important ways with respect to the volunteer and the nonprofit organization receiving assistance (Table 1). One factor, in particular, that distinguishes the two types of volunteering is the involvement in pro bono work of a third party—the volunteer's employer—in the traditional two-party volunteer-host organization relationship. In firms committed to pro bono, the employer acts as a "broker" to try to arrange a suitable match between attorney and nonprofit that yields benefits to all three parties.

The employer is not the sole entity that plays the role of broker in pro bono volunteering. In the legal profession, at least three additional brokers exist. Volunteer centers—community-based organizations that facilitate volunteer recruitment, training, assignment, and related activities—also place attorneys with nonprofits, although the pro bono field does not constitute a large part of the activities of these general purpose volunteer clearing houses. The Internet is another broker, performing the function of matching the business attorney with nonprofit organization at a distance. Finally, a new set of organizations known as "pro bono business law intermediaries" has arisen specifically to create a more efficient market for "buyers"—nonprofit groups and organizations wanting to enlist highly professional volunteer assistance—and "sellers"—prospective volunteers from the legal community. Table 2 provides a comparative analysis of these four intermediary mechanisms in pro bono volunteering.

Although research and practice in pro bono volunteering have developed largely in isolation from the literature of volunteer administration, those with responsibility for arranging pro bono assignments and those who administer more traditional volunteer programs would seem to have much to learn from one another. Effective pro bono work depends on careful screening, matching, and placement of volunteers with high levels of expertise within nonprofit organizations that need but cannot afford this assistance. These practices are longtime staples of traditional volunteer administration and have received substantial coverage in the literature (Hager and Brudney, 2004). Also crucial to the success of pro bono work is evaluation of volunteer assignments, which can stimulate learning and progress toward meeting the goals of all the parties involved. Traditional volunteer administration similarly endorses and details evaluation practices. Research suggests, however, that evaluation is not conducted as regularly or as fully as these other recommended practices in either pro bono work (Table 2) or the typical volunteer program (Brudney, 2005). In this area, especially, the management of both traditional and pro bono volunteering would benefit from upgrading.

Pro bono arrangements likewise have much to offer administrators of traditional volunteer programs. Model pro bono programs emphasize careful design and preparation of work assignments for volunteers before they are recruited, orientation of volunteers to the assignments for which they have been enlisted, clear delegation of tasks to volunteers, and the provision of ongoing support and guidance as necessary. These aspects receive attention in the literature of volunteer administration as well, but some observers worry that lack of support resources combined with an increasing number of volunteers and an escalating volume of work can overwhelm the "volunteer management capacity" of host organizations, thereby jeopardizing the quality or amount of services they are able to deliver (Urban Institute, 2004). Perhaps because the volunteer, the nonprofit organization, and the employer place a high valuation on the volunteer's time—and the pro bono intermediaries have an interest in the volunteer returning for additional projects or assignments—pro bono programs strive to make sure that the time donated by volunteers is used well. By contrast, a national survey commissioned by the UPS Foundation in 1998 of a national sample of more than 2,400 Americans showed that two out of five volunteers claimed to have stopped volunteering for an organization at some time because of one or more poor volunteer management practices. The reasons for stopping included the organization not making good use of a volunteer's time (mentioned by 23 percent of the volunteers), or good use of their talents, skills, or expertise (mentioned by 18 percent); or that volunteer tasks were not clearly defined (16 percent) (UPS Foundation, 1998, p. 15).

Another important area in which pro bono volunteering can help to inform practice in more traditional volunteer programs is in the use of intermediaries to help arrange and negotiate volunteer service to nonprofit organizations. The model underlying most traditional volunteer programs conceives of the volunteer as interacting directly with the host organization in the work assignment, with the latter responsible for all facets of volunteer administration from marketing to recognition. Increasingly, however, intermediaries stand between the volunteer and the host organization and intervene in this relationship. In the area of pro bono volunteering in the legal community, for example, employers, volunteer centers, pro bono intermediary organizations, and the Internet play this role. As discussed above, business attorneys interested in pro bono work seem rarely, if ever, to approach recipient nonprofit organizations directly, but instead are recruited, selected, referred, and perhaps even managed for this purpose by an intermediary. In more traditional volunteer programs, the intermediaries again include employers such as businesses and government, volunteer centers such as those affiliated with the United Way and the Points of Light Foundation, and the Internet. They also include religious institutions (churches, synagogues, and mosques), schools at all levels, civic associations, retirement communities, and so forth. These intermediaries recruit and mobilize volunteers sometimes for their own purposes but more often to assist nonprofit organizations in meeting service needs. They identify worthwhile projects and organizations for their volunteers, provide referrals to these entities, and may assist with other typical volunteer administration tasks such as orientation, training, and supervision.

As intermediaries assume this larger role in traditional volunteer programs, the field of volunteer administration will likely undergo substantial change. First, although many volunteers will continue to seek out host organizations on their own, volunteer administrators will come to rely more on intermediary institutions for volunteer referrals and placements, because they can be more efficient sources of volunteers. Second, the rise of the intermediaries will put pressure on volunteer administrators to develop jobs and opportunities for volunteers that will make their programs stand out from the rest to capture the interest of the go-betweens. Third, since the intermediaries may be able to deliver a collection of volunteers who want to volunteer *en masse,* such as employees of a particular business, or students from the same school, or congregants from the same house of worship, volunteer administrators will need to identify and organize projects suitable for group-based volunteering (for example, refurbishing a building). Fourth, they will need to become more accustomed to the "episodic volunteer," that is, one who serves the organization briefly but often intensely and then departs. Finally, as it has in so many other areas of social life, the Internet will effect changes in volunteering as well, in many cases reducing distance as an impediment to service.

We have only begun to think about these exciting changes and their implications for volunteer administration. They merit the attention of practitioners and researchers in the area of pro bono activity as well as more traditional volunteering.

References

Bromberger, A. R. 2002. "When Help Is Hard to Find." *Business Law Today,* 12 (1), September/ October. Available at www.abanet.org/buslaw/blt/2002-09-10/bromberger.html. Accessed March 22, 2004.

Bromberger, A. R. 2003. *Why Nonprofits Need Lawyers.* New York: Power of Attorney.

Brudney, J. L. 2005. "Designing and Managing Volunteer Programs." In Robert D. Herman (ed.), *The Jossey-Bass Handbook of Nonprofit Leadership and Management.* Second Edition, pp. 310–344. San Francisco: Jossey-Bass.

Brudney, J. L., with the assistance of D. Kim. 2003. *The 2001 Volunteer Center Survey: A Report on Findings and Implications.* Washington, DC: Points of Light Foundation.

Chen, V. 2003. "Pro bono: Thanks to a slowdown in deals work and more complex projects, a growing number of transactions lawyers are signing on for pro bono work." *The American Lawyer,* September, pp. 94–95, 119.

Cravens, J. 2004. "Pro Bono/In-Kind/Donated Services for Mission-Based Organizations: When, Why and How?" Available at www.coyotecommunications.com/probono.html. Accessed March 15, 2004.

Hager, M. A., and J. L. Brudney. 2004. *Volunteer Management: Practices and Retention of Volunteers.* Washington, DC: The Urban Institute.

Lardent, E. F. 2000. *Making the Business Case for Pro Bono.* Washington, DC: Pro Bono Institute, Georgetown University Law Center.

Lardent, E. F. 2001. "For the Public Good: Pro Bono in the Aftermath of September 11th." *What's New in Law Firm Pro Bono.* Georgetown University Law Center, Issue #39, November/December, pp. 5–8. Available at www.probonoinst.org. Accessed July 5, 2004.

Lardent, E. F. 2002. "Trends in Law Firm Pro Bono: Pro Bono in Turbulent Economic Times." *What's New in Law Firm Pro Bono.* Georgetown University Law Center, Issue #40, January/February, pp. 5–8. Available at www.probonoinst.org. Accessed July 5, 2004.

Marron, B. R. 2002. "From Database to Dedication: Linking Lawyers with Good Causes." *Business Law Today,* 12 (1), September /October. Available at www.abanet.org/buslaw/blt/2002-09-10/marron.html. Accessed March 22, 2004.

McCurley, S. 2003. "A Look at Employee Volunteerism." *e-Volunteerism,* 3: 3 (April–June). www.e-volunteerism.com/subscriber/quarterly/03apr/web3cfull.html?URX=175829. Accessed March 21, 2004.

Meijs, L. C. P. M., and E. Hoogstad. 2001. "New Ways Of Managing Volunteers: Combining Membership Management And Programme Management." *Voluntary Action,* 3 (3), pp. 41–61.

Press, A. 2003. "The A-List: Who Are the Nation's First-Tier Law Firms?" *The American Lawyer,* September, pp. 84–87.

Pro Bono Institute. 1998. "Leveraging Larger Firm Resources." Paper prepared for the "Program on Securing Commitments from Law Firms." Washington, DC, April 29. Available at www.probonoinst.org/pdfs/leveragingresources.pdf. Accessed July 25, 2004.

UPS Foundation. 1998. *Managing Volunteers: A Report from United Parcel Service.* Available at http://www.community.ups.com/downloads/pdfs/1998_survey.pdf

Urban Institute. 2004. "Volunteer Management Capacity in America's Charities and Congregations: A Briefing Report (February). Washington, DC: The Urban Institute. Available at www.nationalservice.org/research/vol_capacity_brief.pdf. Accessed March 22, 2004.

Visser, Joanna, and Nadya K. Shmavonian, 2004. "The Profiles Project: A Study of Pro Bono Business Law Intermediaries in the U.S." New York: Power of Attorney. Available at www.powerofattorney.org. Accessed July 24, 2004.

Walsh, Erin. 2003. "Some Call It eLawyering: Is It a Brave New World or an Ethical Quagmire?" *Business Law Today,* 12 (3), January/February. Available at www.abanet.org/buslaw/blt/2003-01-02/walsh.html. Accessed July 25, 2004.

Weitzman, M. S.; N. T. Jalandoni, L.M. Lampkin, and T. H. Pollak. 2002. *The New Nonprofit Almanac And Desk Reference.* New York: John Wiley and Sons.

Zeisel, G., and R. Estes. 1979. "Accounting and Public Service." *The Accounting Review,* LIV (2), April, pp. 402–408.

13

Market Engagement and Competition: Opportunities, Challenges, and the Quest for Comparative Advantage

Kevin P. Kearns
Graduate School of Public and International Affairs
University of Pittsburgh
Pittsburgh, PA

Introduction

Recently, several prominent scholars have given us a broad view of the nonprofit sector in the U.S., focusing on emerging challenges and opportunities facing the sector (Salamon, 2002a; Light, 2000, 2002; Hasenfeld, 1996; Ryan, 1999; Rosenman, 1998; Firstenberg, 1996; O'Connell, 1996). The consistent theme in nearly all of these commentaries is that the boundaries that formerly separated the domains of government, business, and nonprofit organizations are rapidly disappearing. Although the emergence of this *seamless* economy has been more than thirty years in the making, its effects on the nonprofit sector as a whole and on individual organizations has only recently been carefully scrutinized.

The federal government has devolved much of the responsibility for domestic programs and services to states and localities which, in turn, are contracting with nonprofit and for-profit organizations for the delivery of those services. Many government programs now encourage true market transactions by giving consumers the right to exercise choice through vouchers and other mechanisms, thereby setting up new types of competition among nonprofit organizations and between nonprofits and for-profit businesses. True to form, businesses have capitalized on this market-friendly environment by finding opportunities to penetrate growth industries, including social services, where they can leverage their core competencies and comparative advantages. Conversely, many nonprofits have turned to entrepreneurial revenue-generating activities, including for-profit subsidiaries, sometimes at the risk of distracting focus from their charitable missions (Dees, Emerson, and Economy, 2001; Dart, 2004). Meanwhile, at the other extreme, some nonprofits have become so dependent on government grants and contracts that they have morphed into "quasi-governmental" agencies, with all of the public sector's bureaucratic characteristics and pathologies (Lipsky and Smith, 1993).

Details regarding these and other trends are addressed in preceding chapters of this book. This chapter broadly explores several arenas in which the nonprofit sector has become engaged with the private marketplace, sometimes by choice but often by necessity. The first section of the chapter focuses on competition for *market share,* for *resources,* for *visibility,* and for *talent.* In some industries, the competitive environment has exposed the vulnerabilities of nonprofit organizations, especially relative to businesses. The second section provides a primer on the concept of *comparative* advantage. This concept helps explain why businesses have successfully penetrated particular industries and markets previously dominated by the nonprofit sector. But nonprofits also have certain comparative advantages over businesses, which might be leveraged in certain commercial and enterprise ventures. The conclusion of the chapter argues that a values-based approach to the concept of comparative advantage can be employed that considers not only core competencies and operational strengths of an organization, but also its culture, values, and historic role in the community.

Arenas for Market Engagement

Market "engagement" can take several forms. First, engagement takes place whenever a nonprofit competes, as a matter of choice or necessity, with another organization for finite resources in a free market environment characterized by rational choice among producers and consumers. For many years, nonprofits have competed with one another for clients (market share), for financial resources, for community visibility, for leadership talent, and for staff and volunteer services. Increasingly, nonprofits are competing with private businesses for most of these same resources. Second, engagement takes place when nonprofits seek out collaborative relationships or even strategic alliances, sometimes with businesses, in order to gain a competitive edge in the marketplace. Finally, nonprofits "engage" the market when they are beneficiaries (or victims) of free market forces beyond their control. Such is the case, for example, when nonprofits must adapt to changing economic circumstances such as energy prices, health care costs, or other business expenses just like any other organization. This chapter focuses on the type of market engagement that deals with competitive behavior.

COMPETITION FOR MARKET SHARE

Nonprofits are beginning to realize that a principal threat of the competitive marketplace is the prospect of losing programs and clients to new competitors, including for-profit firms. Lester Salamon (2002b) notes that between 1982 and 1997 nonprofit employment relative to for-profit employment fell precipitously in child day care (-27%), home health (-53%), and kidney dialysis centers (-32%). During roughly the same time period, the number of nonprofit providers fell significantly in health maintenance organizations (-60%), rehabilitation hospitals (-50%), home health agencies (-48%), dialysis centers (-45%), and residential treatment facilities for children (-22%).

For-profit firms are flexing their muscles in these and other industries that reward core competencies like cost control, information management (Te'eni and Young, 2003), process management, exploiting economies of scale, and the ability to manage decentralized (sometimes franchised) systems of service delivery. Typically, businesses enjoy a comparative advantage over nonprofits and governments in these skills because they are essential to achieving and maintaining high profit margins. Business leaders and their staffs and boards often have advanced academic training in these strategies and also have the benefit of decades of research on competitive strategies coming out of first-rate business schools around the world. They have fine-tuned these skills through years of experience in a variety of competitive contexts.

Also, the fields in which nonprofits have lost market share tend to favor organizations that have easy access to large sums of investment capital needed to acquire property, equipment, and personnel. Here again, the advantage seems to be on the side of for-profit firms, which typically have greater access to capital markets than nonprofits. Many businesses can generate huge sums of investment capital by selling shares of stock, or seeking other readily available sources of venture capital. Governmental jurisdictions have ready access to capital markets through the issuance of bonds and other mechanisms, and their assistance may ultimately be needed to maintain a significant nonprofit presence in some industries. While some capital markets have become more open to nonprofits in recent years, they still operate at a tremendous disadvantage relative to private businesses in generating venture capital for growth or investment in operational efficiencies.

As a result of these and other competitive pressures, many nonprofits are exploring ways to generate more earned income from fees, memberships, or commercial enterprises. But their quest for earned revenue and market share is tempting some nonprofits to give priority to clients who have the ability to pay over those who are dependent upon charitable services. In an example from the child care field presented later in this chapter we will see how a reputable nonprofit agency refused to yield to this pressure, but ultimately lost its battle for survival in competition with for-profit providers.

COMPETITION FOR CHARITABLE RESOURCES

A by-product of market engagement in the nonprofit sector is a new kind of competition for charitable resources. Nonprofits have always competed with each other for a finite supply of charitable gifts, but today the competition has become more intense and more fragmented (Hodgkinson, Nelson, and Sivak, 2002).

A vivid example of fragmented giving is provided by the various types of donor choice programs that many United Way affiliates have adopted (see, for example, Brilliant and Young, 2004). United Way affiliates began implementing donor choice programs in the mid-1990s in an effort to appeal to people who wanted more control over their charitable contributions and to reverse the cycle of declining donations from people who had lost trust in that organization following the scandals of the early 1990s. Donor choice was an instant hit. In fact, some United Way affiliates were caught off guard by how quickly donor choice programs began to drain them of discretionary funds. As more and more contributors tagged their donations to specific purposes rather than communitywide needs, the role of some United Way affiliates began to shift from social service planner and gatekeeper to fundraising intermediary—a kind of philanthropic middle man— that no longer plays a significant role in communitywide planning, needs assessment, and resource allocation. In an effort to recapture some discretionary funds, the United Way of Allegheny County recently resorted to a tax on donor choice contributions to cover its administrative expenses and create a special discretionary fund. Early reaction to the tax among donors and among member agencies has been mixed at best.

Similarly, community foundations are feeling the pressure from a growing number of donors who want to give only to selected causes (Kerkman and Lewis, 2004). Just like United Way affiliates, community foundations have watched with concern as their discretionary authority has been steadily eroded by donor-directed and donor-advised funds. Highly trained program officers who once wielded substantial influence in community planning and resource allocation have seen their role reduced to a kind of philanthropic "account manager" with greatly reduced discretionary power. Moreover, community foundations are facing intense competition from private sector alternatives, such as the Fidelity Charitable Gift Fund, that provide a level of customer service and sophisticated account management that few foundations can match. Another aspect of this trend is the emergence of *venture philanthropy* as a vehicle to give donors more control over their philanthropic investments (Letts, Ryan, and Grossman, 1997).

In the long term, the phenomenon of fragmented giving and consumer-oriented philanthropy may alter the traditional roles of organizations like United Way affiliates and community foundations. More immediately, this trend toward treating donors like consumers or social *investors* has already intensified the competition among nonprofit organizations for a slice of the charitable pie. There is the risk that only mainstream and relatively sophisticated nonprofits will succeed in this new environment, which rewards core competencies in marketing and compelling missions that appeal broadly to diverse groups of donors. This may leave small or fringe organizations or those that address less "popular" social problems to scramble for alternative survival strategies (see for example, Lune, 2002). In Pittsburgh, several far-sighted members of the philanthropic community have noticed this trend and have commissioned a study to determine if small nonprofits need assistance in learning how to appeal directly to individual donors, thereby reducing their reliance on foundation funding.

Moreover, as the e-commerce approach to philanthropy matures as an industry, we can expect new entrants and even more competition from for-profit firms that will try to mimic the strategies of pathbreaking organizations like the Fidelity Charitable Gift Fund. For-profits are familiar and philosophically comfortable with the notion of *return on investment* and they know how to convey this notion to potential customers. Also, they typically enjoy advantages in marketing, customer relations, and in adapting information management tools like e-commerce to the field of philanthropy (Te'eni and Young, 2003).

COMPETITION FOR VISIBILITY AND CREDIBILITY

In many competitive arenas, visibility and public image are essential ingredients for organizational success. This is especially true for any service in which consumers have a choice and in services where the consumer of the service is also the buyer. As noted above, the playing field is not quite level because for-profit firms generally enjoy significant comparative advantages in marketing, public relations, and communication strategies.

But even when nonprofits acquire these skills, they can pay an unexpected price for higher public visibility. In competitive environments, the public image of nonprofits can easily be intermingled with for-profit firms, resulting in public cynicism, loss of distinctive identity, and culture clashes within organizations. Salamon (2002b) detects an emerging identity crisis within the nonprofit sector produced by the tension between the market characteristics of the services provided by the sector and the charitable missions and cultures of the institutions providing those services.

An anecdote from the health care field illustrates the point. The chief of transplant surgery at a prestigious university-based health system resigned in the summer of 2004 because he perceived that the priorities of the organization had shifted from research and teaching to a "bottom line" orientation that used market share and financial profit as its primary metric of organizational performance. In a front-page news story he was quoted as saying, "It's not like it used to be, which was a much more collegial academic environment" (Snowbeck, 2004). The next day the senior vice chancellor and dean of the medical school vigorously defended the organization's business-oriented approach, noting that profits subsidize the organization's charitable and teaching activities (Spice, 2004). The dean noted that market pressures have been building in the health care industry for decades, and he applauded his institution's ability to remain financially solvent during turbulent market shifts. Clearly, market pressures have affected the organizational cultures of many nonprofit organizations, especially those in health care. As illustrated here, these pressures can easily exacerbate the "staff versus line" tensions that already exist in any organization.

Also, some nonprofit leaders confuse community *need* with market *demand,* which can create other image problems in a competitive environment. Again, an example from the Pittsburgh community illustrates the point. In the mid-1990s the United Way of Allegheny County launched the Early Childhood Initiative (ECI), an impressive and well-intentioned effort to improve preschool educational programs for children in eighty at-risk neighborhoods in the Pittsburgh area. The program had widespread support from community leaders, with multimillion dollar investments from foundations and corporations. The money was used to renovate facilities and to hire and train professional child care workers in accordance with best practice approaches to early childhood education. The ECI program was based on solid research, painstaking plans, and impressive public/private partnerships. The social *need* for the program was well-documented and widely acknowledged.

Despite the need for the ECI, a variety of circumstances conspired to produce a massive miscalculation of the actual *demand* for the program by families in the target communities. First, despite extensive efforts to build support in target neighborhoods, it turned out that many families preferred to have their children cared for by neighbors or relatives, not by professional child care workers. The public image of the ECI in some neighborhoods was that of an elitist outsider, trying to impose a professional model of child care on a community that preferred the familiarity and security of home-based care over the professionalism and state-of-the-art facilities of the ECI. Also, the ECI bypassed some existing neighborhood child care centers and other familiar community facilities, such as churches, preferring to create new facilities. This strategy further tarnished the public image of the ECI and alienated some consumers. Moreover, the business plan of the ECI was based on a half-day model of child care, which did not accommodate consumer *demand* for full-day care following the welfare to work provisions of the welfare reforms of 1996. The costs of the program escalated, while participation waned. Ultimately, the ECI was reduced to a skeleton program in two neighborhoods. A post-mortem report by the RAND Corporation described the program as a "noble bet" (Gill, Dembosky, and Caulkins, 2002). Everyone associated with the Pittsburgh ECI recognized the *need* for better early childhood education, but the *demand* for such a program had subtle nuances that were not anticipated.

THE RACE FOR YOUNG TALENT

There was a time when the competition for managerial talent was relatively clear cut. Graduates of business management programs went to work in the for-profit sector while students with degrees in public administration and social work sought employment opportunities in government or the nonprofit sector. In the new environment, the choices are not so clear cut, and the nonprofit sector may lose the battle for top talent. Some students coming out of public service training centers now have career choices other than government or nonprofit organizations. Even students who are committed to public service can work in consulting firms or private businesses that have a social service portfolio. The catch is that the private sector not only offers higher pay and better benefits, but also better professional development programs and sometimes even higher quality of work life.

Available research tells us that today's young professionals are looking for several things from their first employer, such as clear career paths, opportunities for professional training and growth, diversity in the workplace, access to high technology, and a relatively clear separation of work life and personal life (Catalyst, 2001). Unfortunately, with some exceptions (Pitt-Catsouphes et al., 2004) the nonprofit sector as a whole seems to be at a comparative *disadvantage* in meeting these expectations of talented young professionals. Because most nonprofits are quite small, they don't offer clear career paths or the opportunity to develop specialized professional skills. Instead, in an organization with, say, five to seven employees, almost everyone has to be a "generalist" and fill in wherever needed. Predictable paths to promotion are nearly nonexistent in such small organizations. The quality of work life is often relatively low due to long hours and stressful environments, especially when working with at-risk populations or in distressed communities (Light, 2002). Finally, most nonprofits are well behind the technology curve, which can be frustrating to young people who have become accustomed to living and working in technologically sophisticated environments.

Focus group research conducted by the Coro Center for Civic Leadership and the Forbes Funds in Pittsburgh suggests that young professionals are rather skeptical of careers in the nonprofit sector (Forbes Funds, 2004). They believe that nonprofits in Pittsburgh do not recruit effectively and that finding employment in the sector seems to be based more on personal networks than on skills and abilities. They worry that nonprofit jobs may lead to a professional dead end because the skills acquired there will not be transferable to other sectors. And, finally, the apparent glass ceiling in the nonprofit sector that affects women and minorities is in glaring contradiction to the espoused values of the sector. Add to this mix the forecasts of an alarming number of nonprofit CEO retirements in the coming ten years and we have a recipe for a leadership crisis in the nonprofit sector—a generation of leaders retiring with an insufficient number of young people in the wings being developed and groomed for these positions (Allison, 2002).

Responsibility for recruiting high-quality talent in a competitive marketplace rests primarily on nonprofit organizations themselves (Hansen, Huggins, and Ban, 2003). For example, emphasizing their positive attributes, nonprofits can boast that they provide young professionals with the opportunity to have significant responsibility early in their careers. Also, they offer work environments that are relatively collegial and informal relative to many business or governmental environments. Moreover, they often have workforces that are more diverse than those found in business or government, and diversity is an attribute that young professionals value. Finally, of course, nonprofits offer young professionals the opportunity for meaningful work in the public interest, which may partially compensate for other shortcomings.

Another human resource dilemma for nonprofits is the added burden that commercialization and market engagement have created for nonprofit executives and trustees. Some experts worry that market engagement has placed unreasonable demands on nonprofit leaders who now must master not only the substantive aspects of their respective fields (e.g., arts) but also the intricate and dynamic details of the industries and competitive markets in which they operate (Salamon, 2002b). But it must be noted that these pressures on nonprofit executives have always been borne by their counterparts in the for-profit sector, and they are no more burdensome in the nonprofit sector than in government or industry. Moreover, there is quite a lot of low-cost management support available to nonprofit organizations. Indeed, in some cities an entire "industry" of capacity-building has emerged to help nonprofit executives cope with the multifaceted challenges they face (see, for example, Kearns, 2004). Also, beginning in the late 1980s and throughout the 1990s, universities responded quite rapidly to the need for management-based education for nonprofit executives (Mirabella and Wish, 1999, 2000).

COMPETITIVE ENGAGEMENTS: ONE COMMUNITY'S PROFILE

In the spring of 2003 the author surveyed nearly 400 nonprofit organizations in Allegheny County, Pennsylvania (Pittsburgh). Among other things, the survey asked respondents whether they competed with other organizations for community visibility and image, for funding or other resources, and for clients (market share). Table 1 summarizes the responses to this question.

TABLE 1. COMPETITIVE PROFILE OF PITTSBURGH'S NONPROFIT SECTOR

Response to survey question: Does your organization regularly compete with other nonprofits, government agencies, or for-profit firms for any of the following reasons? (Check all that apply.)

		Arts (n=53)	Education (n=54)	Health and Related (n= 55)	Human Services (n=154)	Public and Societal Benefit (n=54)
Competition for community visibility and image	Regularly compete with other nonprofits	76.3%	41.2%	76.3%	63.2%	56.2%
	Regularly compete with government agencies	2.0%	17.2%	11.2%	12.9%	7.8%
	Regularly compete with for-profit businesses	22.5%	17.1%	20.0%	19.3%	15.0%
Competition for funding and other resources	Regularly compete with other nonprofits	84.3%	66.7%	85.2%	80.1%	80.6%
	Regularly compete with government agencies	24.5%	27.6%	17.5%	32.4%	25.5%
	Regularly compete with for-profit businesses	15.4%	23.2%	13.8%	20.9%	23.6%
Competition for clients (market share)	Regularly compete with other nonprofits	58.5%	39.6%	65.2%	49.5%	38.8%
	Regularly compete with government agencies	4.6%	22.5%	9.8%	18.5%	13.6%
	Regularly compete with for-profit businesses	30.4%	32.0%	24.1%	22.5%	21.7%

Table 1 suggests that in the Pittsburgh area the most consistent competition for visibility, for funding, and for clients comes from other nonprofit organizations. However, it is clear that the nonprofit respondents to this survey perceive the emergence of significant competition from for-profit firms, especially for visibility and for market share. In these two domains, for-profit firms are mentioned ahead of government agencies as organizations with which respondents "regularly compete."

Competition with other nonprofit organizations is most consistently mentioned by respondents from the health care fields, followed by the arts and then human services. Competition with public sector agencies is most frequently mentioned by respondents from the field of education, followed by human services. And, finally, competition with for-profit firms is most frequently cited by respondents from the fields of education and the arts, followed by human services and public benefit organizations.

The Concept of Comparative Advantage

It is evident that the nonprofit sector is engaged in the marketplace, sometimes by choice but often by necessity. Can the nonprofit sector compete effectively in market-driven competitive environments? *Should* the nonprofit sector compete when there are other options such as collaboration or even abandonment of the market? Are competition and collaboration mutually exclusive strategies? Probably not, so nonprofits must also be able to respond to market situations where they must simultaneously compete and collaborate. Universities in a metropolitan region, for example, certainly compete to some extent for students and for public visibility, but they also collaborate for the good of the region because a vibrant local economy will work to their mutual advantage.

The concept of *comparative advantage* can be useful in addressing these questions. Definitive work on this concept has been done by Michael Porter (1980, 1985, 1990) who argues that comparative advantage is the key determinant of a firm's performance.

A widely used business text says that an organization has a comparative advantage "whenever it has an edge over rivals in securing customers and defending against competitive forces," such as producing a higher quality product, providing superior customer service, achieving lower costs in production, or having a more convenient location (Thompson and Strickland, 1992, p. 102). This definition, while intuitively appealing, offers only a partial understanding of the concept of comparative advantage because it focuses almost exclusively on an organization's strengths or core competencies, while ignoring the crucial point that an organization's capabilities (even relative to its competitive rivals) are meaningless unless they are strategically leveraged against a corresponding *opportunity* or *threat* in the external environment. Indeed, an organization that focuses too much attention on its strengths, however impressive they may be, can be lulled into a false sense of security, ignoring external events or dynamic market trends that can render those strengths irrelevant.

An example is a college or university that proudly boasts of its long history of academic excellence, comparing its reputation to Ivy League schools. But what if the institution has become infatuated with its own demonstrated excellence without keeping an eye on changes in the competitive environment? What if its leaders fail to notice or simply ignore the fact that prospective students and their parents are increasingly interested in quality of campus life, superior housing and recreational facilities, personalized student support services, and career counseling programs? Or what if the institution compares itself with the wrong competitors as a result of arrogance, ignorance, or sheer force of habit?

For example, many of us in higher education smugly dismissed the University of Phoenix when it was founded as a for-profit university in 1976. Some thought that it was a novelty, a passing fad. Others perceived it as nothing but another "mail order diploma factory." Soon, however, the University of Phoenix began to capitalize on demographic trends that were largely ignored by traditional, research-oriented universities. It carved out a market niche in adult education, especially in the management sciences. The University of Phoenix built its competitive strategy around high-quality teaching, a focus on developing practical skills, convenient locations in shopping malls and suburban areas, online student support and advising services, and effective distance learning models. Today, the University of Phoenix is the largest accredited university in the nation and poses a significant competitive threat to some mainstream colleges and universities across the nation, especially those that previously enjoyed significant market share in adult education.

This case vividly illustrates that the threat of new entrants into seemingly mature and stable industries, especially in niche services and markets, is significant when established institutions believe they have a monopoly or at least sustainable market power. In this case, established universities largely ignored the emerging market for continuing adult education, a strategic error that the University of Phoenix was happy to exploit.

Table 2 illustrates four types of strategic choices that emerge when an organization successfully assesses its internal strengths and weaknesses relative to threats and opportunities in the external environment (Kearns, 1992). This conceptual framework is similar to portfolio models of strategy design that have been used in industry (Hedley, 1977) and in nonprofit applications (MacMillan, 1983; Gruber and Mohr, 1982; Roller, 1996).

TABLE 2: STRATEGIC CHOICE ANALYSIS

	Opportunities in the External Environment	**Threats in the External Environment**
	Examples:	Examples:
	• Emergence of new funding opportunities	• Reductions or cessation of funding
	• Expansion of consumer needs/markets	• Contraction of consumer needs/markets
	• Changes in competitors' strategies	• Changes in competitors' strategies
	• Demographic shifts	• Demographic shifts
Organizational Strengths	**Comparative Advantage**	**Mobilization**
Examples:	When internal strengths exceed those of the competitive rivals and can be leveraged to exploit external opportunities, then the organization enjoys a true comparative advantage. The organization should carefully nurture, protect, and invest in its comparative advantages and build its competitive strategy around them.	When internal strengths can help protect the organization against external threats, they must be mobilized to avert the threat or even convert the threat into a strategic opportunity.
• Unique skills, competencies		
• Distinctive products / services		
• Slack resources for investment		
• Technological advantage		
• Production and quality control		
• Ideal location		
• Track record and reputation		
Organizational Weaknesses	**Invest, Divest, or Collaborate**	**Damage Control**
Examples:	When internal weaknesses prevent the organization from exploiting an external opportunity, then it faces a vexing problem. It can invest in the weaknesses to try to turn them into strengths, which is risky. It can divest or abandon its weaknesses in order to reallocate resources toward its strengths, which is difficult. Or, it can seek out partners who can bring assets and capabilities to a collaborative relationship that might, in turn, create a comparative advantage.	When internal weaknesses are particularly germane to external threats, then the organization faces the most threatening of competitive situations. It is vulnerable to the competitive threat and may have no choice but to control the damage through evasive maneuvers, stabilization strategies, turnaround strategies, or market abandonment.
• Lack of skills, competencies		
• No distinctive products / services		
• Financial constraints		
• Outdated technology		
• Poor location		
• No or poor track record		

In consulting assignments, the author has found that nonprofit trustees and executives respond very well to the conceptual framework provided in Table 2. Even in abbreviated strategic planning retreats, the framework gives leaders a way to assess their competitive environment and formulate strategic questions for more probing scrutiny later. But in order to be most useful, this framework should be accompanied by a thorough scan of the competitive environment, including economic trends, competitive trends, and overall driving forces in the organization's domain of activity, whether it's child care, human services, crisis intervention, or other nonprofit "industries." The boundaries of an organization's competitive environment are usually delineated by other organizations that offer:

- *Related* goods and services, such as suppliers, distributors, accrediting agencies, oversight agencies, and so on.

- *Substitutable* goods and services that offer to consumers and stakeholders reasonable substitutes.

- *Competing* goods and services that are similar to those offered by your organization and are in direct competition with you for market share, visibility, and resources.

A few simple questions can offer valuable insights into an organization's comparative advantages and can also help clarify issues and choices related to the other cells in Table 2. For example:

- Does the organization possess certain demonstrable strengths that can help it seize an existing or emerging opportunity in the external environment? If the answer is yes, then the organization enjoys a comparative advantage with respect to that opportunity and should do everything possible to protect, nurture, and sustain that comparative advantage. Aggressive growth strategies are usually justified under these circumstances (MacMillan, 1983).

- Does the organization possess certain demonstrable strengths that can help it avoid or mitigate existing or emerging threats in the external environment? If the answer is yes, then the organization should try to mobilize those strengths as quickly as possible to avert the threat or at least minimize the damage from the threat. Aggressive defensive posturing may be called for under these circumstances. If possible, the threat should be transformed into an opportunity.

- Does the organization have certain weaknesses that are preventing it from seizing existing or emerging opportunities in the external environment? If the answer is yes, then the organization has a difficult choice to make. It can try to invest in its weaknesses in order to turn them into strengths. It can divest its weaknesses by abandoning poorly performing programs or markets. Or, it can seek out a collaborative arrangement or strategic alliance with another organization in order to compensate for its own weaknesses. Either way, the organization is likely facing the prospect of significant resource reallocation.

- Does the organization have certain weaknesses that make it especially vulnerable to existing or emerging threats in the external environment? If the answer is yes, then the organization is facing a very dangerous situation. It must try to identify a damage control strategy that will minimize the impact of the external threat, recognizing that it may not be able to avoid the threat completely.

These questions, if posed carefully and answered candidly, can provide nonprofit executives and trustees with valuable insights regarding their prospects for success in a competitive environment.

ORGANIZATIONAL AND PRODUCT LIFE CYCLES

Every organization and every product has a life cycle. They are born, they develop and grow, they mature, and they may eventually decline and die as new goods and services arise to take their place. Different types of organizations have comparative advantages at each stage of the product life cycle (Hofer, 1975). In the early stages of a product or program life cycle, small and nimble organizations often are the first to detect and respond to new consumer needs and demands. They secure a foothold in emerging markets because of their ability to act quickly with goods and services that consumers want and need. It is reasonable to suggest that many nonprofit organizations have a comparative advantage in emerging social programs because they are typically small, community-based organizations that can quickly detect changing needs and respond effectively to meet those needs.

But as demand for the new program or service grows, the comparative advantage can quickly shift to larger organizations that have slack resources or can secure the investment capital needed to ramp up production to meet the growing market needs and demands. This is called *going to scale*. Growth industries tend to favor organizations that can achieve a cost or quality advantage, including firms that do little more than imitate the goods and services of the pathbreaking organizations that first responded to consumer needs. Here we see the incursion of for-profit firms in child care, home health care, ancillary health care, and other growth industries. Going to scale may represent the greatest challenge to nonprofit organizations that are experimenting with various types of social enterprise. It is one thing to penetrate a new market with a creative good or service that meets a need. It is quite another to defend that market share against imitators and latecomers who can capitalize on the innovations developed by trailblazers.

Mature programs and services sometimes favor large organizations that have a comparative advantage in the large-scale and efficient production of goods and services and in marketing and distributing to vast and diverse audiences. Thus, it is easy to understand the continuing trend toward concentration in the field of primary health care as smaller community-based hospitals yield to large health "systems" that can achieve economies of scale in purchasing, production, and distribution. This also explains why competition for market share is so intense among nonprofit organizations in the health care field (see Table 1 above).

Finally, in declining industries the comparative advantage may shift back to the organizations that are happy to exploit markets and serve needs that are abandoned by other organizations. Nonprofits should carefully watch industries that are abandoned by the for-profit sector or by large nonprofits. They may be able to capitalize on residual opportunities that may arise in declining industries. For example, Employee Assistance Programs (EAPs) are used by some firms to provide counseling and treatment to employees who have stress-related problems, especially those involving drug or alcohol abuse. The EAP industry contains both for-profit and nonprofit providers. In some regions, however, the EAP industry is declining because employers are reducing their health care benefits to employees. If nonprofits see that large for-profit firms are abandoning this particular industry (or a particular marketplace), then they might be able to find fruitful niche markets that are sustainable and even profitable.

ENTRY AND EXIT BARRIERS

It has become painfully apparent that the entry barriers in many nonprofit industries are not as formidable as we once believed. For example, entering the health care field requires huge investments in equipment, facilities, and personnel as well as a high level of trust from consumers as well as from medical professionals and insurers who are the gatekeepers to the health care system. These entry barriers once gave nonprofits a clear comparative advantage because of the conventional wisdom that mature industries are difficult to penetrate. However, during the 1990s, for-profit firms proved that they could quickly capture market share in primary health care by simply buying and converting financially troubled nonprofit hospitals, sometimes for pennies on the dollar. Today for-profit firms are capturing market share in many ancillary health services that are less risky. Entry barriers may also be crumbling in areas like child care, job training, higher education, and a variety of other industries formerly dominated by nonprofits. As the prevailing political climate of the country continues to gravitate toward pro-business and anti-government policies, we can expect that entry barriers in the form of government regulations will continue to subside in many industries.

Conversely, many nonprofits find that there are substantial *exit barriers* that prevent them from abandoning or even downsizing their operations in response to competitive threats. For nonprofits it may be difficult, if not morally reprehensible, to abandon clients who depend on them. Also, they may be legally bound by their missions and mandates and by the implicit contract they have with donors who have made charitable contributions. Moreover, even if nonprofits are able to abandon (divest) existing programs and services, they may not have access to the investment capital needed to shift their focus to a new and more promising domain of activity. For-profit firms often have the comparative advantage when it comes to divesting or downsizing in response to new market realities. Through the process of conglomerate diversification, for-profit firms can enter and leave industries more or less at will, and unlike nonprofits, they can quickly gain access to the investment capital necessary to enter new industries. However, for-profit firms are not immune to the hazards of diversifying into industries where they lack the expertise needed to survive and succeed. For example, the ultimate downfall of the Westinghouse Corporation in the 1990s has been attributed to its forays into real estate investment, an area in which it lacked a comparative advantage. Its core business units in electronics and communication remained relatively strong, but bad investments in unrelated industries brought about its demise. Today's business climate appears to be much more skeptical of conglomerate diversification as a business strategy.

REVENUE AND COST STRUCTURE OF THE INDUSTRY

The revenue and cost structure of an industry is usually related to its stage in the life cycle and is always a dynamic variable that can shift very quickly. In child care, for example, the public subsidies for needy families rarely cover the full cost of services. Nonprofits are morally and legally obligated to serve needy families, but in many states they lose money for every such family they serve. Philanthropic contributions are available to nonprofit child care programs, but often they don't bridge the fiscal gap between costs and revenues. Again, the comparative advantage in this industry seems to be shifting to for-profit providers who: 1) are under no moral or legal obligation to serve families that cannot afford the full cost of tuition, and 2) would not accept below market public subsidies unless the marginal revenue exceeded their marginal cost. Fixed costs, variable costs, profit margins, and breakeven points are the *mantra* of any business executive, but nonprofit leaders are just beginning to test these principles in their domains of activity.

THE BASIS OF COMPETITION

Organizations compete with each other in several ways. As indicated above, perhaps the most typical kind of competition relates to cost control and achieving production and distribution efficiencies that give an organization a comparative advantage. But firms also compete on the basis of *product differentiation* with the claim that their good or service has a certain special attribute that consumers and stakeholders value. Firms also compete for market niches, which is called a *focus* strategy (Porter, 1980, 1985). Often nonprofits can gain and keep a comparative advantage if the competition is based on product differentiation and focus. Most nonprofits, for example, are small and they tend to serve specific community needs and demands. They can tailor their services to meet those demands and can focus their energies on relatively discrete communities. However, comparative advantage is not *exclusive to* nonprofits. As illustrated above, the University of Phoenix has focused on the adult education market with a curriculum that is clearly differentiated from what most major research universities offer.

BARGAINING POWER OF CONSUMERS AND OTHER STAKEHOLDERS

Finally, astute leaders must constantly assess changes in the power of consumers and other stakeholders to dictate major organizational strategies and tactics. There is no doubt, for example, that the power balance in health care has now completely shifted from doctors to insurance companies and health maintenance organizations. Their bargaining power in the health care industry is now unquestioned. But bargaining power is also shifting in the human services from providers to consumers. Some nonprofits are having difficulty adjusting to the new market-driven mechanisms of government funding that give individuals and families a choice in the types of social programs and services they receive and a choice over providers of those services. Vouchers and other mechanisms give consumers substantially more power in the market transaction, forcing nonprofits to compete among themselves and with for-profit firms to secure and retain consumer loyalty. Again, the comparative advantage in this environment would seem to be with the for-profit sector, which has vast experience in monitoring consumer needs and demands and responding accordingly. In some industries, nonprofits have historically benefited from "captive audiences" who had little choice but to receive services from them. For example, until the incursion of for-profit hospitals, the health care industry was dominated by nonprofits, giving consumers little choice. Consumer loyalty is especially difficult to retain when the so-called "switching costs" are low. When consumers see short-term gains to switching providers while incurring little or no additional cost, then competition will be quite high. Competition among credit card companies, mortgage companies, auto insurance, and long-distance telephone service providers represents a prime example of intense competitive behavior when switching costs for consumers are low or nonexistent.

AN ILLUSTRATION OF COMPARATIVE DISADVANTAGE IN A HOSTILE COMPETITIVE ENVIRONMENT: CHILD CARE IN PITTSBURGH

The notions of comparative advantage and industry analysis are more than mere theoretical meanderings. They can provide significant insight into specific cases of organizational growth or, in the case study below, demise and death (see, for example, Bielefeld, 1994). Whenever a nonprofit organization engages the market, there is always the prospect of ultimate failure and collapse.

To illustrate, the Pittsburgh nonprofit community recently mourned the death of Louise Child Care, a ninety-eight-year-old agency that was once a national leader in early childhood research, practice, and training for child care professionals. Table 3 provides a brief examination of the child care industry in Pittsburgh, vividly illustrating many of the theoretical concepts discussed above. A careful reading of Table 3 reveals the ultimately unforgiving competitive environment that contributed to the demise of Louise Child Care.

TABLE 3. CASE STUDY OF ORGANIZATIONAL DEMISE:
A BRIEF ASSESSMENT OF THE CHILD CARE INDUSTRY IN PITTSBURGH

Competitive Characteristics of the Industry

- **A crowded and growing market:** 396 day care centers, 166 established since 1997, with 28,000 children in all facilities.

- **Entry barriers:** Strict state licensing requirement (ratios of caretakers to children) and even stricter accrediting standards. Only 55 centers are accredited by the National Association for the Education of Young Children, the gold standard for accreditation.

- **Exit barriers:** Difficult to close centers due to client and community dependence.

- **Competition from for-profit firms:** Emergence of more for-profit centers that offer comparable tuition with better cost control due to operational efficiencies and economies of scale. These organizations compete for mainstream markets on the basis of cost control and quality control.

- **Competition from other nonprofits:** Emergence of university-based centers that offer cutting-edge early childhood teaching methods, research, and training of child care professionals. Tuition is high and access to these centers is limited. These organizations compete for niche market segments on the basis of high product quality and differentiation.

- **Market segmentation and criteria for consumers:** Basis for competition in the child care industry varies according to market segments:

    - Cost control and tuition reduction (for-profit firms have a comparative advantage)

    - Product differentiation and quality (university-based centers have a comparative advantage)

    - Convenience—downtown location dominated by for-profit provider, another for-profit making inroads in the suburbs

    - Perceptions of trust—safety, cleanliness, professionalism.

- **New political realities:** Department of Public Welfare gives consumers a choice, including in-home provider (family members, neighbors) if they meet licensing standards.

Economic Characteristics of the Child Care Industry

- **Revenue structure of the industry:** Average 75% of revenues from fees for service. Higher than most human service organizations.

- **Subsidies and pressure to focus on paying customers:** Public subsidies for needy families do not cover true cost of services. For example, the infant subsidy for needy families in Pennsylvania is approx. $600 per month, but the true cost of infant care ranges from $690 to $828 per month. Thus, agencies need to balance subsidized enrollments with full tuition enrollments to break even.

- **Operational constraints:** 59% of child care personnel earn less than poverty level for a family of four, turnover rate of 25% among skilled professionals

Summary

- Intensely competitive industry
- Boundaries between government, business, and nonprofits rapidly changing
- Pressure on nonprofits to serve primarily paying families, minimize subsidized enrollments
- Narrow margins of "profit" reward efficiency and cost control
- Political forces: Welfare reform, vouchers, subsidy rates below market value.

The author is grateful to Mary Ann Hvizdos, a child care consultant, for providing data for this assessment.

As indicated in Table 3, the child care industry in Pittsburgh (and in many other cities) is turbulent for any nonprofit provider. There are many reasons why Louise Child Care was unable to survive in these new market realities, despite its distinguished track record of accomplishment. First, true to its charitable mission and mandate, the organization continued to enroll a large number of children from needy families, even though state subsidies were not sufficient to cover the true cost of service. Second, when Louise Child Care lost its statewide contract to train child care providers, it had difficulty "divesting" and scaling back its operations to match its reduced revenue streams. It could not easily abandon neighborhoods and families that it was committed to serve. When it finally began closing some of its five neighborhood centers, it lost the confidence of the philanthropic community. Fourth, when university-based programs appeared, Louise Child Care lost its distinctive comparative advantage with the market segment that valued high-quality, professional child care in a research and teaching environment. Thus, the organization became caught between market segments with no distinctive identity, no comparative advantage, and no ability to compete against organizations that had honed their programs and services to appeal to specific populations. Finally, when major foundations in the community saw changes in the market combined with the precarious position of Louise Child Care, they could no longer justify a high-risk investment in the organization. Thus, in June of 2002, Louise Child Care closed its doors forever. This case illustrates that in the new competitive marketplace, the threat of extinction is quite real.

Do Nonprofits Have Any Comparative Advantages?

So far this chapter has presented a sobering, if not pessimistic, assessment of the competitive environment facing nonprofit organizations in the new seamless economy. They face formidable competition from each other as well as from businesses for market share, for resources, for visibility, and for leadership talent. In many arenas they appear to be losing ground in the competitive race. The question is: Do nonprofits still enjoy any comparative advantages in today's competitive environment?

It is difficult to provide a precise answer because, as we have argued, the assessment of comparative advantage must take place on a case-by-case basis, taking into account dynamic industry trends in conjunction with the organization's distinctive characteristics and capabilities. Still, some general propositions or hypotheses might be made, some of which will require further research and testing.

Proposition 1: Nonprofits should be able to exploit comparative advantages in fields where consumers need and demand customized programs and services.

The vast majority of nonprofit organizations are relatively small and community-based. In theory, they should be able to exploit their "local knowledge" to tailor programs and services to meet the needs and demands of consumers. They must, however, master the ability to distinguish between social *needs* and consumer *demands* (see discussion above). Their tradition of innovation and flexibility should give nonprofits a comparative advantage over government agencies and their intimate connection to the communities they serve should provide an edge over many businesses. Just a few examples of industries in which "local knowledge" should provide a comparative advantage include neighborhood development, crime prevention, and youth programs.

Proposition 2: Nonprofits should be able to exploit comparative advantages in emerging industries.

In emerging fields of charitable activity that do not require massive investments of venture capital or research and development, nonprofits should be able to compete head-to-head against for-profit firms. Foundations are often a source of venture capital for nonprofits. Foundations are often able to invest in innovative programming and they are in a position to tolerate risk better than many business investors. Moreover, they do not generally demand partial ownership of intellectual property or other dividends that may result from experimental programs. These factors, in combination with the substantial benefits of tax exemptions, may give nonprofits a reasonable comparative advantage—or at least a level playing field—relative to business in emerging industries such as health promotion and wellness, preventive health care, nutritional education, and organic food development.

Weisbrod (1975) provides historical evidence that voluntary organizations often have been first to meet emerging consumer demand for public goods, such as schools, fire fighting, public parks, canal construction, wharf and harbor construction, libraries, and many other activities that government could not or would not provide early in the product development life cycle. Nonprofits have traditionally excelled in meeting the emerging demands of consumers for goods and services that later in their life cycle are widely acknowledged as public goods, and as such, become the responsibility of the government to provide or at least subsidize.

Proposition 3: Nonprofits might find intriguing opportunities when for-profits abandon industries.

We noted earlier that large firms may abandon declining industries when they can no longer leverage their comparative advantage in mass production and distribution. These declining industries sometimes provide intriguing opportunities for smaller organizations that are willing and able to capture residual markets abandoned by the larger firms. These fields are particularly attractive if the decline is expected to have a reasonably long tail, thereby providing some security that there will be at least niche markets for the programs or services for the foreseeable future. As noted earlier, in some communities the EAP industry displays these characteristics.

Proposition 4: Nonprofits will find comparative advantages in any industry that provides significant rewards for tax exemption and for volunteer labor.

Two very valuable assets that for-profit firms will never be able to match are the various tax exemptions enjoyed by nonprofits and their access to volunteers who provide the equivalent of nearly six million full-time employees nationwide. The general exemptions for corporate income tax and for state sales taxes are valuable assets in any field of endeavor. Exemptions from property taxes are valuable only to nonprofits that own land and facilities, such as YMCAs and universities. Access to volunteer help is more valuable in some industries, such as preventive health care and wellness programs, than in others such as acute health care. The sector, with its historical roots in volunteerism, continues to offer the promise of building *social capital* and *civic engagement* at a time when government has become increasingly removed from the needs of grassroots communities and, indeed, is looking for help from citizens in addressing the needs of our nation.

Proposition 5: Nonprofits will enjoy comparative advantages in industries that require high levels of public trust.

Finally, of course, there is the famous theory of contract failure (Hansmann, 1980), which suggests that nonprofits should have a comparative advantage in any industry where information asymmetries require higher levels of trust between providers and consumers. Nursing homes and other services to the aging or the infirm are frequently used examples in which consumers may not be able to judge if the provider is skimping on quality in order to maximize financial gain. In such circumstances, the removal of the profit motive is expected to give nonprofits an inherent comparative advantage over businesses.

Conclusion: A Values-Based Approach to Comparative Advantage

Lester Salamon (2002b) reminds us that the nonprofit sector has traditionally played unique roles in society and continues to have comparative advantages in its:

- *Service role:* Any field that demands quality services free of the profit motive.

- *Advocacy role:* Identifying unmet social needs and advocating approaches to meet those needs.

- *Expressive role:* Providing a forum for the expression of ideas and impulses, thereby enriching society and enlivening civic discourse.

- *Community-building role:* Building communities through collective action and mediating conflict.

- *Guardian role:* Guarding key cultural and national values and freedoms.

Admittedly, it is not immediately obvious that these are comparative advantages in the types of market engagement we have discussed in this chapter. Yet in today's polarized political and socioeconomic climate, they are assets that the nonprofit sector would be wise to strengthen and leverage against the competitive incursions of for-profit firms. But in order to do so, there must be a collective reaffirmation of the values and ideals upon which the nonprofit sector was built (Rosenman, 1998).

Nonprofit leaders cannot allow the focus on consumerism and commercialization to distract them from their core missions and values. Similarly, nonprofits cannot allow the trend toward professionalization of the sector lock out the important role of volunteers and grassroots engagement. Nonprofits are not in business to make money or even to sustain themselves indefinitely, but to identify and meet needs in their community and the world. Certainly, the nonprofit sector has much to learn from business in areas like market analysis, comparative advantage, and investing in research and development. But management tools developed for use in the private sector cannot be simply transplanted to the nonprofit sector without substantial modification (Ring and Perry, 1985; Oster, 1995; Kearns, 2000).

In the for-profit sector the motive for competition is always survival and growth of the organization to the benefit of employees and owners. Customer satisfaction and meeting community needs are means to that end, not ends in themselves. In the nonprofit sector, the motivation to compete must be just the opposite. The first objective must be to enhance services to the community, to fill gaps not adequately or appropriately addressed by either business or government. If that community objective is best achieved through the nonprofit's survival and growth, then competition is fully justifiable and any competitive edge that the nonprofit can exploit is legitimate.

After considering all of the issues and analytical techniques outlined in this chapter, the decision by a nonprofit organization to compete or not to compete must give primary consideration to whatever decision is in the best long-term interests of the community and its citizens who, in the final analysis, are the only legitimate "shareholders" of any nonprofit corporation.

References

Allison, M. 2002. "Into the Fire: Boards and Executive Transitions," *Nonprofit Management and Leadership,* Summer, 12 (2), pp. 341–351

Bielefeld, W. 1994. "What Affects Nonprofit Survival?" *Nonprofit Management and Leadership,* Fall, 5 (1), pp. 19–36.

Brilliant, Eleanor, and Dennis. R. Young. 2004. "The Changing Identity of Federated Community Service Organizations," *Administration in Social Work,* 28 (3), pp. 23–46.

Catalyst. 2001. *The Next Generation: Today's Professionals, Tomorrow's Leaders,* New York: Catalyst, Inc. (www.catalystwomen.org)

Dart, R. 2004. "The Legitimacy of Social Enterprise," *Nonprofit Management and Leadership,* Summer, 14 (4), pp. 411–424.

Dees, Gregory; Jed Emerson, and Peter Economy. 2001. *Enterprising Nonprofit: A Toolkit for Social Entrepreneurs.* New York: John Wiley and Sons.

Firstenberg, Paul B. 1996. *The Twenty-First Century Nonprofit: Remaking the Organization in the Post-Government Era.* New York: The Foundation Center.

The Forbes Funds. 2004. *Look Here! Attracting and Developing the Next Generation of Nonprofit Leaders.* Pittsburgh, PA: The Forbes Funds.

Galaskiewicz, J., and W. Bielefeld. 1990. "Growth, Decline, and Organizational Strategies: A Panel Study of Nonprofit Organizations 1980—1988." in *The Nonprofit Sector (NGOs) in the United States and Abroad: Cross-Cultural Perspectives.* Washington, DC: Independent Sector.

Gill, Brian; Jacob Dembosky, and Jonathon Caulkins. 2002. *A Noble Bet in Early Care and Education: Lessons from One Community.* Santa Monica: RAND Corporation.

Gronbjerg, K., and L. M. Salamon. 2002. "Devolution, Marketization, and the Changing Shape of Government-Nonprofit Relations." In Salamon, L. M. (ed.), *The State of Nonprofit America.* Washington, DC: Brookings Institution Press.

Gruber, R. E., and M. Mohr. 1982. "Strategic Management for Multipurpose Nonprofit Organizations." *California Management Review,* 24 (3), pp. 15–22.

Handy, F., and N. Srinivasan. 2004. "Valuing Volunteers: An Economic Evaluation of the Net Benefits of Hospital Volunteers." *Nonprofit and Voluntary Sector Quarterly,* March, 33 (1), pp. 28–54.

Hansen, S.; L. Huggins, and C. Ban. 2003. *Explaining Employee Recruitment and Retention.* Pittsburgh, PA: The Forbes Funds, 2003.

Hansmann, H. 1980. "The Role of Nonprofit Enterprise," *Yale Law Journal,* 89 (5), pp. 835–901.

Hasenfeld, Y. 1996. "The Administration of Human Services—What Lies Ahead?" In P. R. Raffoul and C. A. McNeece (eds.), *Future Issues for Social Work Practice.* Boston: Allyn and Bacon.

Hedley, B. 1977. "Strategy and the Business Portfolio." *Long Range Planning,* 10 (1), pp. 9–15.

Hofer, C. W. 1975. "Toward a Contingency Theory of Business Strategy." *Academy of Management Journal* 18 (4), pp. 785–810.

Hodgkinson, Virginia A.; Kathryn E. Nelson, and Edward D. Sivak, Jr. 2002. "Individual Giving and Volunteering." Chapter 12 in Lester M. Salamon (ed.), *The State of Nonprofit America.* Washington, DC: The Brookings Institution Press.

Kearns, K. P. 1992. "From Comparative Advantage to Damage Control: Clarifying Strategic Issues Using SWOT Analysis." *Nonprofit Management and Leadership,* 3 (1), pp. 3–25.

Kearns, K. P. 2000. *Private Sector Strategies for Social Sector Success.* San Francisco: Jossey-Bass.

Kearns, K. P. 2004. "Management Capacity Building in the Pittsburgh Region," *Nonprofit Management and Leadership,* Summer, 14 (4), pp. 437–452.

Kerkman, L., and Lewis, N. 2004. "Donor Funds Are On The Rise Again," *Chronicle of Philanthropy,* May 27, pp. 21–24.

Letts, C.; W. Ryan, and A. Grossman. 1997. "Virtuous Capital: What Foundations Can Learn from Venture Capitalists." *Harvard Business Review,* March–April, pp. 36–44.

Light, P. 2000. *Making Nonprofits Work: A Report on the Tides of Nonprofit Management Reform.* Washington, DC: Brookings Institution Press.

Light, P. 2002. *Pathways to Nonprofit Excellence,* Washington, DC: Brookings Institution Press.

Lipsky, M., and S. Smith. 1993. *Nonprofits for Hire: The Welfare State in the Age of Contracting.* Cambridge: Harvard University Press.

Lune, H. 2002. "Weathering the Storm: Nonprofit Survival Strategies in a Hostile Environment," *Nonprofit and Voluntary Sector Quarterly,* December, 31 (4), pp. 463–483.

MacMillan, I. C. 1983. "Competitive Strategies for Not-for-Profit Organizations." *Advances in Strategic Management,* Vol 1. Tucson, AZ: JAI Press.

Mirabella, R., and N. Wish. 1999. "Perceived Educational Impact of Graduate Nonprofit Degree Programs," *Nonprofit Management and Leadership,* Spring, 9 (3).

Mirabella, R., and N. Wish. 2000. "The 'Best Place' Debate: A Comparison of Graduate Education Programs for Nonprofit Managers," *Public Administration Review,* May/June, 60 (3).

O'Connell, B. 1996. "A Major Transfer of Government Responsibility to Voluntary Organizations? Proceed with Caution." *Public Administration Review,* 56 (3), pp. 222–225.

Oster, S. 1995. *Strategic Management for Nonprofit Organizations.* New York: Oxford University Press.

Pitt-Catsouphes, M.; M. Swanberg, J. Bond, and E. Galinsky. 2004. "Worklife Policies and Programs: Comparing the Responsiveness of Nonprofit and For-Program Organizations," *Nonprofit Management and Leadership,* Spring, 14 (3), pp. 291–312.

Porter, M. E. 1980. *Competitive Strategy.* New York: The Free Press.

Porter, M. E. 1985. *Competitive Advantage: Creating and Sustaining Superior Performance.* New York: The Free Press.

Porter, M. E. 1990. *The Competitive Advantage of Nations.* New York: The Free Press.

Ring, P. S., and J. L. Perry. 1985. "Strategic Management in Public and Private Organizations: Implications of Distinctive Contexts and Constraints." *Academy of Management Review,* 10 (2), pp. 276–286.

Roller, R. H. 1996. "Strategy Formulation in Nonprofit Social Services Organizations: A Proposed Framework." *Nonprofit Management and Leadership,* 7 (2), pp. 137–153.

Rosenman, M. 1998. *Nonprofit Sector Issues.* Washington, DC: The Union Institute, April.

Ryan, W. P. 1999. "The New Landscape for Nonprofits." *Harvard Business Review,* January–February, pp. 127–136.

Salamon, L. M. (ed.). 2002a. *The State of Nonprofit America,* Washington, DC: Brookings Institution Press.

Salamon, L. M. 2002b. "The Resilient Sector." In Salamon, L. M. (ed.), *The State of Nonprofit America,* Washington, DC: Brookings Institution Press.

Snowbeck, Christopher. 2004. "Transplant Chief Fung Discusses His Reasons for Leaving UPMC." *Pittsburgh Post-Gazette,* July 8, vol. 77, no. 343, pp. 1, 3.

Spice, Byron. 2004. "UPMC Official Defends Bottom Line Focus." *Pittsburgh Post-Gazette,* July 9, vol. 77, no. 344, pp. 1, 7.

Te'eni, D., and D. Young. 2003. "The Changing Role of Nonprofits in the Network Economy." *Nonprofit and Voluntary Sector Quarterly,* September, 32 (3), pp. 397–414.

Thompson, Arthur A., and A. J. Strickland. 1992. *Strategic Management: Concepts and Cases.* Boston: Irwin.

Weisbrod, B. 1975. "Toward a Theory of the Voluntary Nonprofit Sector in a Three-Sector Economy." In Edmund S. Phelps (ed.) *Altruism, Morality, and Economic Theory,* New York: Sage.

14

Issues for Research

Dennis R. Young
Bernard B. and Eugenia A. Ramsey Professor of Private Enterprise
Andrew Young School of Policy Studies
Georgia State University
Atlanta, GA

Introduction

The theme running throughout this book is that contemporary nonprofit organizations in the United States exist in a rapidly shifting and uncertain environment, and if they are to remain viable and effective, they must learn to cope in a more sophisticated manner with risk and change. The authors have drawn on a broad spectrum of theory, research, and practical experience to delineate the issues associated with this dynamic context, and they have suggested important ways to think about and address the resulting challenges. In the process, tentative recommendations and solutions have been offered, including some tested in practice by experienced practitioner-authors or collaborators. However, all would readily admit that our knowledge of this field is tentative and incomplete. Indeed, the chapters of this book are laced, implicitly and explicitly, with elements of a robust research agenda for the future—one that can inform practice as it advances theory and can expand the knowledge base on which future nonprofit decision-makers will rely. The purpose of this chapter is to suggest how this research agenda could be structured and what some of the specific research questions can be. The emphasis is explicitly on "applied research" of direct relevance to future practice, although academic researchers will hopefully find plenty of red meat to whet their appetites for theoretical and empirical research of a more general nature as well.

The discussion is divided into six categories which are intended to capture what needs to be better understood in order to improve the ability of nonprofits to cope effectively with the rapidly changing and uncertain world which they inhabit. While there are substantial interfaces among these categories, they form somewhat of a logical progression: First, what exactly is the nature of the changing environment? What are the trends and the risks that are fundamentally important? Second, what is it about nonprofit organizations that limits their ability to cope with such an environment in the most productive ways? What cultural, value-based, structural, or procedural issues need to be examined and addressed? Third, what kinds of analytical and informational tools do nonprofits need to better understand and deal with the challenges posed by an uncertain and dynamic environment? Fourth, how can nonprofits obtain the resources they need to adapt to change, manage risk, and best support their missions over time? How can they make better use of the resources they have? Fifth, how can nonprofits best position themselves in the emerging economic and political landscapes? What should be the nature of their future relationships with government and business and what will be their comparative advantages vis-à-vis these potential competitors and collaborators? Finally, how can nonprofits manage and manipulate their environments to make them less unstable and more predictable? What sorts of cooperative arrangements and political activity might facilitate such aspirations?

The Nature of Change and Uncertainty

Various chapters in this book document trends in the nonprofit environment, relative to such issues as the sources of financial resources and volunteer support, competition and collaboration with the business sector, developments in philanthropy and public policy, and in management practices. These trend analyses, while based on the most recent data and available reports, paint only a broad and misty picture of the nonprofit environment, and fail to pinpoint information that would be most relevant to nonprofits in particular situations. For example, behind aggregate economic trends for the nonprofit sector as a whole—or even broad subsectors such as health, the arts, or education—lies substantial variation, associated with industries within subsectors (for example, home health care within the health care sector, or theaters within the performing arts), and by geography (e.g., regions, states, and localities). Such variation suggests two lines of important future research. Obviously trends need to be discerned for smaller aggregates of interest to nonprofit decision-makers working within their local contexts. More than this, some sense of the overall variations around aggregate trends needs to be developed. If, for example, there is increasing dependence on commercial sources of revenue in the nonprofit sector and in broad subsectors therein, to what degree is this trend homogeneous? Is there large variation around this trend, and if so, where are the largest variances? By locality? By size of organization? By field of service? To be relevant to nonprofit decision-makers, the latter must know not only if the trend applies to their particular context, but also the likelihood that it applies to them within that context. The pioneers in documenting nonprofit sector data and broad patterns and trends, such as Virginia Hodgkinson, Murray Weitzman, Elizabeth Boris, and Lester Salamon, have done a monumental job over the past twenty-five years to bring us to our current state of knowledge of how the nonprofit sector is evolving and how its environment is changing. Future researchers will have to build on this foundation to obtain a more finely grained picture.

Which brings us to the question of risk. Scanlan and Dillon-Merrill argue in Chapter 4 that nonprofit decision-makers often poorly perceive the actual risks that they face. Hence, they tend to make inordinately conservative, necessarily inefficient decisions. This view is implicitly supported by Levy in Chapter 2, who argues for nonprofits to take a more entrepreneurial approach, involving greater risk-taking. Levy and Scanlan are seasoned practitioners who should know. But part of the problem is informational. If the variations in environmental trends are undocumented or poorly articulated, nonprofit decision-makers will not be able to fully appreciate the risks they actually face. Ignorance can breed timidity (or recklessness). Hence research on variation as well as average and aggregate trends seems important as a prerequisite to more sophisticated decision-making in the face of uncertainty.

A further informational issue affecting risk concerns the possibilities for catastrophic change. Such change by definition breaks with existing trends and falls outside observed ranges of historical variation. But catastrophic change happens, perhaps all too frequently. Recent experiences with the September 11th attacks, the tsunami of 2004, and the Gulf Coast hurricanes of 2005 bear grim witness to this fact. Sharp changes in the economy or sudden shifts in political administrations can deliver similar shocks. How can nonprofits better assess these kinds of risks in order to prepare for them in some way? This too seems an appropriate area for research. Clearly the insurance industry deals with questions of this sort all the time. We don't know when or where catastrophic changes will occur but we do know they will happen. Having a sense of what their nature and magnitude could be would be helpful information to nonprofits in developing protective strategies and arrangements. For example, understanding the ripple effects of a calamitous event in one part of the nonprofit sector on another would have been helpful in coping with the aftermath of 9/11. Few understood the shifts that could take place in displacing philanthropy from one subsector to another, or how such an attack could echo through the economy in other ways that created additional demands and resource problems for nonprofits. As Zietlow suggests in Chapter 6, some of these new demands can be quite surprising, such as the difficulties associated with investment or expenditure of windfall donations.

The foregoing brings to mind one additional focus for future research. In portfolio theory, financial analysts distinguish between *systematic* and *unsystematic* risk. Roughly speaking, the former is variation that is correlated across all relevant categories, whereas the latter is uncorrelated variation. The significance of this distinction is that decision-makers can use diversification strategies to address the latter but not the former. Thus, for instance, in the nonprofit sector it would be useful to know how variations in donated revenues are correlated with revenues from fees for services over time, so that decision-makers can design their revenue strategies to cope with overall financial risk. Research that would clarify such correlations therefore could be immensely useful.

Finally, the case for studying variations in aggregate trends and developing a better understanding of catastrophic changes does not reduce the importance of further analyzing the implications of known trends. This too needs to be a priority for research if nonprofits are to cope well with these trends. Several authors here have made reference to large intergenerational transfers of wealth in coming years, but we do not yet understand how this is likely to affect nonprofits in different fields and circumstances. Authors here have also cited other known trends such as the increasing inequality in the distribution of wealth in the U.S., the changing demographic profiles in the workforce and in the population at large, rapidly evolving information technologies, continued devolution of government financing through demand-side subsidies, and accumulating government deficits that are likely to constrain discretionary spending or precipitate further changes in the tax structure. All these developments can have serious implications for nonprofit decision-makers. The more that research can provide an understanding of the implications of these developments on nonprofit organizations in different circumstances, the better these decision-makers will be able to make efficient, well-informed choices.

The Internal Workings of Nonprofit Organizations

In order for nonprofit organizations to take advantage of better information and research about the nature of change and uncertainty in their environments, they need to be inclined to do so. Several authors have suggested that this will require changes in organizational culture, structure, and focus. Levy, for example, calls for a stronger entrepreneurial bent in considering new ventures in the marketplace and in charitable fundraising. Reid suggests the same for seeking change in the policy arena, while Smith calls for entrepreneurial leadership in forging collaborative arrangements, overcoming more provincial tendencies that inhibit collective action among nonprofits. Scanlan and Dillon-Merrill argue for a diminishing of risk avoidance behavior overall, while Mesch and McClelland, as well as Levy, suggest that nonprofit decision-makers need to become more focused on outcome and performance measurement and remain vigilant about potential compromises between output focus and important organizational values such as hard-to-measure aspects of mission achievement. Mesch and McClelland also emphasize the need to connect organizational reward systems to performance and to adopt the principles of a "learning organization," so that nonprofits can continuously adapt to change.

One part of a future research agenda can be to verify and refine some of the premises on which these recommendations are based. To what degree are nonprofit decision-makers excessively risk averse and in what circumstances? To what extent is risk averseness built into the cultures of nonprofit organizations? And to what extent has risk averseness limited the effectiveness of nonprofit organizations and their ability to adapt to change?

Overall, prescriptions for internal change require a richer knowledge base to guide transformations that will render nonprofit organizations more sympathetic and capable of constructive change. A number of research themes emerge from this agenda. Studies of the labor market and nonprofit human resources policies are needed to determine how entrepreneurial leaders can be attracted to nonprofit work in larger numbers. Studies of nonprofit governance can ask what changes need to be made in order for boards to encourage entrepreneurial behavior in their organizations, and be willing to take greater risks themselves. Case studies of organizational decision-making can discern where performance orientation and reward systems, and entrepreneurial mind-sets, bump up against difficult value questions in the nonprofit context. And studies of nonprofit organizations that have implemented performance measurement systems can determine how these systems help to change the organizational culture and support a more entrepreneurial orientation. Finally, research can inquire into what particular circumstances performance measurement and reward systems threaten to compromise the integrity of a nonprofit organization and therefore dampen an organization's inclination to adopt them.

In summary, we still have much to learn about how nonprofit organizations work in circumstances requiring change: how they handle the tensions between implementing systems to help them adapt and change and how they maintain their core organizational values; how they succumb to the inertia of tradition and bureaucratic thinking, and how they embrace renewal as a means to better address their missions; how they manage the sometimes conflicting interests and propensities of manifold and diverse stakeholder groups, and how they forge fresh relationships to enable movement in new directions.

Analytical and Informational Tools and Methods

Even if the nature of environmental change and uncertainty are better understood and nonprofit organizations become more adaptive and willing to be prudent risk-takers, these organizations will still need information, usefully framed, in order to act effectively. Authors here have considered several different parts of this informational elephant. Mesch and McClelland, in Chapter 3, have focused on outcome and performance measurement systems that would produce the feedback that nonprofits need to determine if they are achieving their goals and what kinds of adjustments they need to make in order to maintain performance in a dynamic environment. Scanlan and Dillon-Merrill, in Chapter 4, offer a methodology for making decisions under risk, using decision trees to determine efficient choices once risks and potential outcomes are assessed. Zietlow, in Chapter 6, describes the model of prudent investing that requires nonprofits to maximize their returns within a carefully established policy of risk tolerance.

In all these cases it is clear that research can contribute to customizing these methodologies so that they are comfortably and effectively used in nonprofit practice, and so that they do not compromise a nonprofit organization's mission or values. For example, how are constructs such as Return on Investment (ROI) or the Balanced Scorecard, drawn from the business sector, best adapted to nonprofits, so that tangible as well as intangible benefits and costs are accounted for? Or, how can cost-benefit analysis, drawn from the public sector, be adapted to account for the particular social benefits and costs associated with the mission of a given nonprofit organization? How can any of these methods be suitably simplified and based on readily available data so that busy nonprofit decision-makers can use them productively, without excessive burdens of time and money?

At a more detailed and technical level, several useful methodological research questions have been suggested in these chapters. For example, what measures best capture the somewhat murky notions of financial health and vulnerability of a nonprofit organization? What kinds of output and outcome measures best capture the performance of nonprofits with different kinds of functions, for example advocacy vs. service delivery vs. financial intermediaries vs. umbrella organizations?

How are different kinds of nonprofit organizations properly benchmarked against one another for particular types of performance measurement? And how can so-called "logic models" best be used to connect an organization's mission, strategies, goals, inputs, and outputs with its short- and long-term outcomes, so that a variety of intermediary measures can contribute to performance assessment and evaluation?

Another important research agenda entails the relationships between performance measurement systems and the character and functioning of the nonprofit organization itself. For example, how can systems of performance measurement support a culture of entrepreneurship within a nonprofit organization? In particular, how can performance management systems encourage prudent risk-taking and embracing of change? How can performance management and outcome orientation become an integral part of a nonprofit organization's culture as a "learning organization"?

It is important, of course, to study how performance measurement systems are actually used and what problems they entail. For instance, how do performance management systems in practice sometimes discourage risk-taking and entrepreneurial behavior? In what ways can outcome measurement systems distort the allocation of resources, and indeed the overall functioning, of a nonprofit organization (for example, by giving implicit priority to measurable objectives) and how can such pitfalls be avoided? Where do ethical questions arise in the design and response to performance measures, and how can such questions be addressed? For example, how can nonprofit performance systems be designed to avoid manipulation, intended to put the best face on performance rather than produce honest assessments? How can an organization's core values be emphasized through various managerial initiatives so as to minimize ethical compromise? What are the roles and responsibilities of the board and top management in developing and implementing a successful performance measurement system? How can the interests of various other stakeholder groups, including external constituencies, be integrated into performance measurement systems so that they are appropriately accounted for in decision-making?

It is not as if there is a complete vacuum of knowledge on these various fronts; indeed, it would take a substantial search of the literature to appropriately acknowledge all the important contributions to these sets of questions. It is fair to say, however, that the relevant research landscape is fairly sparse, and that much remains to be done to customize and evaluate these methodologies and measurement approaches with the particular needs of practicing nonprofit decision-makers in mind.

Resource Mobilization and Capital Formation

Responding to change and uncertainty is never cheap. It takes resources to develop and support information systems that gather and analyze the necessary information; it requires investment capital to undertake new initiatives; and of course it requires resources to make adjustments in organizations so that they are suitably adapted to their changing environments over time. In one way or another, most chapters here have dealt with resource issues associated with nonprofits' adaptation to, and management of, change. For example, in Chapter 2, Levy points to the marketplace and to the pending intergenerational transfers of wealth as potential sources of additional resources for nonprofit development and sustenance in the future. In Chapter 3, Mesch and McClelland allude to the resources necessary to develop and implement new systems of performance assessment. In Chapter 5, Lane addresses the strategies that nonprofits need to consider when resources are inadequate to support current operations and changes must be implemented to ensure future viability. In Chapter 6, Zietlow considers how efficient investment management can enhance and sustain a nonprofit organization's financial resources. In Chapter 7, Smith considers alternative strategies for funding nonprofit collaborations in order to maintain the viability and efficiency of these arrangements. In Chapter 8, Reid discusses the tensions between advocacy work and the ability to raise charitable funds. Similarly, in Chapter 11, Louie and Brooks examine the interactions between a nonprofit's investment in a corporate partnership and its stream of charitable contributions. In Chapter 12, Brudney implies that investment in intermediary institutions may be a good way to attract and ensure efficient use of pro bono volunteers. In Chapter 13, Kearns considers how nonprofits must sometimes compete for capital with profit-making businesses in newly emerging areas of competition, and how this affects their competitive advantage in various markets. Chapters 9 and 10 by Ferris and Cantori, respectively, are about foundations as social investors, and various tools, frameworks, and strategies that can help foundations make effective social investments in their nonprofit grantees.

In other words, issues of resource development and utilization pervade the consideration of nonprofit organizations' successful adaptation to uncertainty and change, suggesting a rich research agenda addressed to helping nonprofit organizations cope more effectively with resource-related concerns. One set of questions has to do with where future resources for nonprofit development will come from. For example, does the anticipated massive intergenerational transfer of wealth suggest that nonprofits should put even more emphasis on planned giving and the building of endowments, even as charitable contributions continue to diminish as a proportion of overall nonprofit support? Alternatively, what is the ultimate potential for earned income, the current growth area? Similarly, what are the long-term prospects for government funding, which in recent years has been the major driver of nonprofit growth in several important areas of nonprofit activity? Are advocacy and collective action strategies by nonprofit organizations, aimed at increasing government support, likely to be effective or should nonprofits continue to turn elsewhere for their sustenance?

Another set of research questions has to do with the policies, strategies, and methods through which resources are developed and allocated within the nonprofit sector. For example, if earned income is to continue as a major resource alternative, what particular pricing and marketing strategies are likely to permit its exploitation without compromising nonprofit missions and values? How are collaborative arrangements among nonprofits best funded, e.g., with large front-end investments or through gradual development of funding streams over time? How should the costs and benefits of collaborations be shared to ensure success of these efforts?

In the realm of government funding, how can nonprofits use the Internet and other avenues of advocacy to build political support for the programs that fund their work? What balance of advocacy and partnership will be most successful in eliciting government funds over time? In the realm of business, how can nonprofits use their market power to leverage greater support from corporations? How does this strategy relate to the notion of working collaboratively with these corporations? And in the area of charitable contributions, how can the "capital market" for nonprofits be made more efficient through systems of information-sharing and better mechanisms to match donor preferences with the needs of nonprofit organizations? And what kinds of tax and regulatory policies are likely to increase, or discourage, charitable giving, volunteering, and the formation of charitable foundations?

A host of research issues arise in the area of foundation funding, especially if foundations continue to gravitate towards the view that they should assume as their primary role the provision of investment capital for the sector. First, to what extent should foundations focus their efforts on nonprofit capacity-building, support of particular programs and projects, investment in sector-level infrastructure, or helping nonprofits engage in the public policy process? Which of these kinds of investments promises the greatest social return and the greatest potential for nonprofit viability and effectiveness over time? For example, would it be more productive to focus on efforts to increase tax incentives for charitable giving than to directly support nonprofit investment projects?

Foundations face other fundamental choices as well. Indeed, to what extent should foundations be exclusively focused on investment compared to funding current needs and shortfalls? Are there differences among types of foundations in terms of these priorities? For example, are community foundations more obligated to help cherished local institutions get through short-term crises than are private foundations? Similarly, foundations must carefully examine their investment and payout policies so that these parameters are selected to best address their social missions, time horizons, and goals of helping operating nonprofit organizations. More generally, as Cantori indicates in Chapter 10, foundations have a wide array of choices in allocating their funds, ranging from grants to loans to "program-related investments." What then is the appropriate use of each tool in maximizing the effectiveness of a foundation's social investment, considering the costs and benefits of each approach? The issue of collaboration among foundations also arises in this context. How can foundations effectively cooperate with one another, in the process of investing their funds, in coordinating the grant applications process, in combining grantmaking resources through collaborative projects, and in other ways?

Finally, resource-related research issues arise in the context of the business cycle. As Ferris points out in Chapter 9, foundations are generally not well positioned to help nonprofit organizations with their fiscal challenges when the economy slows, because their own assets and in-flows of contributions are likely to decline at the same time. Moreover, foundation funding represents only a small fraction of overall nonprofit revenue. However, one may ask whether a restructuring of foundation policies might help selectively in this domain. For example, could foundations be of greater countercyclical assistance if they disciplined themselves, or if they were guided by law, to restrict their spending during prosperous times so that more was available during periods of recession? Certainly there have been outcries from critics during recent crises and recessionary periods that foundations should "do more," including increasing their payout rates. But the implications of such recommendations have never been carefully studied.

Business-cycle issues arise in other areas of nonprofit resource management as well. For example, Brudney points out in Chapter 12 that the availability of pro bono resources rises and falls with the economy, providing a helpful boost to nonprofits in slow times. Is pro bono volunteering unique in these countercyclical benefits or are there other such sources to which nonprofits can turn in times of economic slowdown? Government used to be an obvious answer, but in this post-Keynesian world that seems no longer to be the case. A reexamination of countercyclical resource mobilization would thus seem to be another productive avenue for future research.

Positioning

A good portion of success in coping with change is being in the right place at the right time. Some authors, including Levy in Chapter 2 and Kearns in Chapter 13, suggest that nonprofits must continue to assess their competitive positions, particularly as the economy changes over time. Others, including Smith in Chapter 7, Reid in Chapter 8, and Louie and Brooks in Chapter 11, ask how nonprofits can position themselves in the context of various coalitions and collaborations with government, business, and other nonprofits, so as to enhance their stability and maximize their options for resource support and social impact.

The very juxtaposition of competition and collaboration begs a basic research issue—how can nonprofit organizations balance these divergent propensities? Is a competitive strategic orientation and an entrepreneurial culture necessarily at odds with a collaborative mentality or can the two be made compatible? What combinations of competition and collaboration allow nonprofits to be most successful in managing risk and adapting to change?

Within this mixed context of collaboration and competition, a number of puzzles arise that might be informed by research. For example, Levy suggests that nonprofits should ask how for-profits succeed in some of the very same markets in which nonprofits require subsidy. No doubt, research could uncover some secrets that might allow nonprofits to exploit some of the techniques that for-profits use to develop earned income streams. A fuller research agenda, however, would also ask what nonprofits must necessarily do differently in order to justify their market share in a "mixed industry." This closer examination is likely to show that nonprofit missions require different pricing and marketing policies that may preclude profitability and which justify subsidy from alternative sources. In any case, given that nonprofits and for-profits continue to make inroads into each others' traditional market territories, research that illuminates these basic questions is likely to provide helpful information for nonprofits seeking to adjust their competitive positions over time.

It is interesting that one mode of protection against competitive pressures is the development of collaborative arrangements. One obvious strategy is the forming of larger, more stable nonprofit entities (through federation or merger, for example) that can mute competition, reduce costs, and command greater market power. However, as authors here have noted, collaborations can help nonprofits deal with uncertainty and change in other ways as well. Nonprofit collaborative arrangements can facilitate risk-sharing, including catastrophic risk that may randomly strike some members of a collaborative effort but not others.

Collaborative arrangements among nonprofits can also provide information services and facilitate organizational learning in a more effective way than most individual organizations can support. And, as discussed below, collaborative efforts can help to stabilize the economic environment of nonprofits by offering greater collective bargaining power with suppliers of input resources, a stronger political voice to influence expenditure, tax, and other government policies, or more reliable support from business or government partners.

Collaborations, as they relate to improving nonprofits' abilities to manage risk and cope with change, point to a substantial underlying research agenda for gaining greater understanding about how these arrangements can be made to work effectively. For example, how can trust among collaborative partners be built up over time so that collaborations remain viable during times of stress? What is the role of entrepreneurial leadership at different stages in the development of collaborative efforts? How can leadership help overcome the parochial interests of prospective partners and facilitate support of collective efforts? How do successful collaborations take account of changes in the character and interests of partner organizations over time? (Indeed, collaborations are themselves dynamic and may constitute part of the turbulent environment with which nonprofits must cope.) What kinds of governance arrangements and sharing of leadership responsibilities help ensure adaptation and growth of collaborative arrangements over time and in changing circumstances? What resource development and sharing policies are most effective in maintaining the viability of collaborations? For example, do successful collaborations require up-front investments by internal or external parties, or can resource commitments be built over time? How can measurement and evaluation practices help keep collaborations together and maintain the commitments of their members? And most importantly from the viewpoint of an individual nonprofit organization, how can the worthiness of a potential or ongoing collaboration best be assessed so as to guide decisions about new or continued membership? In particular, how can the transaction costs associated with collaboration be appropriately weighed against the prospective collective and agency-specific benefits produced by the collaboration?

In sum, productive research would address three challenges facing nonprofit organizations seeking to position themselves effectively within their competitive environments and networks of potential collaborative partners. First, how can one define and design a maximally viable competitive position within a chosen field of service? Second, what collaborative arrangements should one join, and under what terms, in order to protect and enhance that competitive position? And third, how can those collaborative arrangements be made most effective in dealing with risk and change over time? While there is much written on these various issues, the general literature only scratches the surface in terms of the specific challenges nonprofits face in positioning themselves effectively in their particular complex, uncertain, and dynamic world of interlaced competition and collaboration.

Managing the Environment

Individual nonprofit organizations can do just so much to improve their decision-making and management capacities in order to deal more effectively with the uncertainties and dynamics of their circumstances. Gaining a greater understanding of the nature of the risks they face, aligning their internal structures and cultures to deal forthrightly with those risks, providing themselves with sophisticated analytical and informational tools to analyze those risks and devise appropriate courses of action, mobilizing resources to support those strategies, and positioning themselves carefully in the fields and networks relevant to their work, are all ways for nonprofits to react smartly to the challenges they face in an uncontrollable environment. That environment will always be substantially uncontrollable. However, the authors here point to a number of ways in which nonprofits can partially ameliorate their uncertainties and impose some limited control over their economic and political settings. For example, in Chapter 6, Zietlow suggests that certain financial management strategies, including revenue diversification and the building of endowments, can insulate nonprofits to some extent from the vicissitudes of their economic environments.

And as considered above, collaborations can play a big role in reducing environmental uncertainty. In Chapter 7, for example, Smith hints that collaborative efforts among nonprofits can provide greater stability through risk-sharing and mutual support. In Chapter 8, Reid implies that through effective advocacy, nonprofits can influence the environment of public funding, perhaps achieving more reliable flows of governmental resources over time. Such advocacy, Reid suggests, can take place at various levels—through the efforts of individual advocacy-oriented nonprofit organizations, through the support of advocacy efforts by grantmaking foundations, and through the collective efforts of nonprofits acting through their associations and coalitions.

In Chapter 9, Ferris indicates that foundations could potentially have multiple stabilizing influences on the nonprofit environment, including support of public policy advocacy efforts, support of the collective organizational infrastructure of various parts of the nonprofit sector, and by improving the efficiency of the capital markets through which nonprofits obtain their philanthropic contributions. While Ferris minimizes the potential for foundations to actually serve in a countercyclical capacity to offset business-cycle-related shortfalls, this too may be a minor contribution of some foundations. Further, in Chapter 10, Cantori argues that foundations can readily offer nonprofits a wider variety of financial and other kinds of support, thus increasing the chances that any given nonprofit under stress could be helped through a crisis by some means of foundation assistance.

In Chapter 11, Louie and Brooks also point to ways in which collaborations with business corporations can help stabilize the nonprofit environment, by cultivating long-term business partnerships strong enough to weather short-term dislocations in the economy. As noted earlier, in Chapter 12, Brudney offers pro bono volunteering as an example of a resource that can indeed be a stabilizing influence on the downside of the business cycle. Moreover he argues that ways can be found to make the market for pro bono services more efficient so that a distressed nonprofit is more likely to find what it needs in a timely fashion. Finally, in Chapter 13, Kearns suggests that by "going to scale" some nonprofits may achieve greater stability through economies of scale and market power that would allow them to build up greater internal reserves. Further, Kearns suggests the intriguing (countercyclical) possibility that by studying the life cycle of service industries, nonprofits can potentially seize opportunities where for-profit business interest is declining yet social needs merit, and could lead to support for, nonprofit expansion.

These various approaches to stabilizing the nonprofit environment also imply a rich and potentially productive research agenda. For example, how can nonprofit organizations successfully diversify their revenue streams, especially where funding in particular fields of service tend to come from a few particular sources? And in what circumstances is it sensible for nonprofits to undertake the building of endowments as a risk management strategy, relative to other uses of contributed or earned funds? How can these endowments themselves be made more stable in circumstances where donor constraints preclude portfolio diversification?

Another set of questions would address what particular insurance or other approaches associations or other nonprofit collaborations can take to providing economic stability for their members. What should federations and nonprofit professional or industry associations be doing along these lines? What are the potential disadvantages of insurance-like approaches, for example, disincentives that might reward poor performance (what economists call "moral hazard")? What other initiatives can nonprofit collaborations and coalitions take to stabilize the nonprofit environment, e.g. , through information-sharing, policy advocacy, educational services, reduction of competition, or sharing of resources to exploit economies of scale and scope? How do these approaches work in practice and how effective can they be? For example, does political advocacy by federations or coalitions invite retribution by government or create divisiveness among members? How can foundations support advocacy without inviting greater government scrutiny?

In terms of the business cycle, research can hopefully illuminate the ways in which some foundation efforts, as well as pro bono volunteer services, can be focused and leveraged for maximum impact in relieving stress on nonprofit organizations in a slowing economy. For example, how would a more efficient market in matching pro bono volunteers to nonprofit organizations actually work? And how can foundations differentiate the impacts of their various assistance tools so that there is better understanding of which approaches can best help relieve nonprofits' stress in a poor economy?

In the realm of business–nonprofit relations, an interesting research agenda arises from the notion that greater stability can be achieved through deeper nonprofit–corporate partnerships that can build trust and integration of mutual interests over time. This idea is somewhat at odds with the conventional paradigm of risk management based on diversification. Hence a worthy line of inquiry would investigate how nonprofits can best design their collaborative business strategies to achieve suitable combinations of stability and benefit. To what degree should nonprofits attempt to diversify their partnerships with corporations versus focusing on building stronger relationships with a few selected partners? To date, the literature is based on relatively few case studies, but more systematic analysis of this issue seems worthwhile.

Finally, a rich research agenda would seem to emerge from issues surrounding the life cycle development of nonprofit organizations and the industries in which they are embedded. On the surface, such study would seem to abstract from the surrounding turbulence in which nonprofit organizations operate, by presupposing that nonprofit organizations and industries go though generic stages of development regardless of what is going on around them. In actuality, the connection between life cycle stages and environmental conditions would in itself be an interesting area of investigation. In addition, a focus on the individual life cycles of nonprofit organizations could throw greater light on the issue of achieving "scale" and the circumstances under which growing larger, or expanding outside the locality in which an organization is initially established, is necessarily an efficiency-achieving and stabilizing experience. Presumably nonprofits in many industries do not experience economies of scale or scope and would be better off taking a different approach to achieving stability (such as joining forces with other organizations). At the industry level, research could illuminate how nonprofit industries tend to grow, what the role of federations and associations are in such development, what the relative roles of nonprofit, for-profit, and government providers tend to be at different stages of development, and where, therefore, nonprofits can best look for opportunities to participate in such collaborations on terms that promise growth and stability.

Final Thoughts

The intent of this chapter is not to prescribe a very specific research agenda, but rather to elucidate a number of areas where research that promises to help nonprofits become more successful in coping with change and uncertainty is likely to be productive. The possibilities would seem to be rich in number, in practical significance, and in intellectual challenge. Research can potentially produce better information about trends and uncertainties, can better characterize the risks that nonprofits actually face, can help nonprofits evaluate these risks with greater prudence, can offer better analytical tools for nonprofits to think through their decisions about change and risk management, can point out how nonprofit organizations may need to reform themselves in order to be more capable and inclined to deal with the uncertainties and dynamics of their environment, can find better ways of mobilizing resources to help them adapt to new and uncertain circumstances, can help them think through their competitive positions and alliances in a more strategic way, and can suggest strategies under which nonprofits may gain greater control of their environments. In turn, researchers have the opportunity to do some very interesting work, with the understanding that some of it will surely be helpful in strengthening the ability of nonprofits to do good work in an increasingly challenging milieu.

Index